IMAGES of America
PLYMOUTH'S AIR RIFLE INDUSTRY

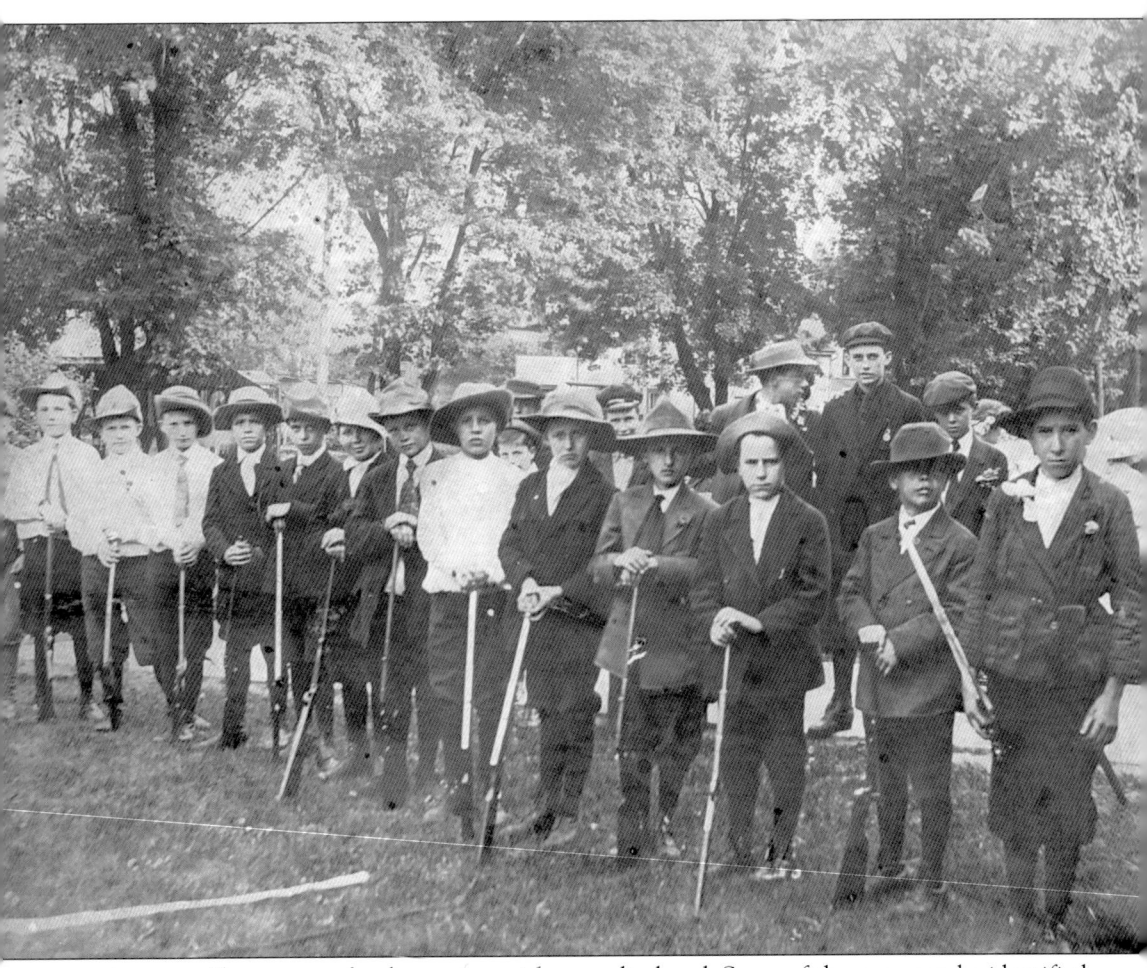

A group of boys pauses for the camera with guns displayed. Some of the guns can be identified: the boy second from the right is holding a Hamilton Rifle No. 15; the boy third from the right is holding a Daisy 20th-century, single-shot air rifle; and the boys fifth and sixth from the right are holding Daisy Bennett air rifles. (Courtesy of Wes Powers.)

ON THE COVER: Taken around 1910, this image shows the assembly department of the Daisy Manufacturing Company at the pinnacle of the competitive air rifle industry in Plymouth, Michigan. In the assembly department, workers assembled the various components of the air guns into the final products ready for testing and, ultimately, shipping. (Courtesy of the Plymouth Historical Museum.)

IMAGES of America
PLYMOUTH'S AIR RIFLE INDUSTRY

Elizabeth Kelley Kerstens

Elizabeth Kelley Kerstens

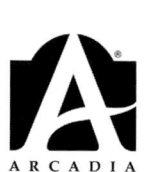

ARCADIA
PUBLISHING

Copyright © 2013 by Elizabeth Kelley Kerstens
ISBN 978-1-4671-1046-4

Published by Arcadia Publishing
Charleston, South Carolina

Printed in the United States of America

Library of Congress Control Number: 2013933772

For all general information, please contact Arcadia Publishing:
Telephone 843-853-2070
Fax 843-853-0044
E-mail sales@arcadiapublishing.com
For customer service and orders:
Toll-Free 1-888-313-2665

Visit us on the Internet at www.arcadiapublishing.com

This book is dedicated to the two visionaries who made this history possible: William F. "Phil" Markham and Clarence James Hamilton.

Contents

Foreword   6

Acknowledgments   7

Introduction   8

1. Markham Dreams of an Air Rifle   9
2. Clarence Invents a Windmill   33
3. The Short-lived Plymouth Air Rifle Company   37
4. "Boy, That's a Daisy!"   45
5. Plymouth's View of Daisy   55
6. Daisy's Inner Strength   67
7. The Essence of Daisy   87
8. Clarence Eyes the Boys' Rifle Market   115

Bibliography   126

About the Friends of the Plymouth Historical Museum   127

Foreword

Detroit may be the Motor City, but Plymouth, Michigan, was once the "Air Gun Capitol of the World." Many recognize Plymouth as the first home (from 1895 to 1958) of Daisy Manufacturing, makers of the world-famous Daisy BB guns. Fewer know that the city was, at one time, home to three highly competitive and interrelated air gun companies.

If you, like most people, took your first shot with a BB gun, you'll enjoy reading this remarkable history. Learn how one small town virtually monopolized the early commercially successful air gun business and consequently put itself on the map. Discover why the creativity of a watch repairman and inventor, the ingenuity of a bucket company, and the potential failure of a windmill company all played integral roles in air gun history.

Elizabeth Kerstens is a diligent researcher and meticulous historian who, with access to an impressive archives of documents and photographs, is uniquely qualified to have researched and written this comprehensive pictorial history of the air guns of Plymouth.

As vice president of marketing for Daisy Outdoor Products, the company's liaison with the non-profit corporation—the Daisy Museum in Rogers, Arkansas, and author of the book *Daisy, It All Starts Here*—I can proudly report that the Daisy management team places a high value on our company's corporate history. It is the foundation of our company's continued success and of the public's unmatched recognition of and respect for our brand.

I'm tempted to describe this book with superlatives such as awesome, excellent, or cool; however, history dictates—and it's only appropriate—that I end this foreword the way it all (for Daisy) began, with a colloquialism of the 1880s: "It's a Daisy!"

—Joe C. Murfin
Vice President of Marketing
Daisy Outdoor Products

Acknowledgments

I would like to thank Arcadia Publishing for the opportunity to tell the story of the guns that put Plymouth, Michigan, on the map. This history could not be told, however, without the painstaking work of historians who have preserved the stories of Plymouth's past. I stand on the shoulders of Sam Hudson, Karl Starkweather, Charles Bennett, Cass Hough, and the countless others who have donated pieces of Plymouth's past to the Plymouth Historical Museum. I am particularly indebted to several individuals who have provided invaluable guidance during the preparation of this book. Wes Powers is a collector-extraordinaire and air rifle historian. Over the years, he has provided a wealth of invaluable information to the museum's archives about the four companies discussed here. Wes generously provided access to his photograph archives, allowing me to use numerous images in this book. And, best of all, he read the manuscript and provided guidance and encouragement along with his vast storehouse of knowledge about Plymouth's air rifles. Jim Perkins is also a collector and historian who has studied and written about Markham and Hamilton. Jim sent a plethora of images, many of which are found in this book. He also read parts of the manuscript and provided helpful suggestions; then, he donated all of the images and his research notes to the museum's archives for posterity. Joe Murfin, vice president of marketing for Daisy Outdoor Products, provided access to some priceless early Daisy documents and provided insight into Daisy Manufacturing while reading the manuscript, as did long-time Daisy employee Orin Ribar. Nathaniel Gibson, a museum volunteer, assisted in writing some of the captions in the book. Heidi Nielsen, the museum's archivist, has cheerfully responded to my unreasonable requests to find needles in our archives haystacks, mustering the help of her volunteers. Kathy Petlewski, Plymouth's genealogy librarian, read the entire manuscript for continuity. And last, but not least, my husband Marty Kerstens once again read my manuscript and added his editorial comments. Thank you all for your help.

Unless otherwise noted, all images appear courtesy of the Plymouth Historical Museum.

INTRODUCTION

In the 1880s, when this story begins, Plymouth was a sleepy little farming community of a tad more than 2,000 people. Sitting about 25 miles west of Detroit, Plymouth Township was founded in 1827 by transplanted New Yorkers who made their way west using the recently opened Erie Canal. The Village Green in the center of town was the gathering place for community events and local gossip. Many residents were part of the Michigan Anti-Slavery Society and participated in the temperance movement. In the Village Green in August 1862, the citizens held a rally in support of Pres. Abraham Lincoln's call for more troops during the Civil War. Plymouth raised a company of men that day—many of them blood relatives—who fought valiantly as part of the 24th Michigan Infantry and the Iron Brigade. At the war's end, surviving veterans returned to their farms and eked out their livings as best they could. With only one factory in town at the time, employment opportunities were very limited. In this unlikely location, men dared to dream, and village residents embraced their dreams. William F. "Phil" Markham turned a wooden water tank and cistern manufacturing company into a company producing the first commercially successful air gun. Clarence James Hamilton, already an inventor when he arrived in Plymouth in 1874, dreamt up some improvements for the windmills he saw dotting the countryside. He found willing investors in town, and together they formed the first publicly held stock company in Plymouth: the Plymouth Iron Windmill Company. One wonders what the gossip must have been in the Village Green when Hamilton left the windmill company after dreaming up some improvements to the air gun that Markham produced. Hamilton and his friend Cyrus Pinckney started the ill-fated Plymouth Air Rifle Company. But Hamilton did not stay there long; he went back to the windmill company with another improvement on an air rifle—one that was ultimately named Daisy. Never content to sit still, Clarence dreamt up improvements to the .22-caliber rifle and opened C.J. Hamilton & Son with his son Coello. All of this dreaming in the space of two decades turned Plymouth into the air rifle capitol of the world; at least until 1958, when Daisy Manufacturing moved to Rogers, Arkansas.

One
MARKHAM DREAMS OF AN AIR RIFLE

The Markham Manufacturing Company, formed in Plymouth by William F. "Phil" Markham, produced wooden water tanks and cisterns about 1879. According to Phil's son Leigh, Phil "envisioned a [toy] gun shooting BB shot, not by gun powder but by compressed air." The company began manufacturing air guns with wooden stocks in 1886 and was renamed Markham Air Rifle Company about 1887, the year Markham received a patent for the invention. The September 16, 1887, issue of the *Plymouth Mail* stated, "The Markham Manufacturing Company, of this place, are taxed to their utmost to fill orders and are some ways behind yet. This is the kind of business we like to see." The Strobel and Wilken Company of Chicago placed a large order for the air guns on the condition that the company would have exclusive rights to the gun in Chicago for five years and that it would be named Chicago. After minor alterations, the first named model was introduced. Markham is considered the first company to create a commercially viable air gun, a couple years before the Plymouth Air Rifle Company and the Plymouth Iron Windmill Company (later Daisy Manufacturing Company). By 1888, Markham had built a new factory on Main Street just east of the Pere Marquette Railroad tracks to handle the demand for his popular invention. He introduced additional models, especially as competition heated up with the other air rifle companies in Plymouth. One of Markham's more popular models was the King, which was a sheet-metal gun with a cast-iron receiver. Phil Markham was a prolific inventor, owning at least 12 patents, along with patents held by his employees. But his company did not have the marketing savvy of his chief competitor, Daisy Manufacturing Company. Advertisements for Markham guns were infrequent and less desirable than those for Daisy, no matter what new gimmick Markham developed. Ultimately, troubles in his personal life would cause Phil Markham to move to California in 1912; the controlling shares of Markham Air Rifle Company were sold to Daisy chiefs Edward Hough and Charles Bennett in 1916.

William F. "Phil" Markham (1851–1930) founded the Markham Manufacturing Company about 1879. The company made wooden cisterns and water tanks for many years, but its best seller was the air rifle, invented by Markham in 1886. This photograph was taken on January 10, 1900.

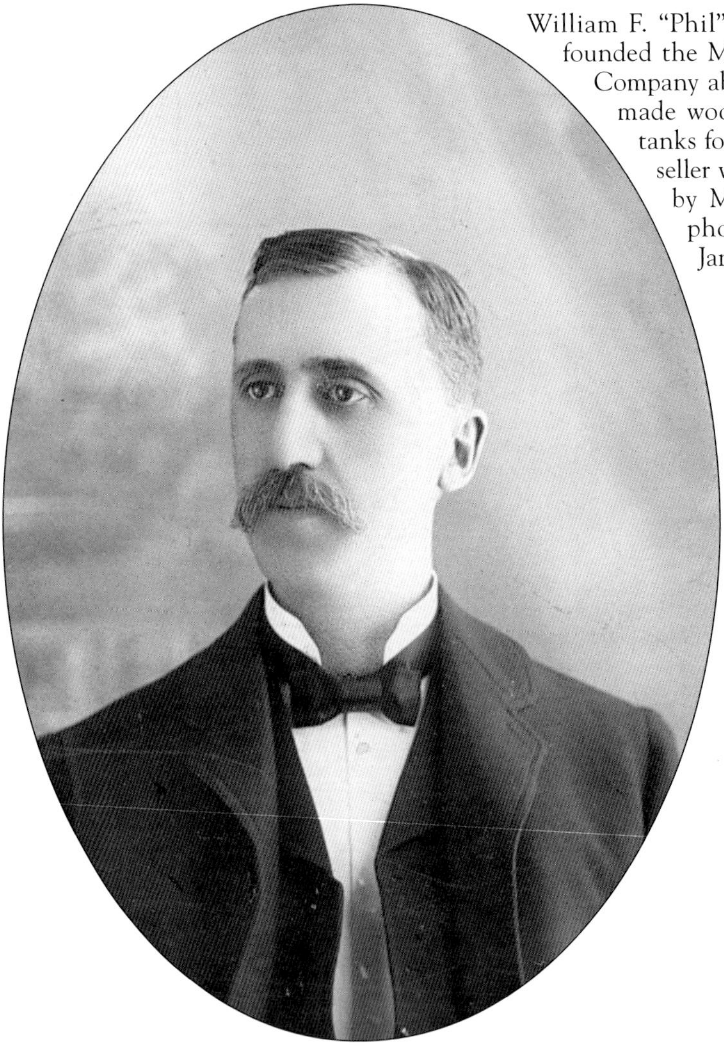

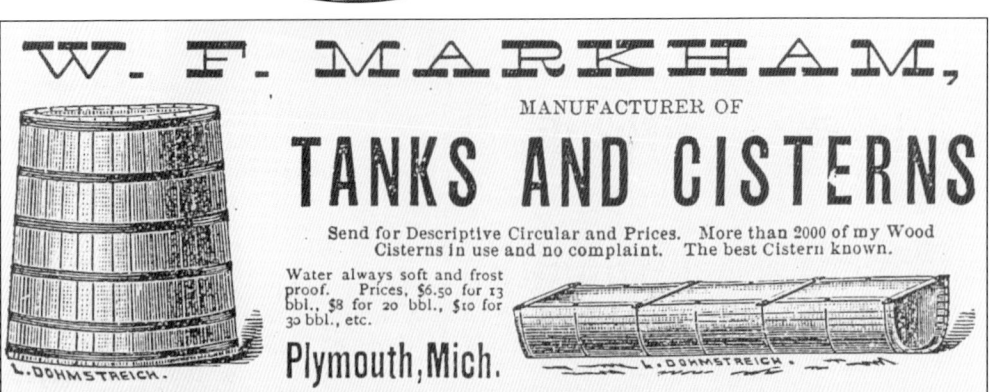

An ad in the 1887–1888 *Michigan Gazetteer* shows images of the water tanks and cisterns made by the Markham Manufacturing Company. The ad appeared about the time that Markham received his first patent for an air rifle.

Markham's first patent for an air gun was granted on October 25, 1887. The gun in the drawings was the prototype for what became the popular Chicago air gun, the first of Markham's mass-produced air guns.

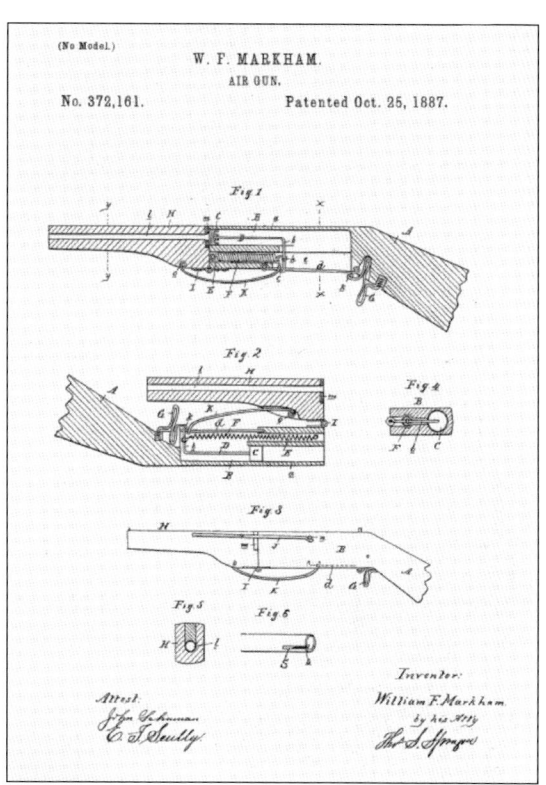

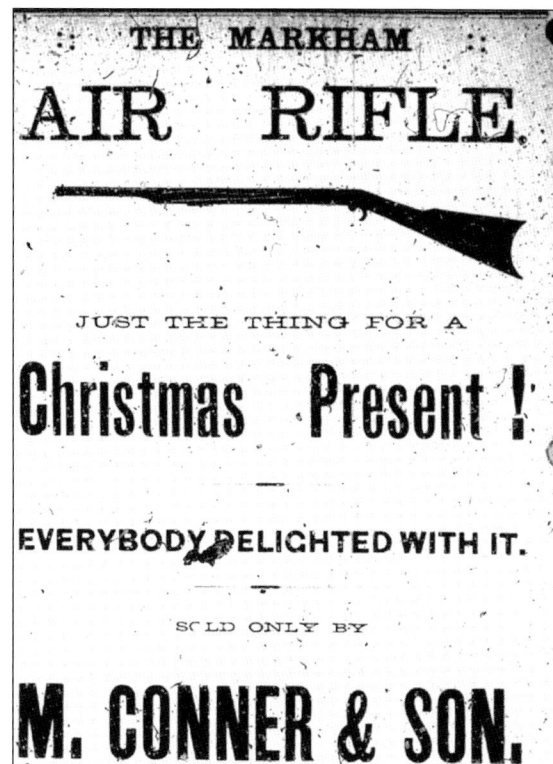

The earliest known ad for Markham's Chicago air rifle appeared in the *Plymouth Mail* on December 9, 1887, only three months after the newspaper began publishing. While difficult to see in this image, the Chicago has a patch box in the stock, a feature that was later discontinued.

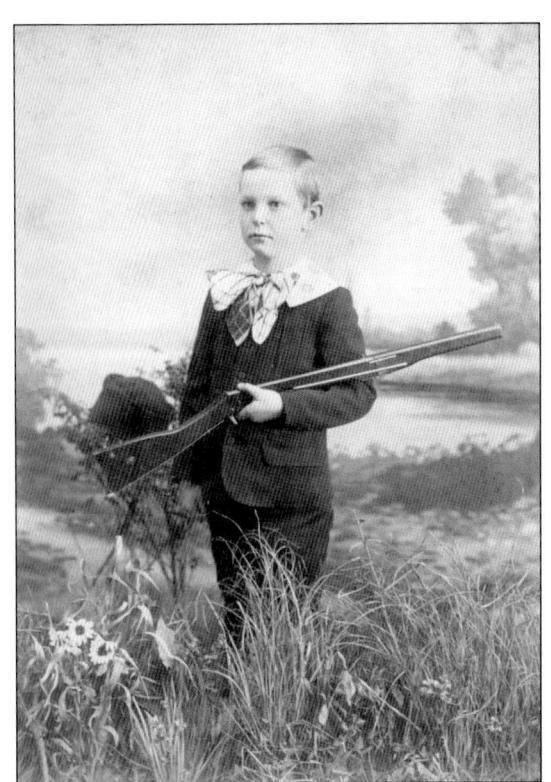

Both boys are showing off their Chicago air guns in these portraits with outdoor scenes as backdrops. The boy on the left, Frank Thomas, was from Norwalk, Ohio. The unidentified boy and his moving dog below were from Wayland, Michigan. The Chicago loaded at the breach and shot BB shot and darts. The outer barrel and stock were made of maple with a mahogany finish. The Chicago was manufactured between 1887 and 1910. (Both courtesy of Wesley Powers.)

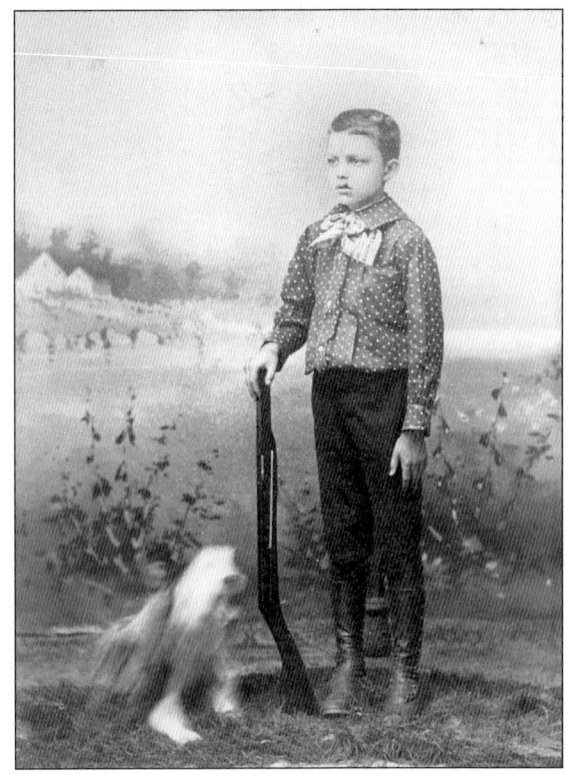

The top building is the Markham Manufacturing Company's first factory, where it began production of the Chicago in 1887; it was a two-story shop measuring 45 feet by 55 feet. The bottom complex, in Markham's heyday, was 65,000 square feet of floor space, with a capacity of 3,000 guns a day.

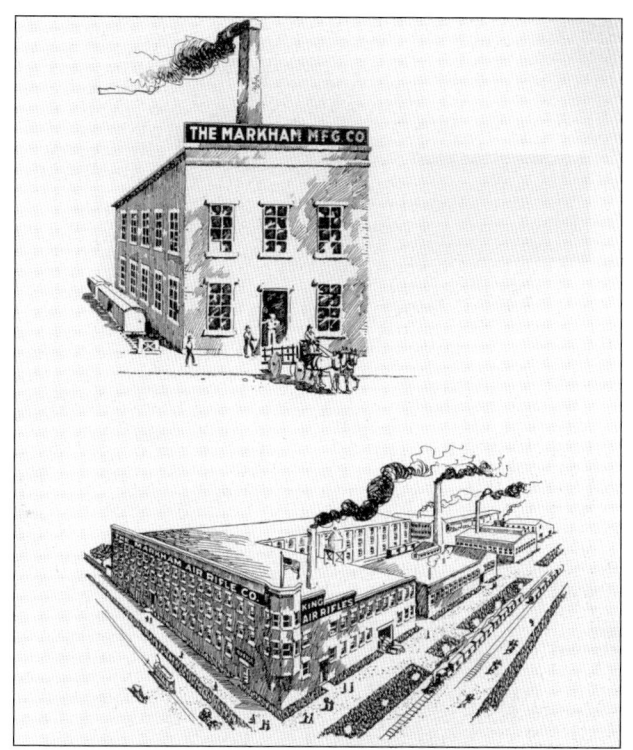

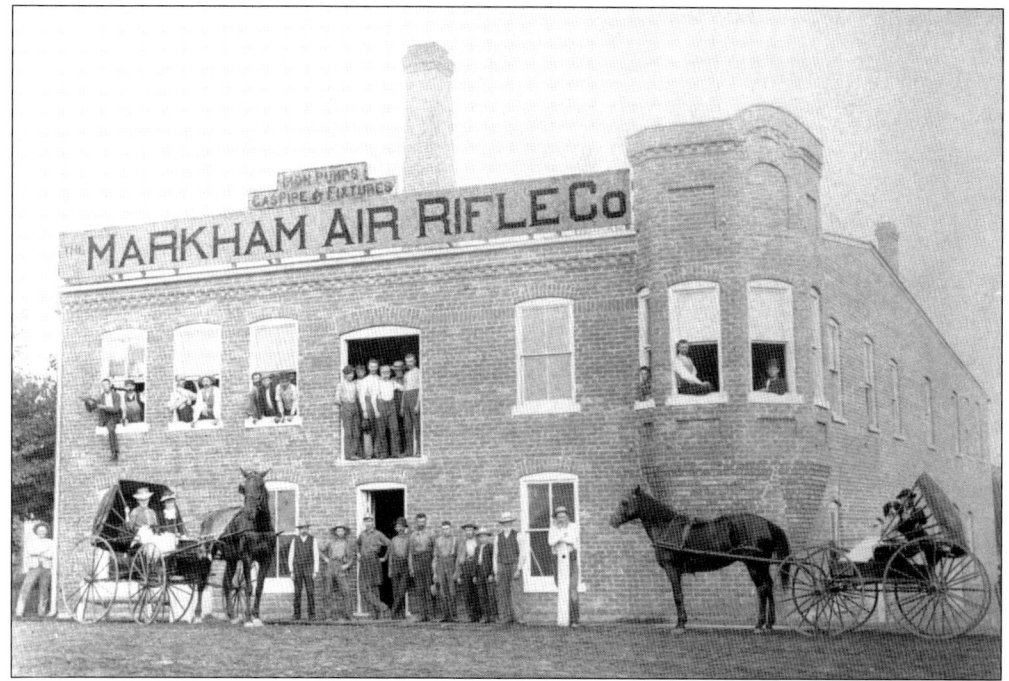

The original factory of the Markham Air Rifle Company was two stories and 45 feet by 55 feet. Phil Markham can be seen in the open window second from the right. His son Harry is in the third open window from the right. The photograph dates to about 1888; the factory had been completed in October 1887.

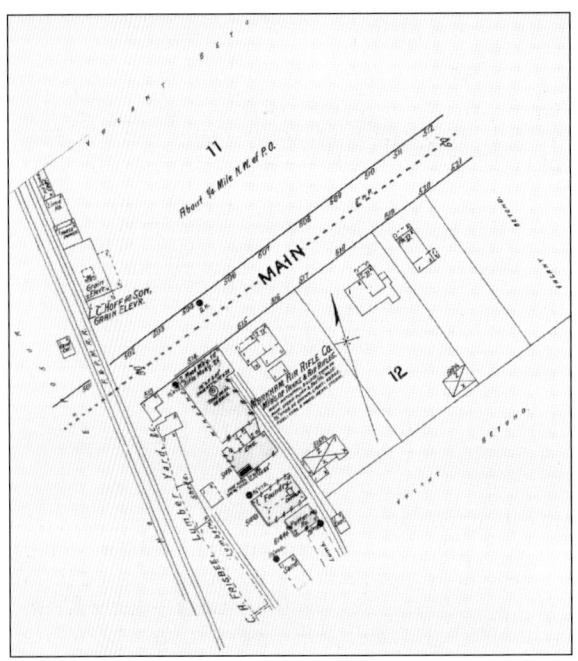

The Sanborn Company has created fire insurance maps since 1866 "to help insurance companies assess the potential risks involved in underwriting policies," states its website. Maps were made for Plymouth beginning in 1893, perhaps because of the three air rifle companies in the village. The 1893 map for Markham (at left) indicates that it used the first floor for manufacturing wood products, while air rifles were produced on the second floor. Across the tracks from Markham were two local competitors, the Plymouth Iron Windmill Co. (later Daisy Manufacturing Co.) and Plymouth Air Rifle Co. By 1899, Markham had grown and was building an addition (below) to be occupied in 1900. (Both courtesy of Environmental Data Resources.)

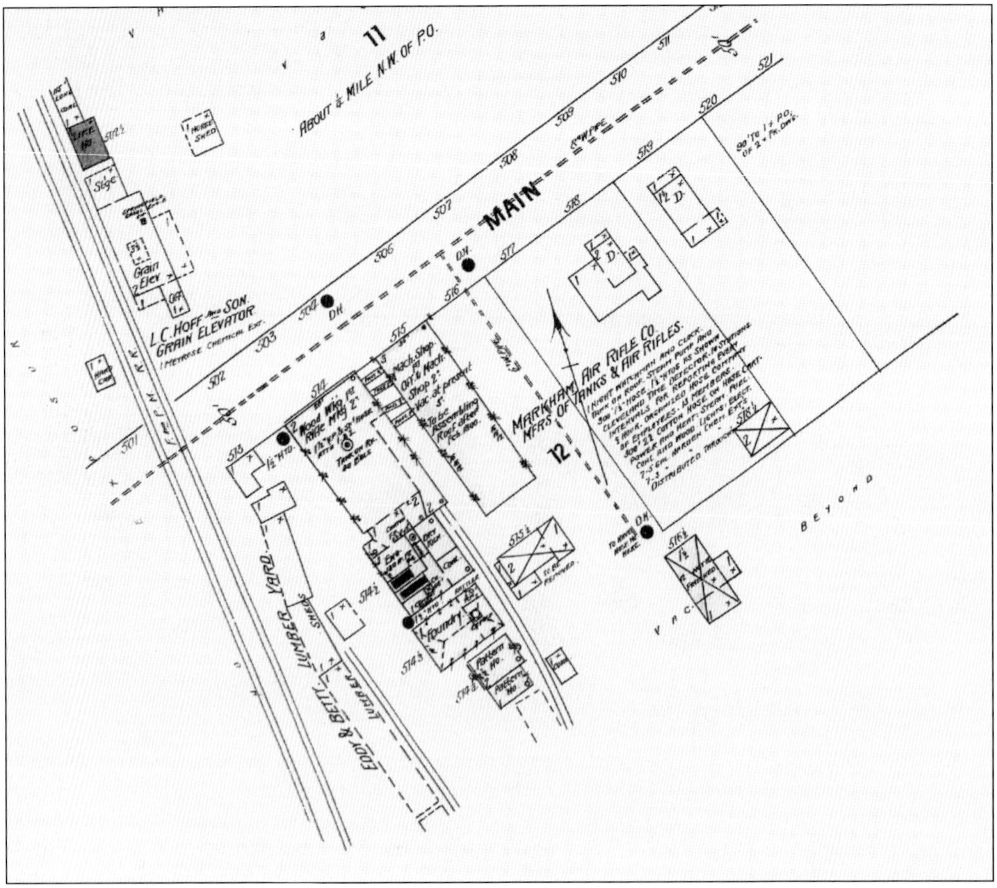

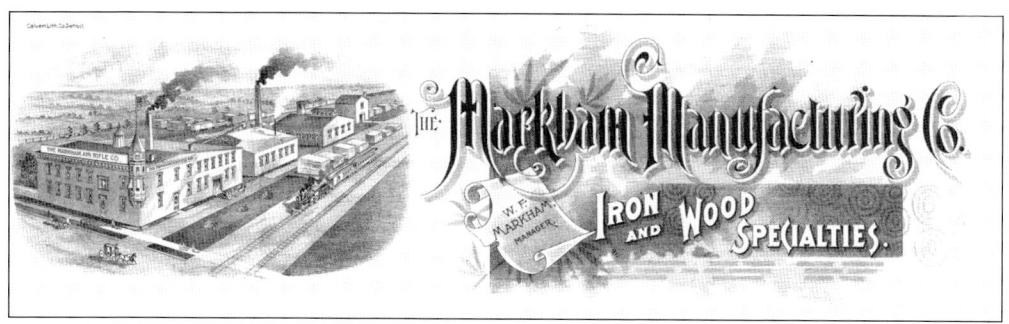

The artist's rendering of the Markham Air Rifle Company's buildings on the 1899 letterhead above shows the buildings before the expansion in 1899–1900 and includes stacks of lumber next to the railroad tracks. The lumber represents the Eddy and Betty Lumberyard, as noted in the 1899 Sanborn map on the previous page, which shows the lumberyard between the tracks and the Markham buildings. Below, an artist's rendering on a company envelope dated 1901 reflects the look of the complex after the additions; however, the artist placed the complex directly adjacent to the railroad tracks, eliminating the lumberyard in between. The lumberyard, later the Plymouth Lumber & Coal Company, remained in its location long after the manufacturing of the Markham products was moved to Daisy Manufacturing Company in the 1930s. (Below, courtesy of Michael Pappas.)

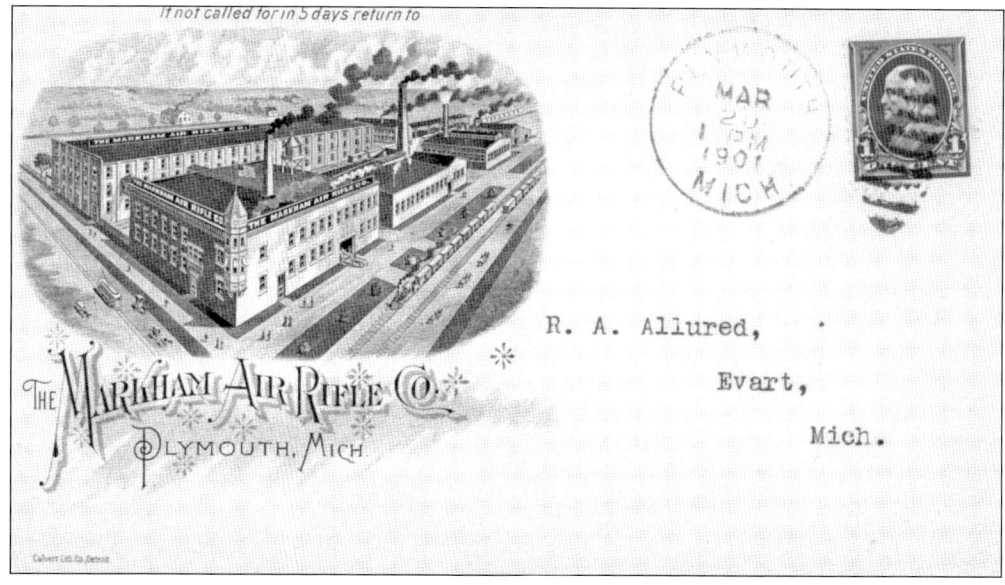

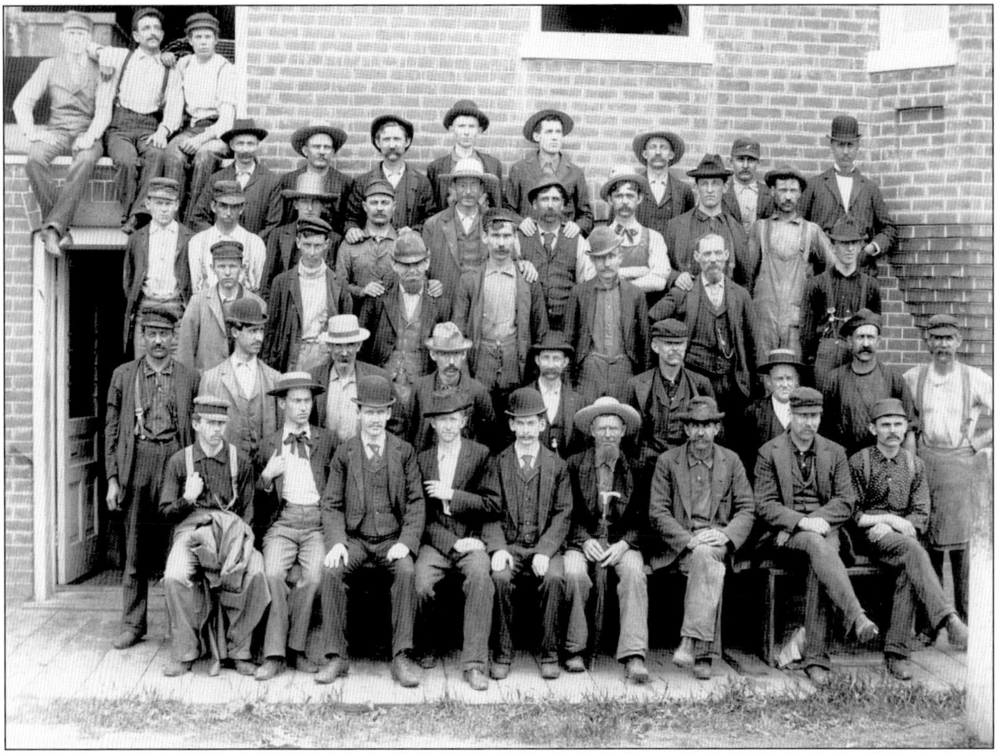

A group of 45 employees of the Markham Air Rifle Company poses for a photograph in 1895, mostly in fancy clothes. In the window on the left sits Ernest S. Roe, one of Markham's inventors and patent holders. Phil Markham is on the far right in the top row. Names of most of the other workers are available at the Plymouth Historical Museum.

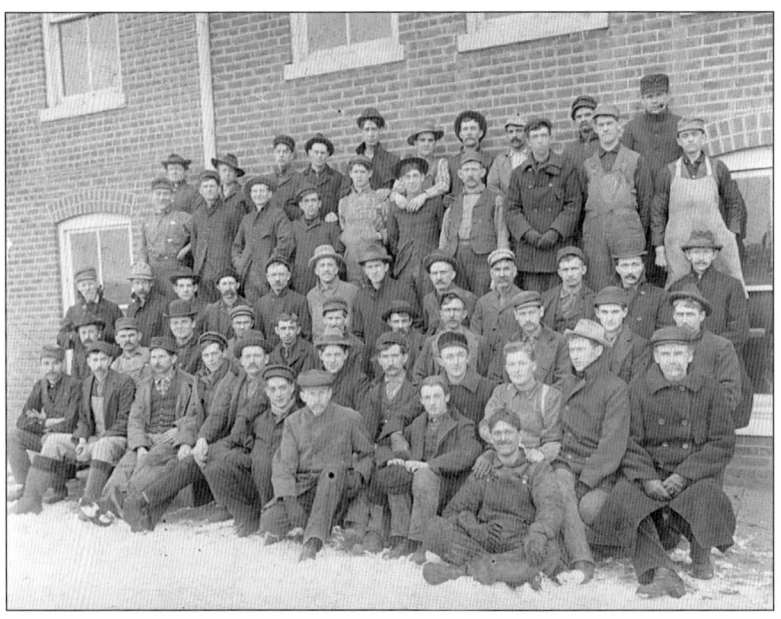

In this 1900 photograph, 58 Markham workers pose during a Michigan winter with snow on the ground. Some of these men are identified on the back of the photograph, including Willard Roe, a Civil War veteran from Company C, 24th Michigan Infantry Regiment, who is in the third row on the far left.

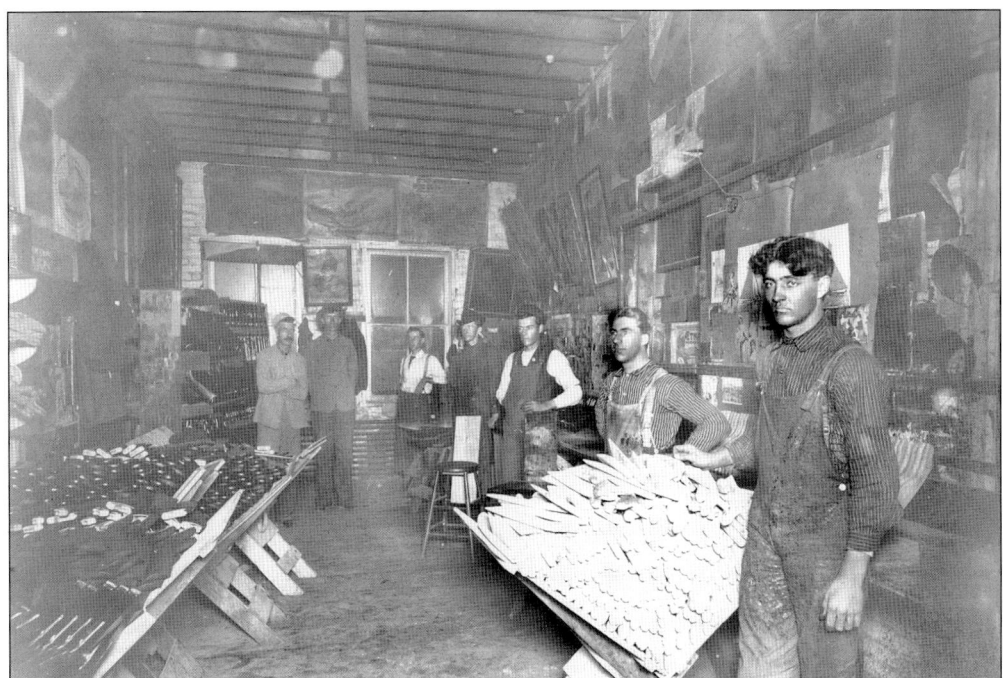

Above, Markham employees are in the second floor woodworking shop in the late 1890s. The shop was where workers turned wood blocks into finished wood stocks. The walls are covered with items ranging from posters for the Detroit International Fair and Exposition of 1891 to photographs of boxers and scantily clad women. Shown below is possibly the finishing room for the wood components, as there are multiple racks of stocks, possibly model 95 Kings. A metal hook was taken out of a barrel, attached to a stock, and then hung on a rack or a conveyer line. The finish was applied either by a spraying or dipping process. The stocks were then left hanging until they were dry. These walls are also covered with photographs of women.

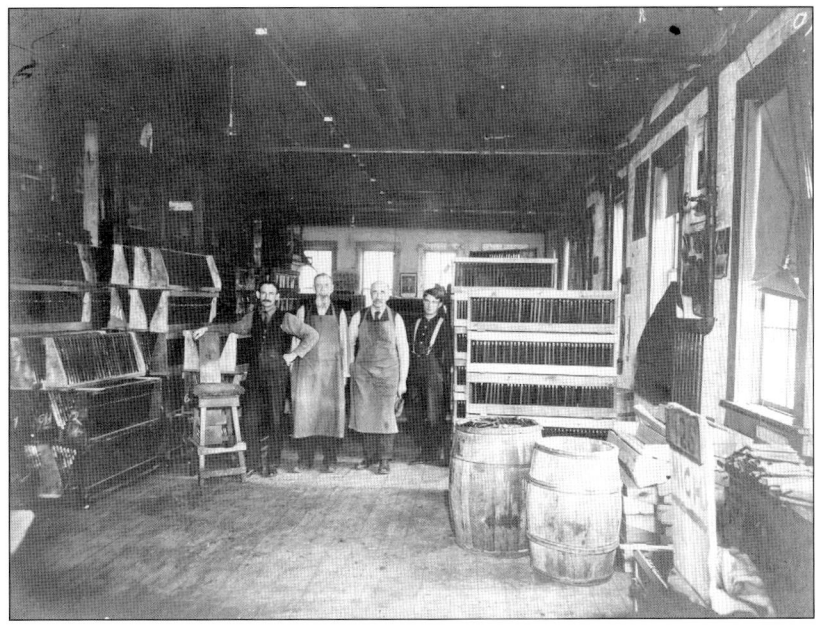

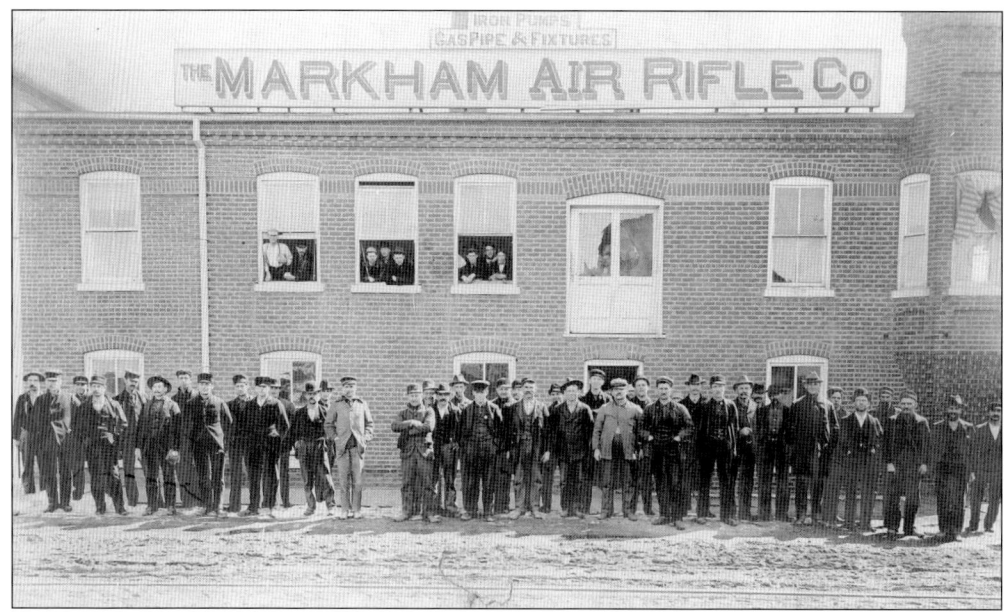

Here is another shot of Markham employees. This c. 1900 photograph was taken from a similar vantage point as the image on page 13; however, the 1900 addition to the original building can be seen. Before the addition, the building ended where the downspout is located here.

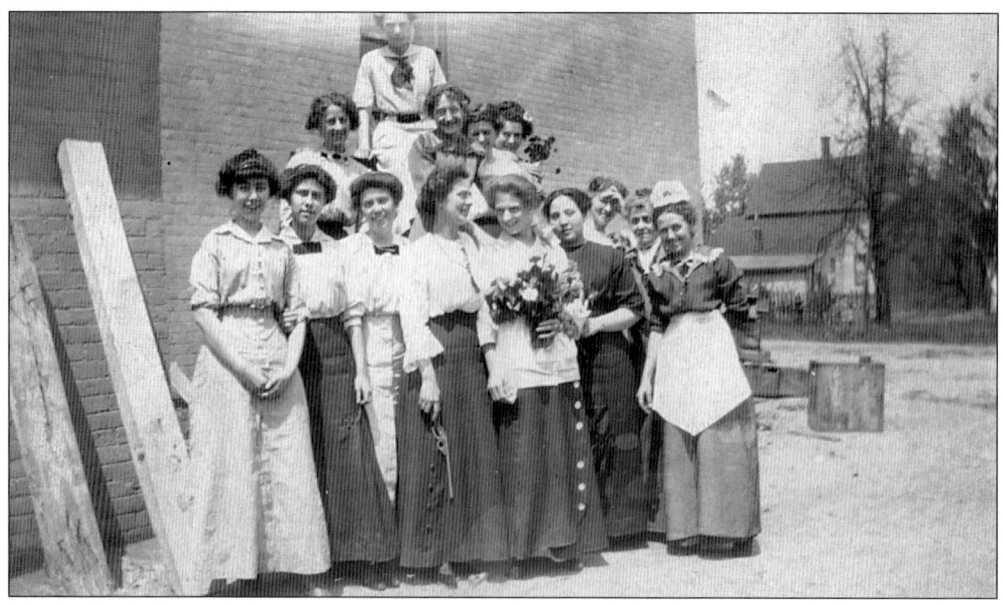

The back of this real photograph postcard merely reads, "The Markham girls." It is unknown what positions women may have filled in the company at this time or if these are wives of some of the employees. Perhaps they were celebrating a special day for the woman holding a bouquet of flowers near the center.

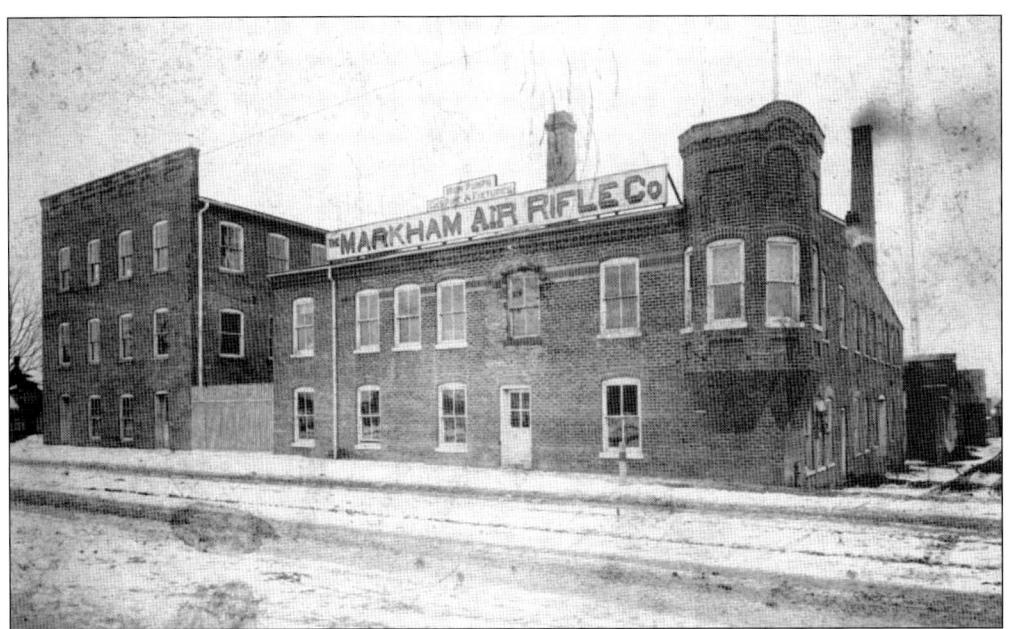

Between 1900, when the first addition was completed, and 1908, when the lumberyard was renamed the Plymouth Lumber & Coal Company, a brick facade was added to the original Markham factory building, joining the old and the new buildings on the Main Street side of the complex. The photograph above shows the original building on the right and the 1900 addition on the left. The photograph below was shot after the facade was added and after the lumberyard was renamed in 1908. Note the train tracks running across the image and the Detroit Interurban Rail lines crossing the train tracks. This spur of the Interurban ran from Northville, through Plymouth, and on to Wayne between 1898 and 1924.

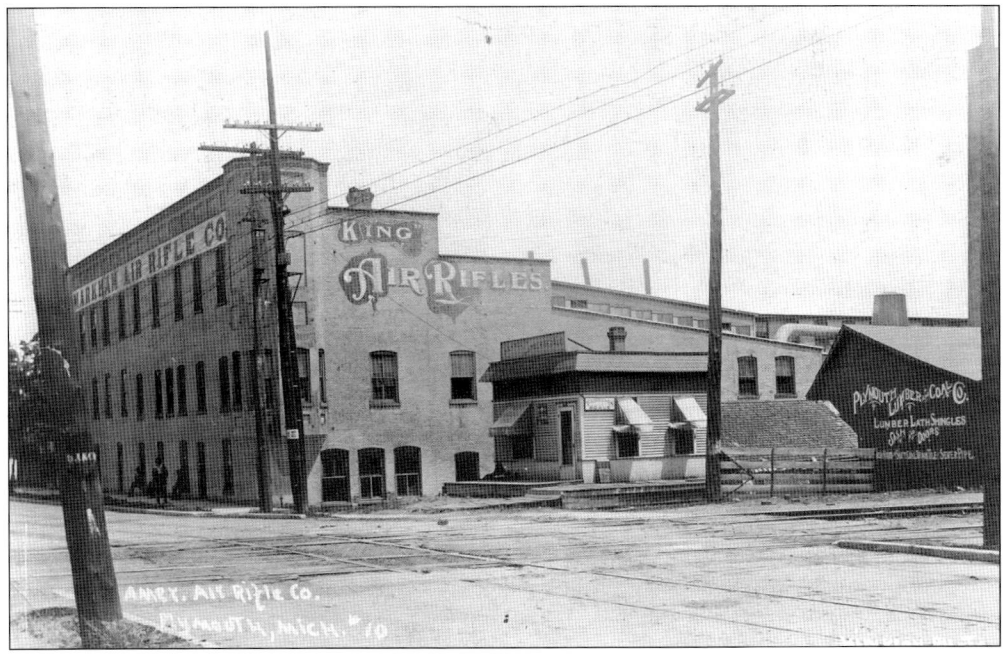

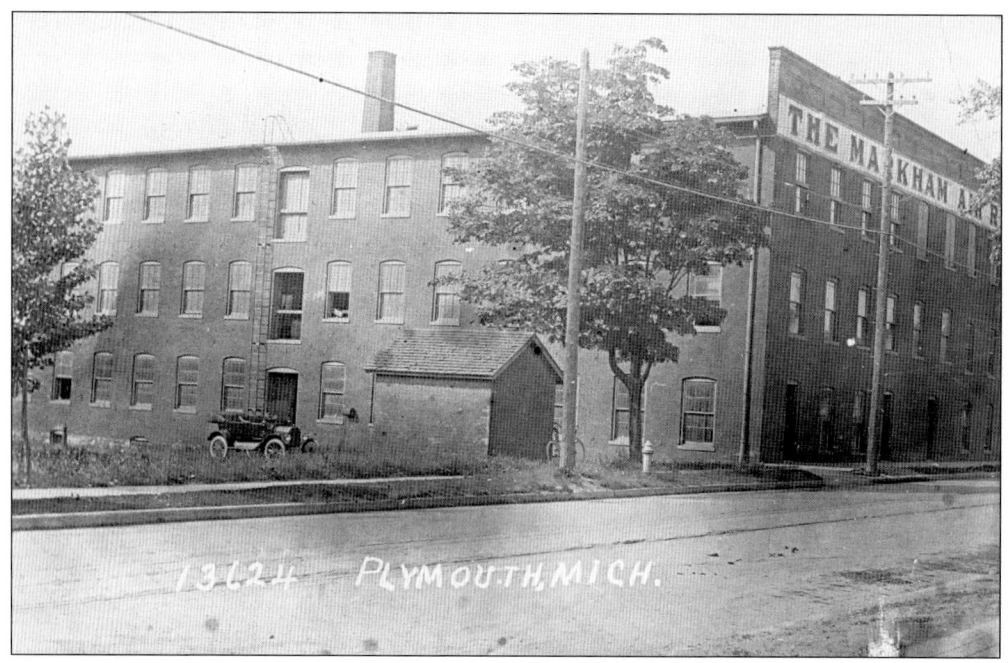

This is a rare view of the north side of the Markham Air Rifle factory around 1915. The structure has the 1900 addition, as well as the facade added before 1908 that joined the two factory buildings.

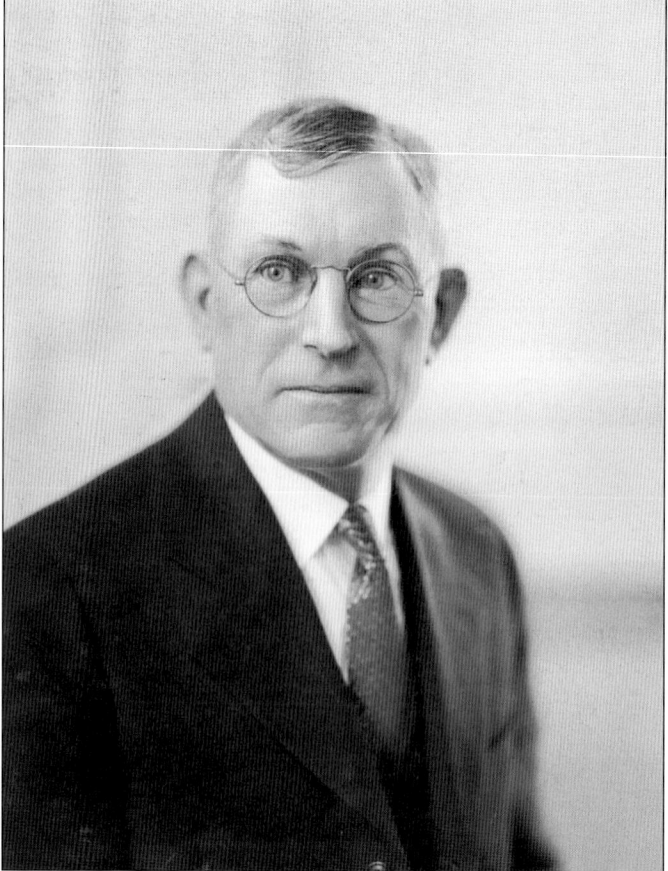

Ernest Roe (1870–1964) started working at the Markham factory in 1887 when he was 17 and retired after 44 years with the company in 1931, when all of the Markham works were absorbed by Daisy Manufacturing. Roe held several patents for designs associated with Markham air guns.

These two photographs are from "The Story of the Air Rifle," a booklet published by the Markham Air Rifle Company around 1913. Both men are operating machinery that cut or stamped out the steel parts for King air guns. The dies had to be accurate to within one one-thousandth of an inch. The machine shops were located on the first floor of the 1900 factory addition according to the Sanborn map of 1899. Markham introduced the King air rifle in 1893.

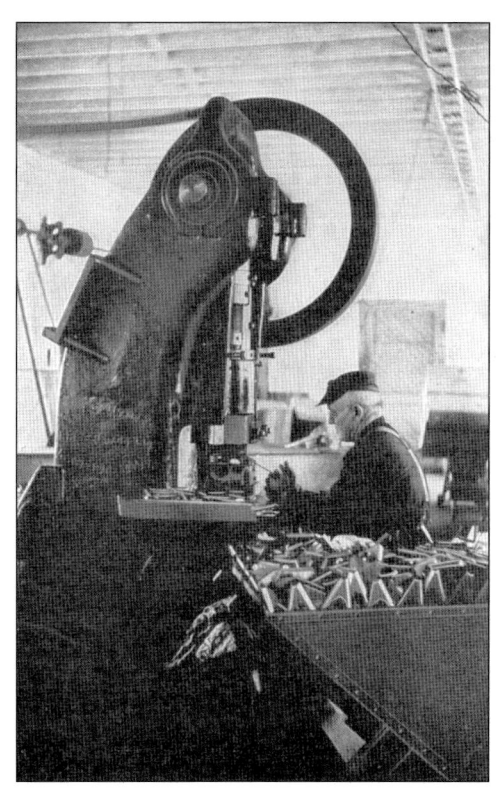

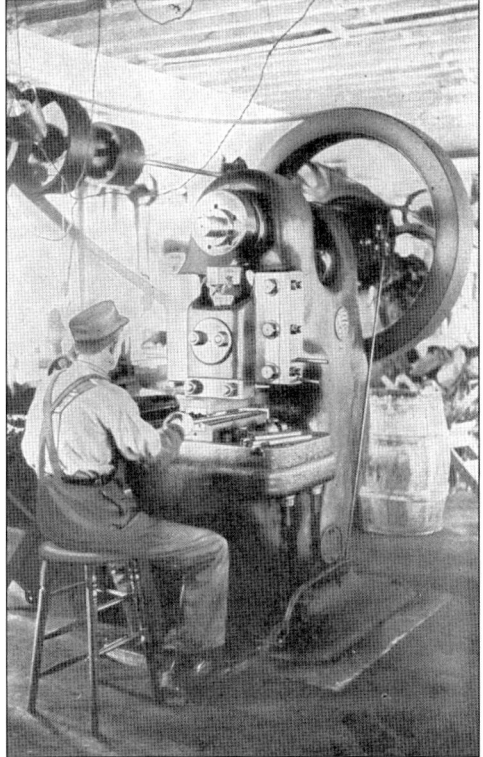

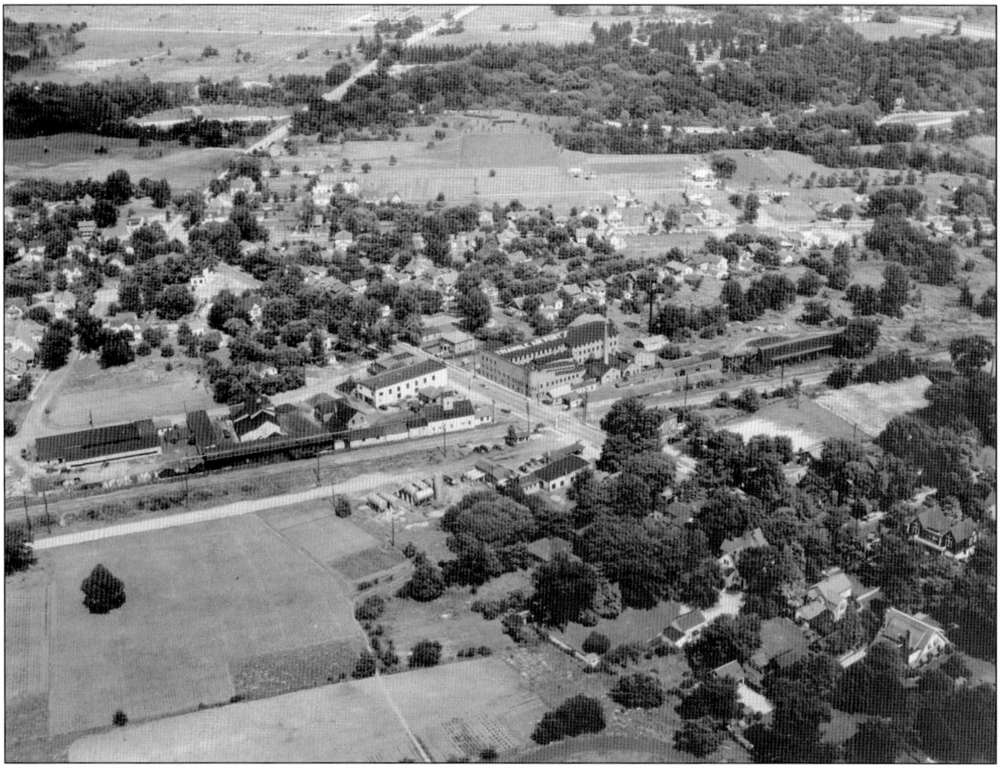

This aerial view of part of Plymouth was taken from Cass Hough's plane in July 1938. Markham was renamed the King Manufacturing Company in 1928. In 1931, Daisy Manufacturing Company moved all of the operations of King over to the Daisy plant. The former King plant is the building with "Triangle Airport" written on the roof. From this angle, it is easy to see the facade that joined the two factory buildings prior to 1908.

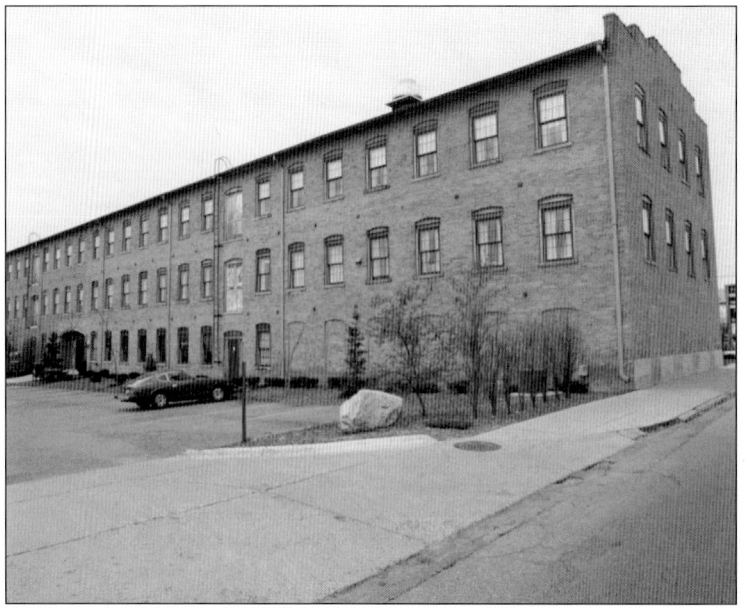

The original Markham factory and several outbuildings were torn down between 1954 and 1976, but the 1900 addition remains today. The structure was revamped as a restaurant and office building in the late 1970s and received a historical marker in 1983, the year of this photograph. The building is still a significant source of commerce in the city of Plymouth.

A family portrait, taken between 1910 and 1920, is completed by the Markham popgun held proudly by this little boy. (Courtesy of Wesley Powers.)

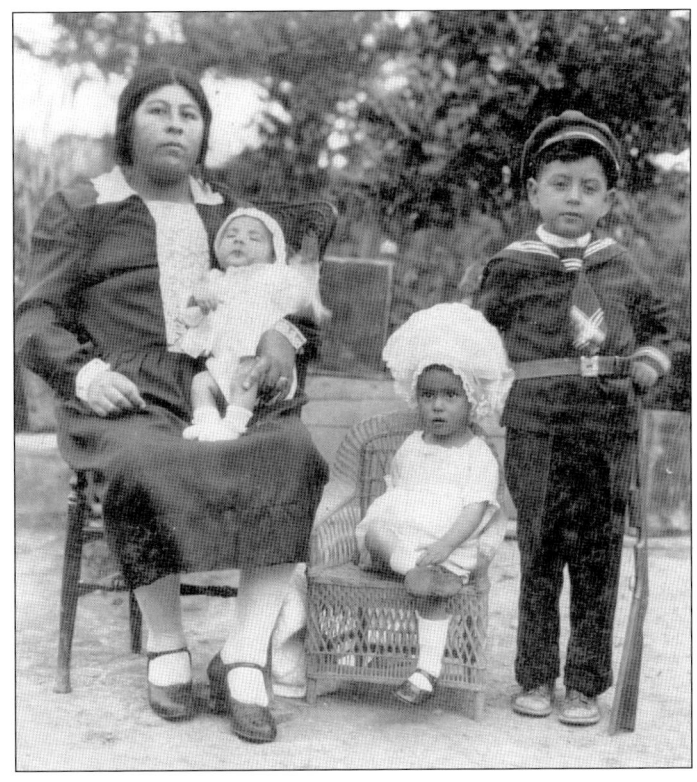

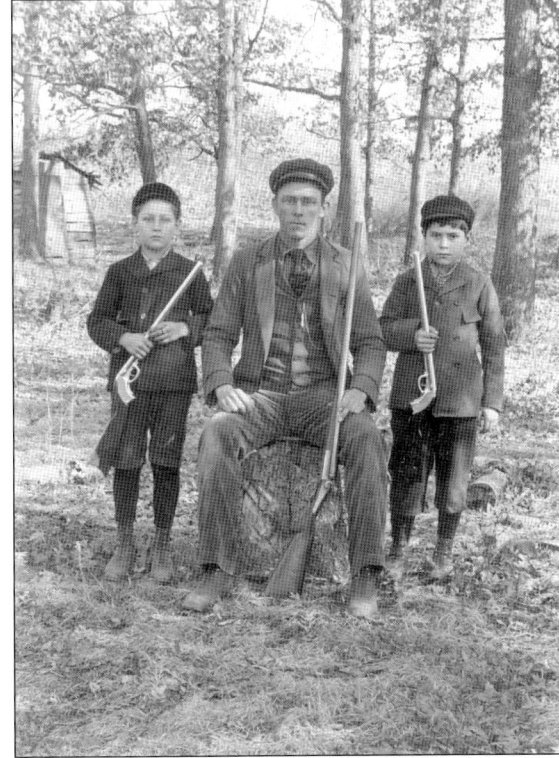

Oscar Burton (left), Ed Phillip (center), and Lou Gullet are out for a day in the woods, perhaps for target practice. Both boys are proudly displaying their 95 Style King Markham air guns, while the man is holding a shotgun. (Courtesy of Wesley Powers.)

Itinerant photographers traveled from town to town with a pony or a donkey, making a living capturing staged photographs of people posed with the photographer's traveling companion. This little boy in his Indian costume is perched on a donkey and holds a Markham air rifle. The image dates between 1910 and 1920. (Courtesy of Wesley Powers.)

Another photograph of a young boy holding a Markham air rifle, enjoying the river scenery with his faithful dog, is seen here between 1910 and 1920. (Courtesy of Wesley Powers.)

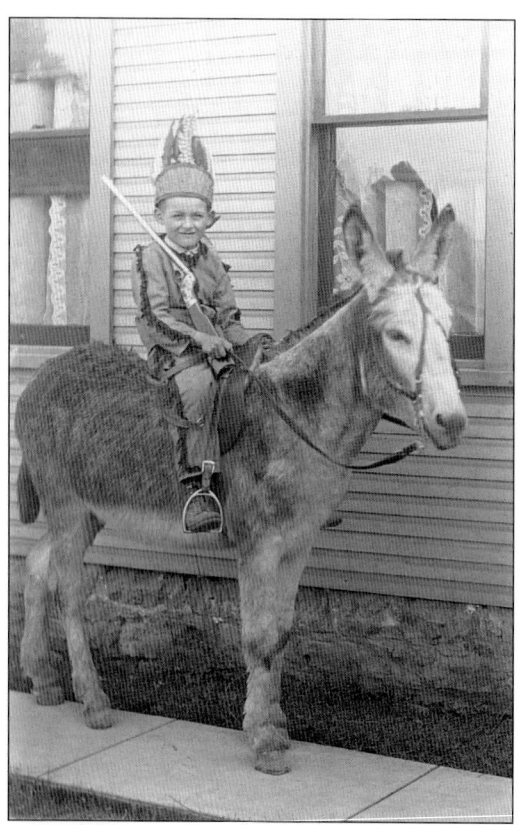

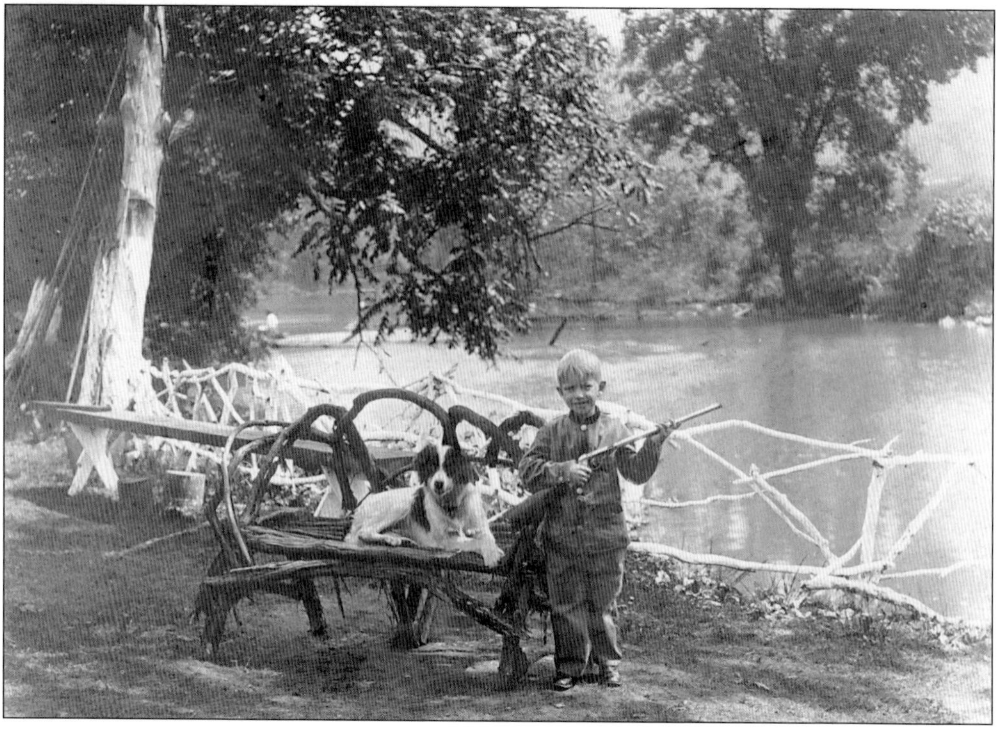

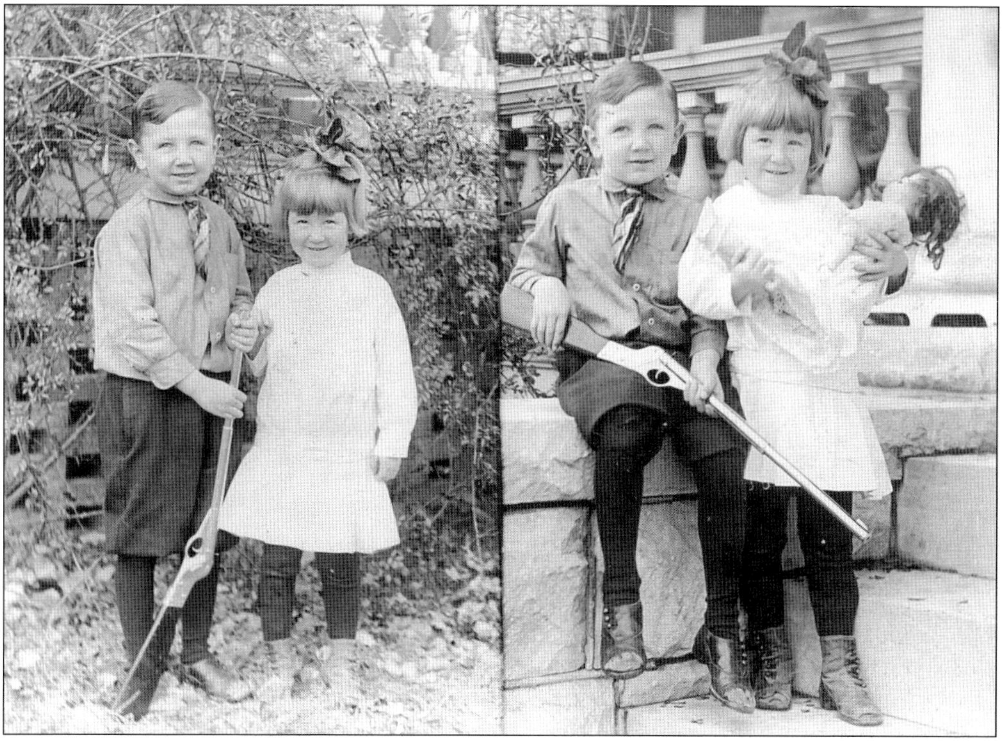

From what is written on the back of this unique double image, "August and Louise" are posing here for the camera. August is holding a Break-open Markham air gun in both shots, while Louise is holding a doll in the image on the right. (Courtesy of Wesley Powers.)

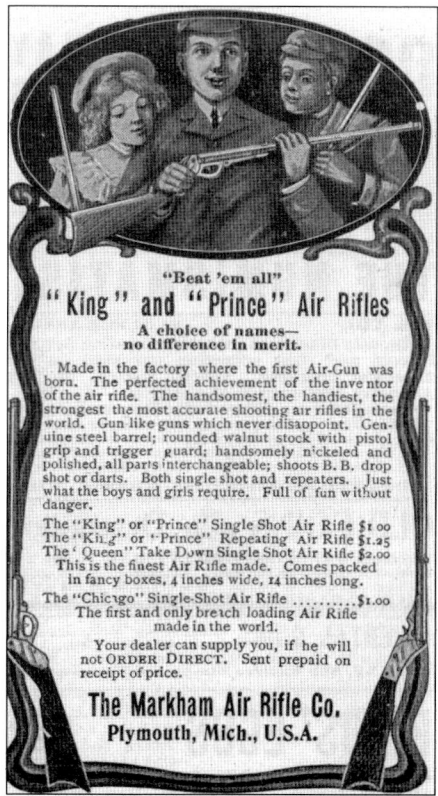

"Beat 'em all"
"King" and "Prince" Air Rifles
A choice of names—
no difference in merit.

Made in the factory where the first Air-Gun was born. The perfected achievement of the inventor of the air rifle. The handsomest, the handiest, the strongest the most accurate shooting air rifles in the world. Gun-like guns which never disappoint. Genuine steel barrel; rounded walnut stock with pistol grip and trigger guard; handsomely nickeled and polished, all parts interchangeable; shoots B. B. drop shot or darts. Both single shot and repeaters. Just what the boys and girls require. Full of fun without danger.

The "King" or "Prince" Single Shot Air Rifle $1.00
The "King" or "Prince" Repeating Air Rifle $1.25
The "Queen" Take Down Single Shot Air Rifle $2.00
This is the finest Air Rifle made. Comes packed in fancy boxes, 4 inches wide, 14 inches long.

The "Chicago" Single-Shot Air Rifle $1.00
The first and only breech loading Air Rifle made in the world.

Your dealer can supply you, if he will not ORDER DIRECT. Sent prepaid on receipt of price.

The Markham Air Rifle Co.
Plymouth, Mich., U.S.A.

A Markham Air Rifle Company ad from a May 1903 magazine brags about the King and Prince air rifles that were made in the same factory where the first air gun was born. The single-shot King or Prince sold for $1, the repeating versions sold for $1.25, the Queen "Take Down Single Shot" sold for $2, and the Chicago single shot sold for $1. (Courtesy of Wesley Powers.)

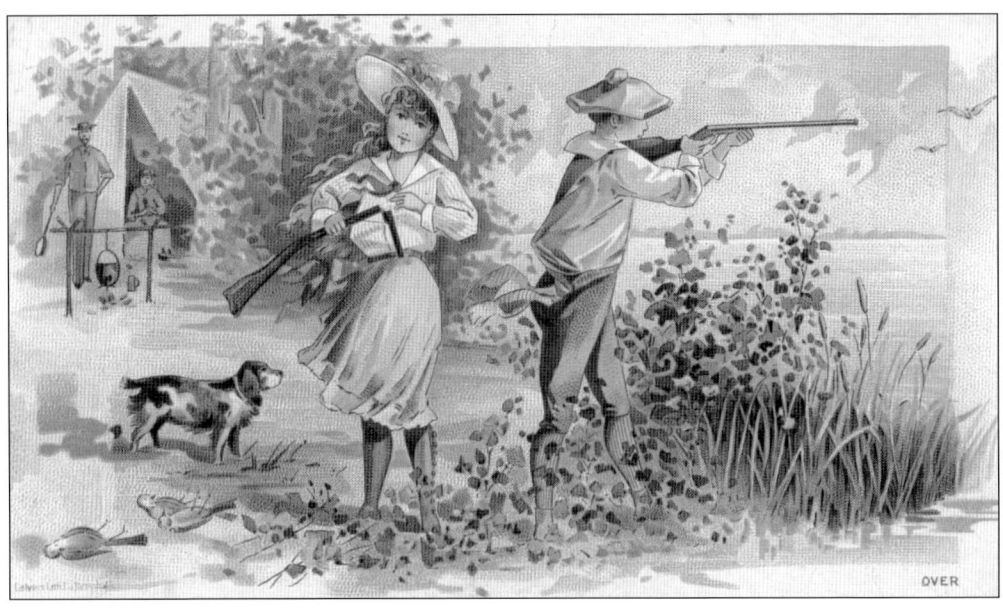

Resellers of the Markham air guns helped to promote the sale of the popular children's toys by printing double-sided advertising postcards. The John P. Lovell Arms Company of Boston was established in 1840 as a weapons manufacturer, as well as a wholesale and retail distributor of firearms and sporting goods. The company was the local distributor of Markham products and would have made these advertising cards available to customers and other interested parties. The ad tried to appeal to boys and girls alike, showing how easy the Chicago was for a girl to operate while depicting the boy aiming his King at some birds. The image above is the front of the card, and the back of the card is depicted below. (Both courtesy of Wesley Powers.)

THE "KING" AND THE "CHICAGO" AIR RIFLES.

This Boy says, there is nothing like his "KING," while the Girl, is equally confident that her "CHICAGO" leads the procession, and beats them all. If you want AIR RIFLES that will sell on sight; that have the talking points as well as the merit, then buy the "KING" and "CHICAGO." They were the *first* in the *race* and are still at the front. The "KING" is made of STEEL AND BRASS, NICKEL PLATED, with Mahogany stock. The "CHICAGO" is too well known to need description, and all we can say is "to see them is to buy them."

FOR SALE BY

JOHN P. LOVELL ARMS CO.,
147 Washington Street, = BOSTON, MASS.

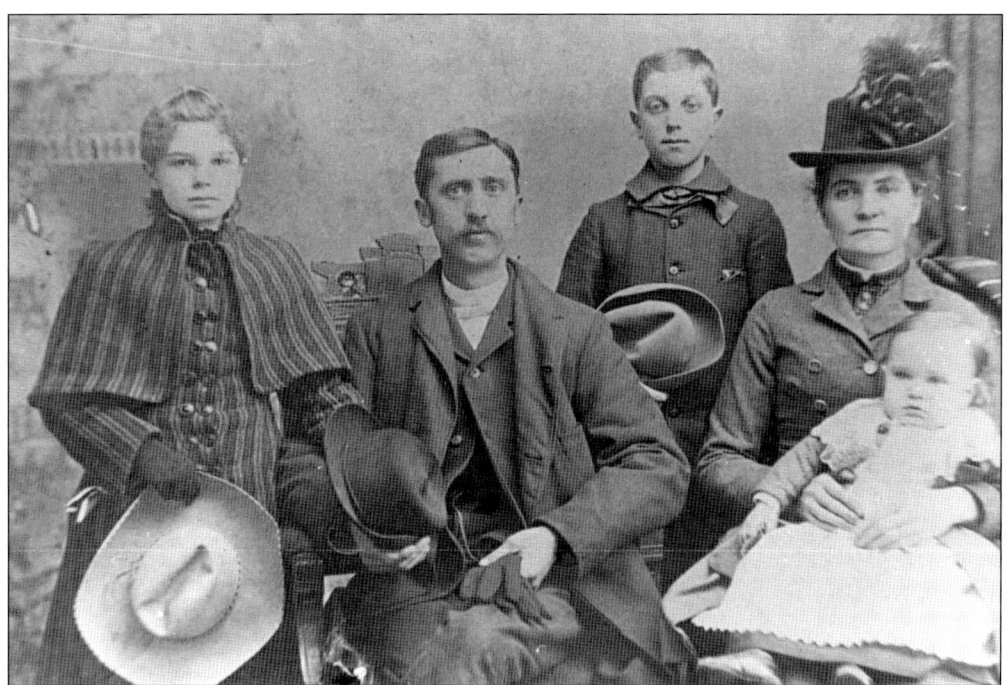

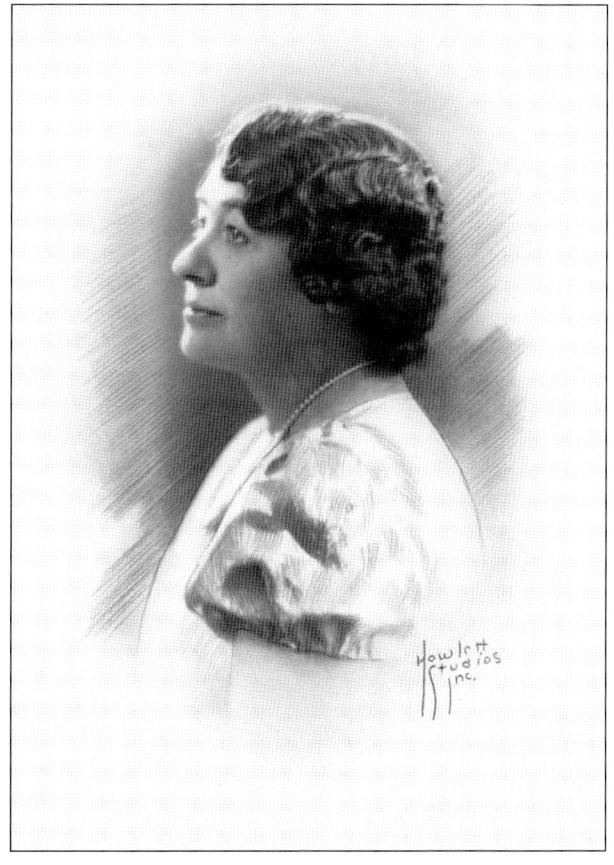

Above, the Markham family poses for a portrait in 1887. From left to right are Maud (1879–1944), Phil (1851–1930), Harry (1875–1895), Carrie (nee Shepard, 1856–1910), and Leigh (1887–1970). This photograph was taken the same year that Markham received his first air gun patent. Ultimately, family conflict pushed Phil out of the air rifle industry and Plymouth, Michigan. In the early 1890s, he hired young stenographer Carrie Blanche Shortman (1870–1937), seen at right, and fell in love with her. Stenographer Carrie quit working at Markham Air Rifle Company in May 1895. But, wife Carrie, a crusader with the Women's Christian Temperance Union, would not grant Phil a divorce. At the time, the family home was at 763 Ann Arbor Trail, right across the street from Kellogg Park in downtown Plymouth. (At right, courtesy of Leonard Burkhart Jr.)

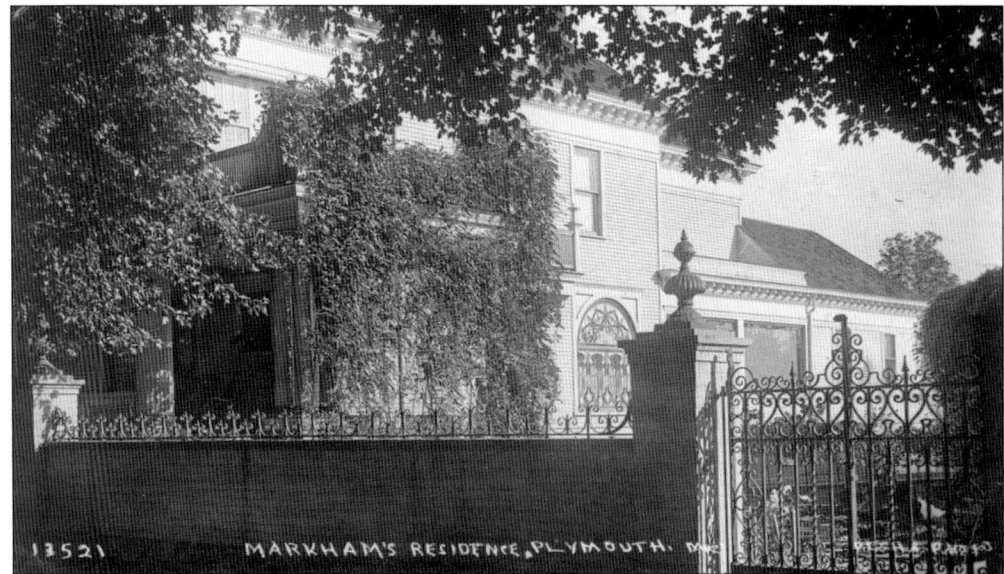

Probably to taunt his wife, Phil purchased property in 1900 on Union and Sutton (now Penniman) Streets—across the park from his family residence—and had a grand home built in 1901 for his mistress, Carrie (also called Blanche). The home (above) was an elaborate, Queen Anne–style mansion complete with columns, ornate decorations, wrought-iron fence, and a luxuriously extravagant garden on a sizable lot (below). Markham designed the home, which contained 17 rooms, including five bedrooms, a conservatory, sitting room, parlor, a large wraparound veranda, and a two-tiered portico. Blanche frequently sat on a swing on the second-floor portico, where she was taunted by local ladies who disapproved of the scandalous affair. Markham eventually had the upper portico enclosed to protect Blanche from the unkind remarks. The beautiful stained-glass window seen in the photograph above is now permanently housed in the Plymouth Historical Museum.

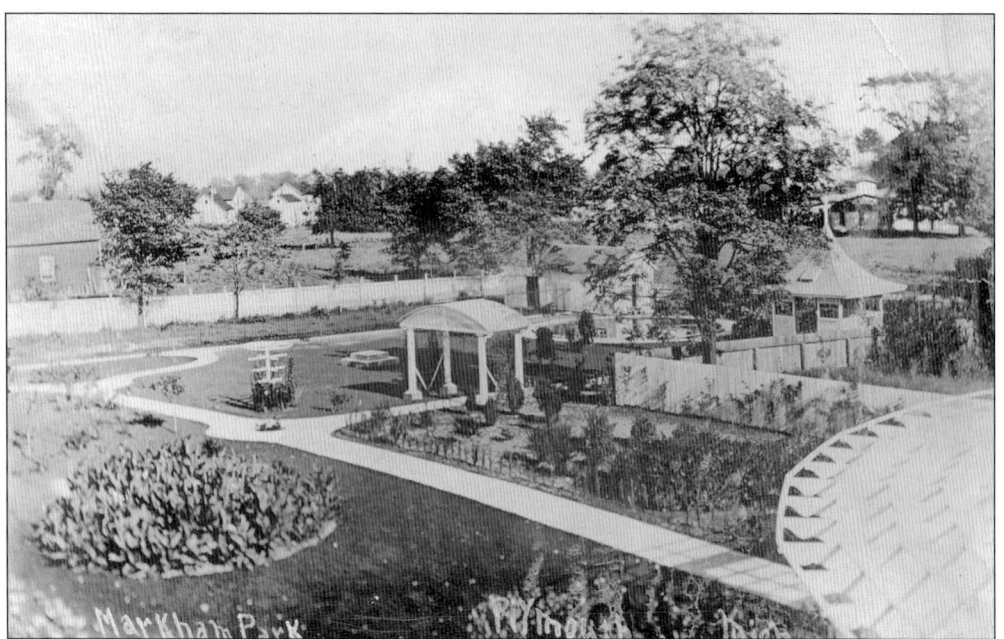

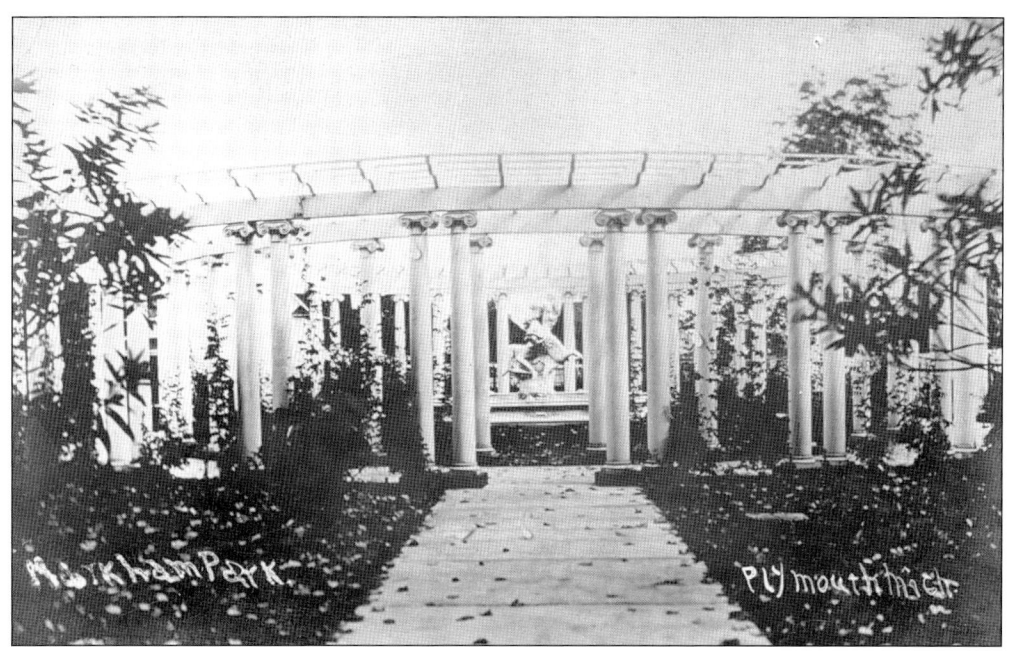

Markham also designed the landscaped garden to accommodate his love of birds. According to a study of the house done by Gregory H. Presley in 1983, "The most prominent feature of the original garden was the pergola [above]. It was about sixty feet in diameter with double wood columns at eight-foot increments marching around both sides of a concrete walkway. The columns supported an architrave and latticework designed for climbing plants. In the center was a beautiful cast metal statue of Atlantis slaying the dragon [below]. The pergola was destroyed by a tornado sometime later and was never rebuilt."

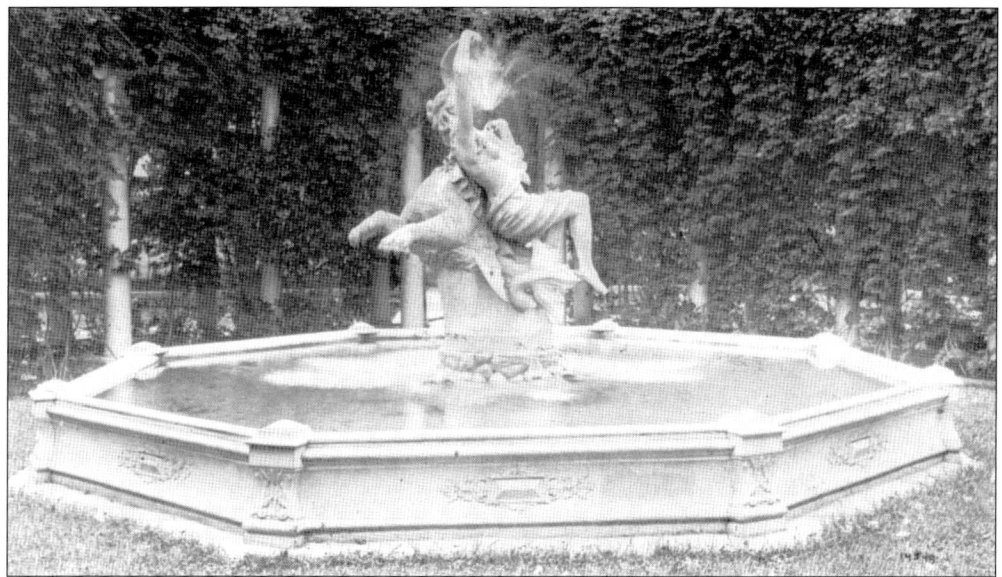

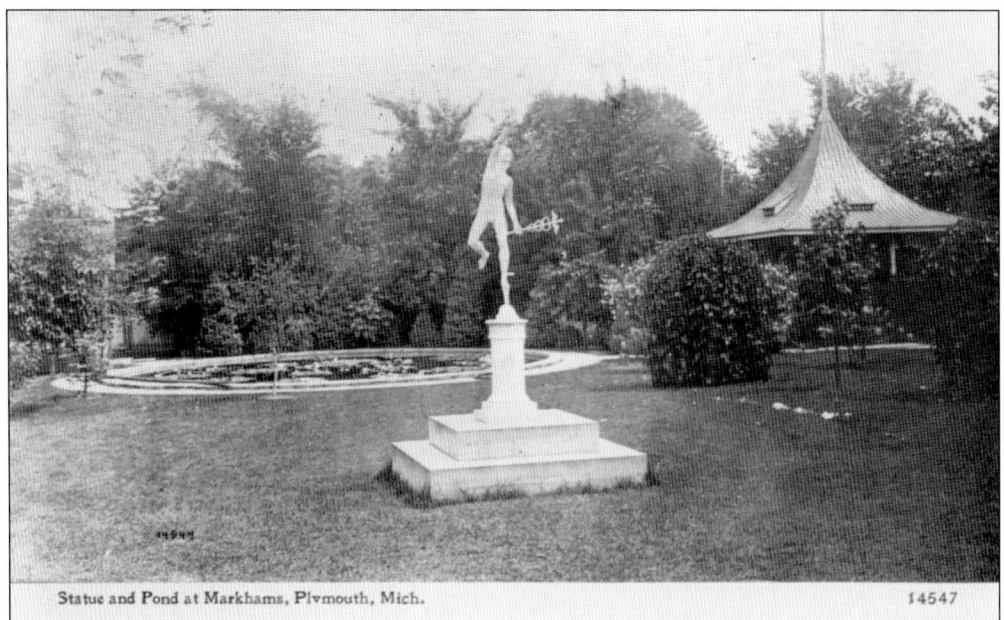

Statue and Pond at Markhams, Plymouth, Mich.   14547

The gardens also contained goldfish ponds, a gazebo, a tool shed, a deer park with three live deer, exotic flowers, and a statue of Mercury near a round lily pond (pictured). Local legend states that when the house was purchased by the Wilcox family in 1911, the naked Mercury statue was covered. The statue was sold by the Wilcox family after World War II and, as of 1975, was at a home in Garden City, New York.

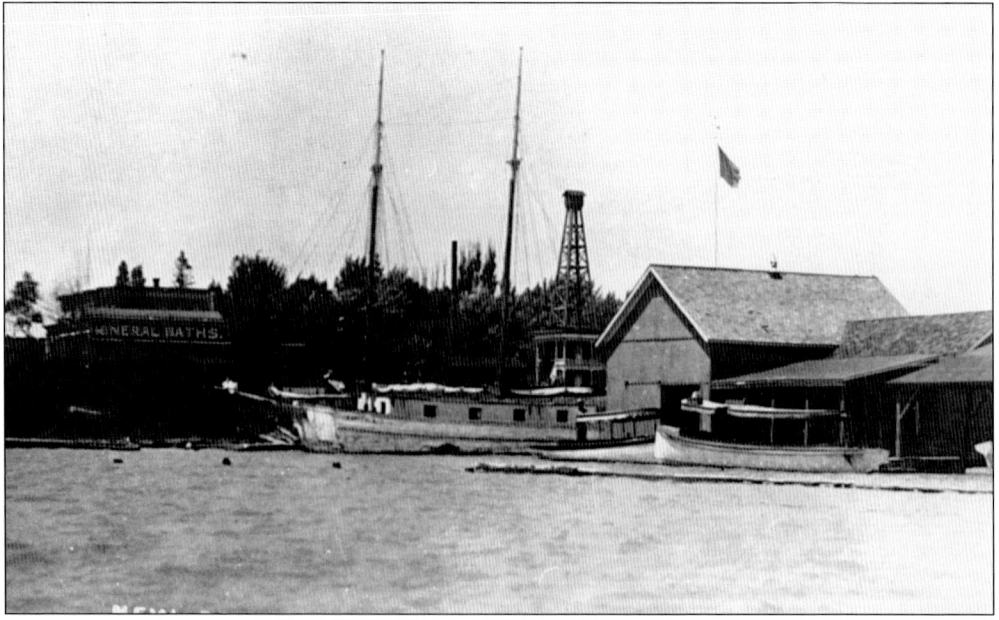

Around 1900, Markham bought waterfront property on Lake St. Clair in the little town of New Baltimore, Michigan. According to his son Leigh, Phil made improvements to the property, including a 900-foot pier and a summer resort home called "Bay Court." He also had a 47-foot cruiser built at his factory and transported to the lake. Because of the yachting cap he sported regularly, he earned the nickname "Captain." (Courtesy of Jim Perkins.)

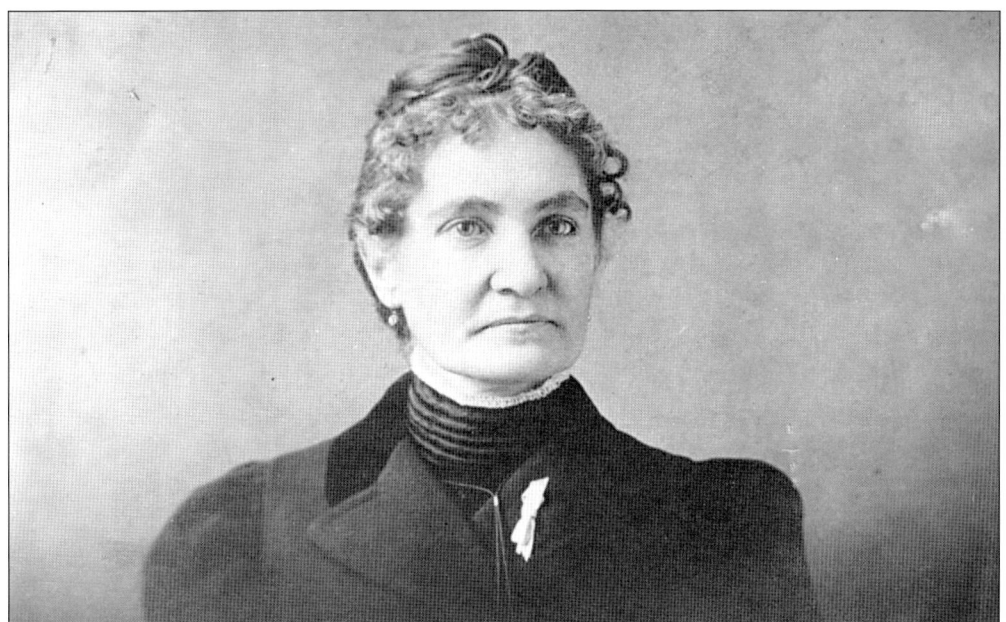

Carrie Shepard Markham (pictured) died on June 10, 1910, freeing Phil to marry his mistress. In October 1910, Blanche resigned as treasurer of the Markham Company; it is unclear when she had returned to work there. The couple wed on June 27, 1911, in Detroit. Regardless of the fact that Phil and Blanche were now legally married, local residents were unforgiving and shunned the couple. They sold both homes on Kellogg Park and moved to Hollywood, California.

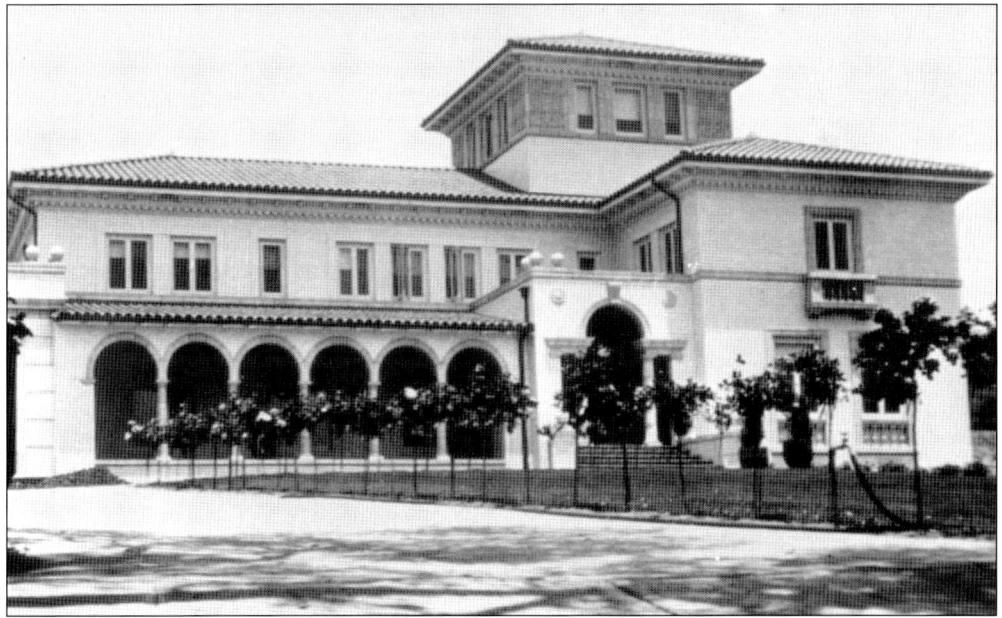

In California, the Markhams purchased vacant property at Hollywood and Vine Streets and built their next home. Phil became a shrewd real estate mogul, selling off property at what became the epicenter of the Hollywood movie industry. In 1927, the Markhams moved into the mansion seen here in Glendale, California. The home, called "Homeland" by the Markhams, was complete with fancy gardens and a bird sanctuary. Phil died here in 1930. (Courtesy of Jim Perkins.)

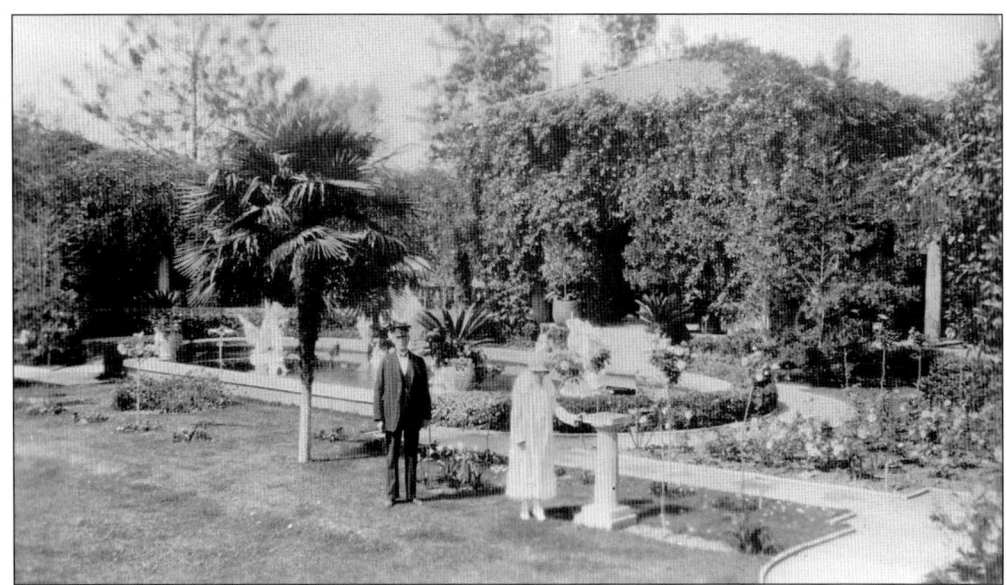

Captain Phil and Blanche Markham enjoy the gardens at one of their California homes. According to the Glendale Register of Historic Places, Phil "allowed his property to become a bird sanctuary where thousands of birds were to eventually find a refuge." It is unknown if this is the house in Hollywood or Glendale. Note the yachting cap atop Phil's head. (Courtesy of Jim Perkins.)

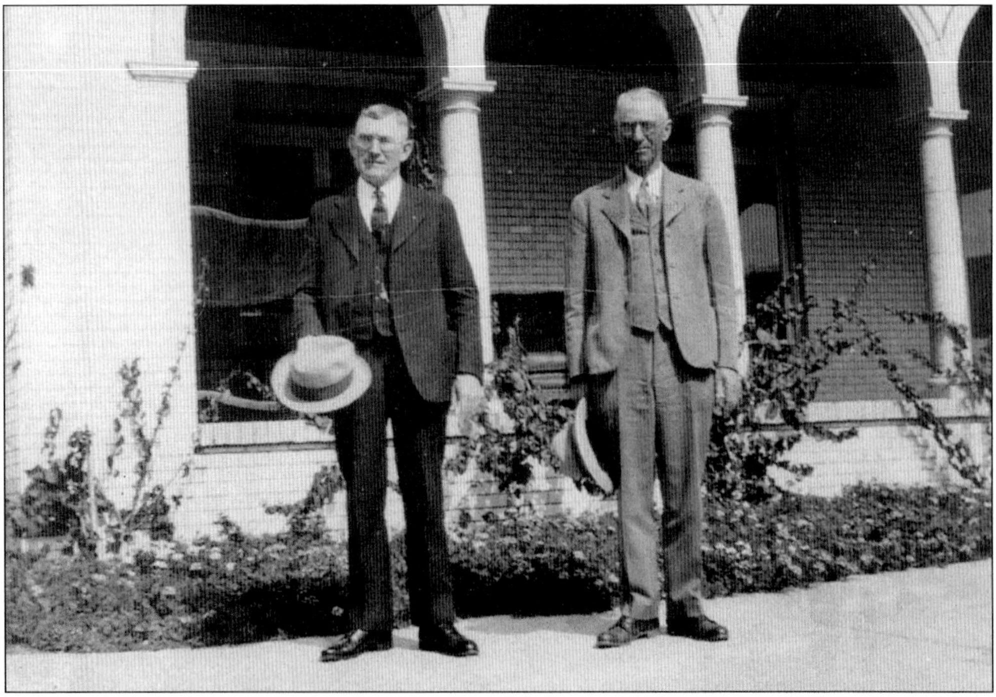

Ernest S. Roe (left) and Phil Markham stand outside Markham's home in Los Angeles. Roe became president of Markham Air Rifle Company after Markham left town and was responsible for negotiating the deal that sold Phil's interest in the company to Edward Hough and Charles Bennett of Daisy Manufacturing Company in 1916.

Two

Clarence Invents a Windmill

Clarence J. Hamilton had "an inventive brain of no mean ability," according to fellow Plymouthite and chronicler Charles H. Bennett. In 1880, Hamilton built a small model of his metal windmill invention to show to prospective stockholders for the first stock-held manufacturing company in Plymouth. While farmers had used windmills for centuries, they were made of wood and often had structural integrity issues. Hamilton's vane-less, all-metal version solved some of the problems inherent in the wooden models. He was producing the windmills on a limited basis in a shop near his home and applied for a patent, receiving it on December 13, 1881. The invention sparked the interest of several Plymouth residents, who put up the $30,000 in capital needed to build Plymouth's second factory building and begin operations. An 8,000-square-foot brick factory was built on 25 acres of land just north of Plymouth's downtown area on Union Street. The Plymouth Iron Windmill Company (PIWC) was incorporated on January 9, 1882. The first stockholders included Roswell L. Root, whose store Hamilton had used for his jewelry and watch repair business; Michael Conner, owner of Conner's Hardware in town and first president of PIWC; Henry W. Baker, the first president of Daisy; Lewis Cass Hough, the company treasurer; and Hamilton, who was named superintendent of works. In a descriptive catalog from the mid-1880s, the company boasted that the windmill's working parts "are made of the best wrought and grey iron and each mill has the personal supervision of the inventor, who is himself a practical mechanic." Unfortunately, sales of the windmill were not as anticipated; in January 1888, the PIWC stockholders met to consider liquidation. The motion was tabled, and a week later the stockholders unanimously voted to continue producing and selling windmills for another year. Later that year, the same inventive genius, Clarence Hamilton, approached the company's board with a design of an all-metal air rifle. Hough test-fired the gun and exclaimed, "Boy, that's a Daisy," a popular expression at the time. This company later became Daisy Manufacturing Company, which will be discussed in chapters five through seven.

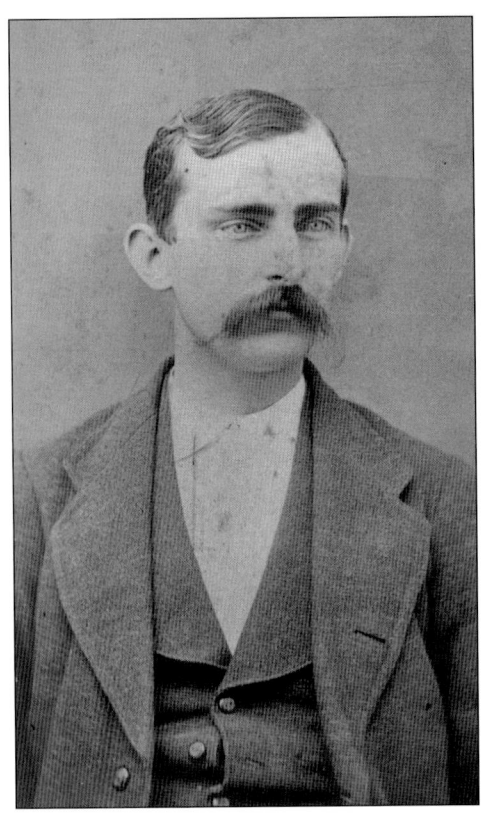

Clarence J. Hamilton (1849–1902) was repairing jewelry and watches when he improved on a design of an iron windmill. While working at the Plymouth Iron Windmill Company, he designed an air gun with a wooden stock. As an employee at the Plymouth Air Rifle Company, he designed an air gun with a wire stock. After resigning from Daisy in 1898, he designed a .22-caliber rifle with his son Coello. (Courtesy of Rosemary Steele.)

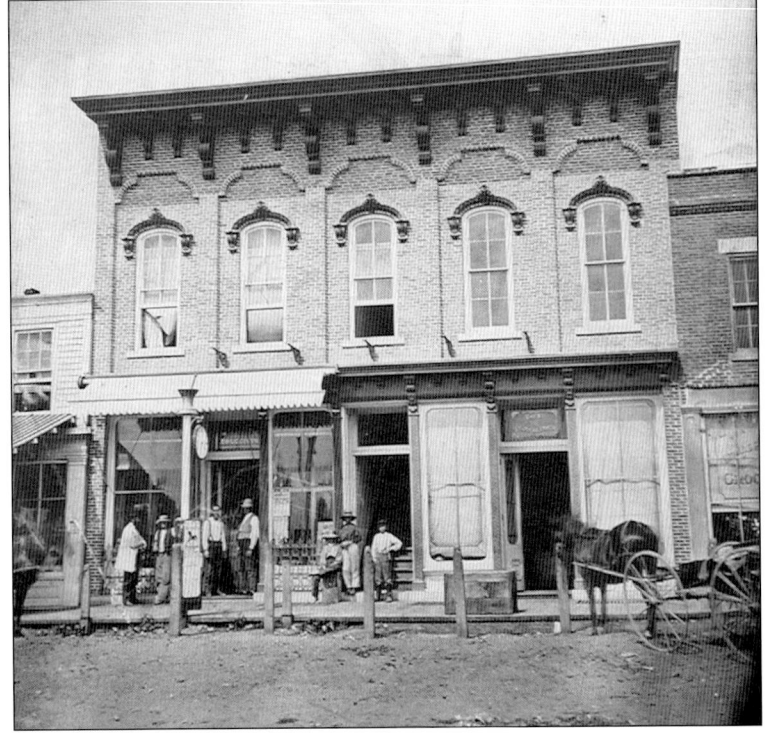

Roswell Root's storefront was in the left lower half of this building in 1869. When Hamilton arrived in 1874, he set up his jewelry and watch repair shop in the left front portion of Root's store. Root was a druggist and Plymouth postmaster and ran the post office behind Hamilton's counter. Across from Hamilton's counter, Root had the only soda fountain in town. The First National Bank was in the back of the building.

Clarence Hamilton applied for his windmill patent on September 14, 1881, stating he invented an improvement in windmills "whereby the sails of the wind-wheel are automatically presented to the action of the wind . . . for throwing the sails out of the wind and . . . various combinations of the parts." He assigned half of the patent to R.L. Root of Plymouth. The patent was granted on December 13, 1881, with patent no. 250,661 (at right). The Plymouth Iron Windmill Company stationery contained a line drawing of the Hamilton windmill in a farm setting (below), as farmers were the primary market for the company's product. The company catalog included a note "to the farmer" claiming "all animals require pure, cool water during the sultry months, as does the human, and while 'God's free winds of heaven' are furnishing the power to produce health-giving water to his stock, the farmer has leisure to improve and beautify his premises."

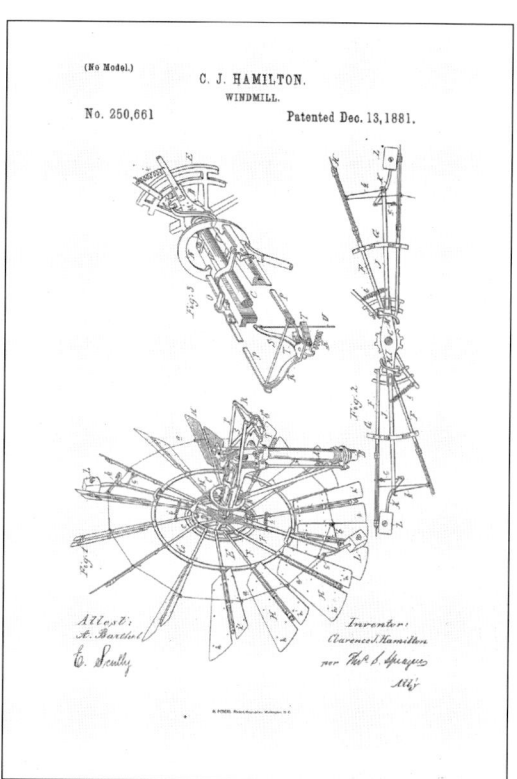

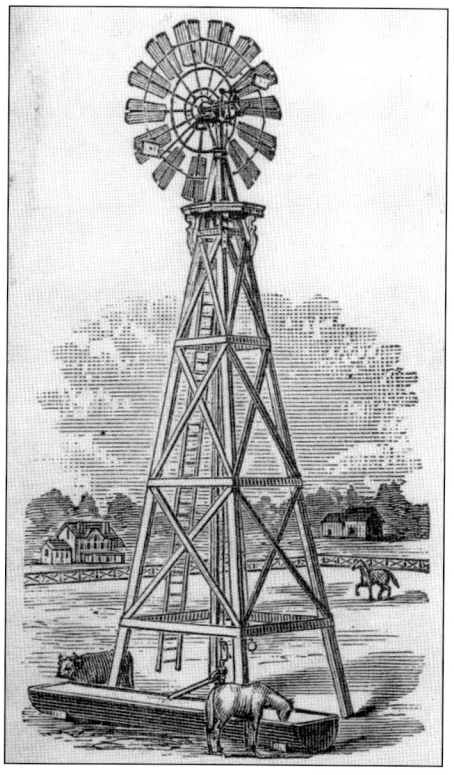

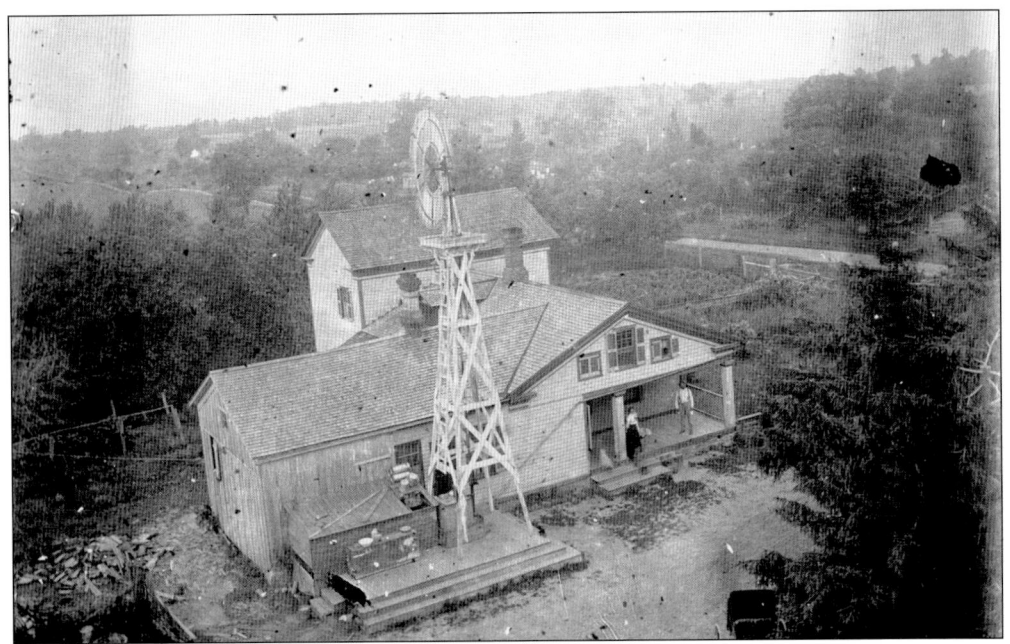

Local Plymouth photographer Charles Draper took this image of a rural farm with what appears to be a Hamilton windmill from the Plymouth Iron Windmill Company. The location of the photograph is unknown, but is likely somewhere within Plymouth Township in the 1890s.

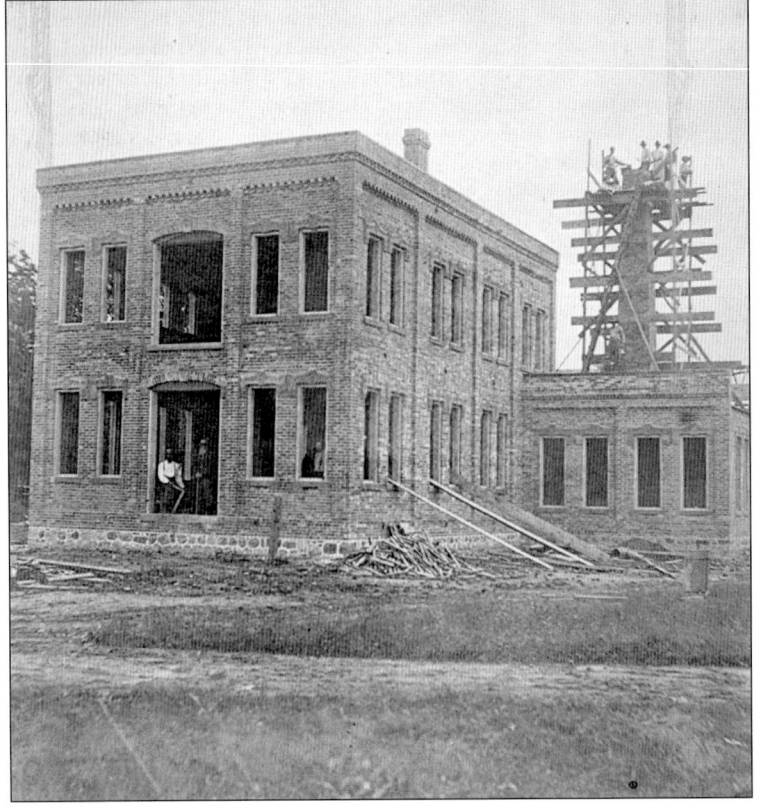

Plymouth's second factory, and first brick factory, was built in 1882 for the Plymouth Iron Windmill Company. The building was two stories, 8,000 square feet, and fronted on Union Street just north of downtown Plymouth.

Three

THE SHORT-LIVED PLYMOUTH AIR RIFLE COMPANY

Phil Markham's invention of the air rifle in 1886 must have whetted Clarence Hamilton's invention appetite, as he was soon at the drawing board again. After developing his own air gun with a wooden stock and an iron barrel, he left the windmill company and convinced friend Cyrus A. Pinckney to sell his Red Front Store and join in a new venture: the Plymouth Air Rifle Company (PARC). In 1888, the partners bought a factory adjacent to the Plymouth Iron Windmill Company, hired salesman Ed Crosby, and began manufacturing their version of the air gun. Hamilton and Pinckney received a patent for the gun on October 2, 1888, about four months after the company sent out its first order of guns. In mid-1888, Markham Air Rifle Company was producing 100 guns a day, while PARC, just across the tracks, was turning out 50 handmade guns daily. In 1888, Hamilton presented another air rifle design to the board of the PIWC, where he still held stock. The board liked what they saw, and Hamilton left PARC to return to his former company. According to the January 25, 1889, *Plymouth Mail*, "This will make three gun factories in Plymouth. At this rate our town can soon be classed with such gun producing cities as Hartford, Springfield, and Ilion!" Four gun models were manufactured by PARC during its short, six-year history: the Plymouth, the Challenge, the Magic, and the Bijou. The company also dabbled in nickel plating, manufactured the Yankee Mole Trap, and had its own band. Railroad strikes in 1894 were the beginning of the end for the Plymouth Air Rifle Company. After months of being shut down, the factory started producing again in September. But, on October 14, 1894, it mysteriously burned down, and the company, being underinsured, was unable to rebuild. An attempt to get funding from the village fell on deaf ears, perhaps because the village common council consisted of a couple men from competing air rifle companies, Roswell Root (PIWC) and Elmer W. Chaffee (Markham).

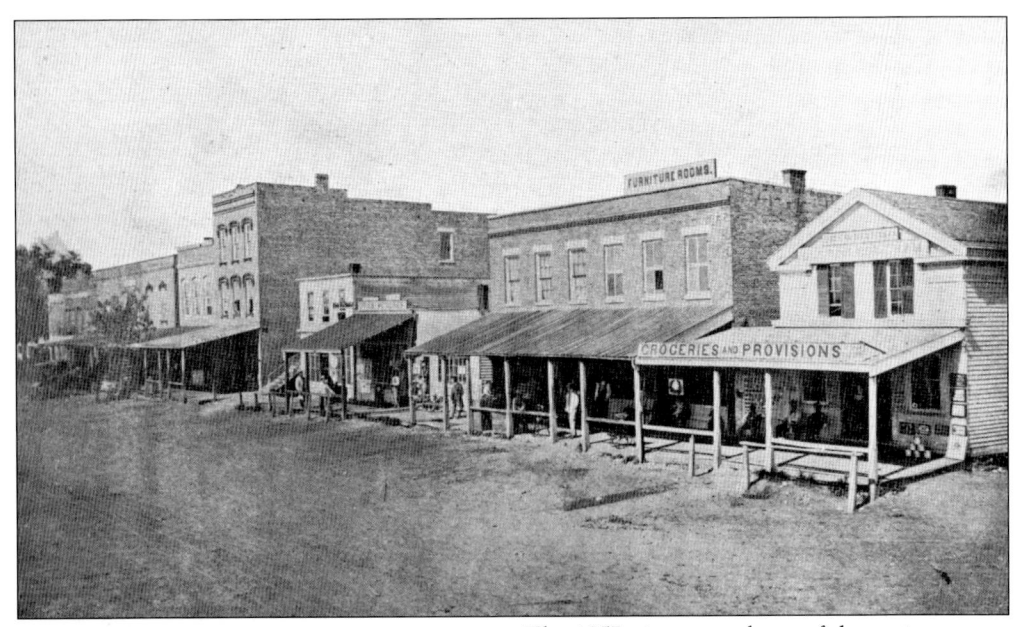

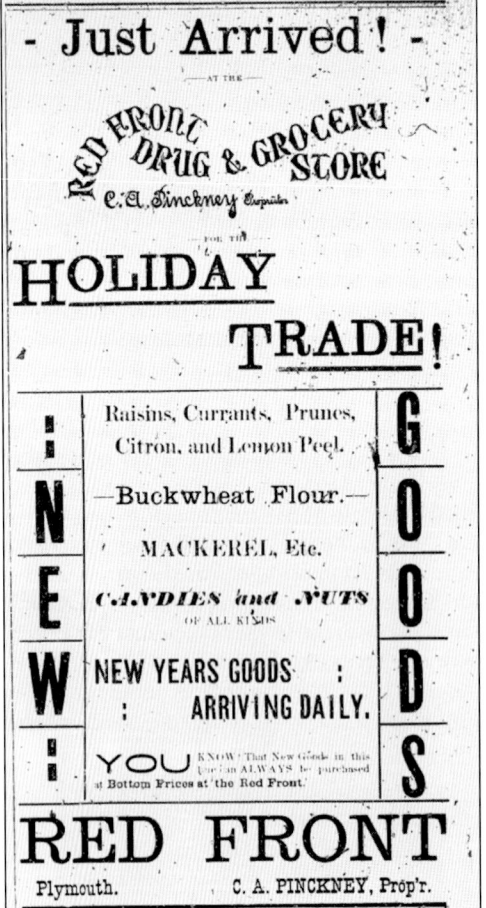

The 1857 view seen above of the main business district of Plymouth includes the white wooden building on the far right that housed A.B. Coleman's Grocery and Provisions Store. Cyrus A. Pinckney, Coleman's nephew and a pharmacist, took over the business around 1880 with partner Elmer W. Chaffee. After a few years, Pinckney bought out Chaffee when he went to work at Markham Manufacturing Company. In March 1888, Pinckney sold the store to his half-brother John L. Gale to get capital to launch the Plymouth Air Rifle Company with inventor Clarence J. Hamilton. Pinckney called the store the Red Front Drug & Grocery Store because, according to Pinckney, "It had a red front." The ad at left appeared in the November 11, 1887, *Plymouth Mail*.

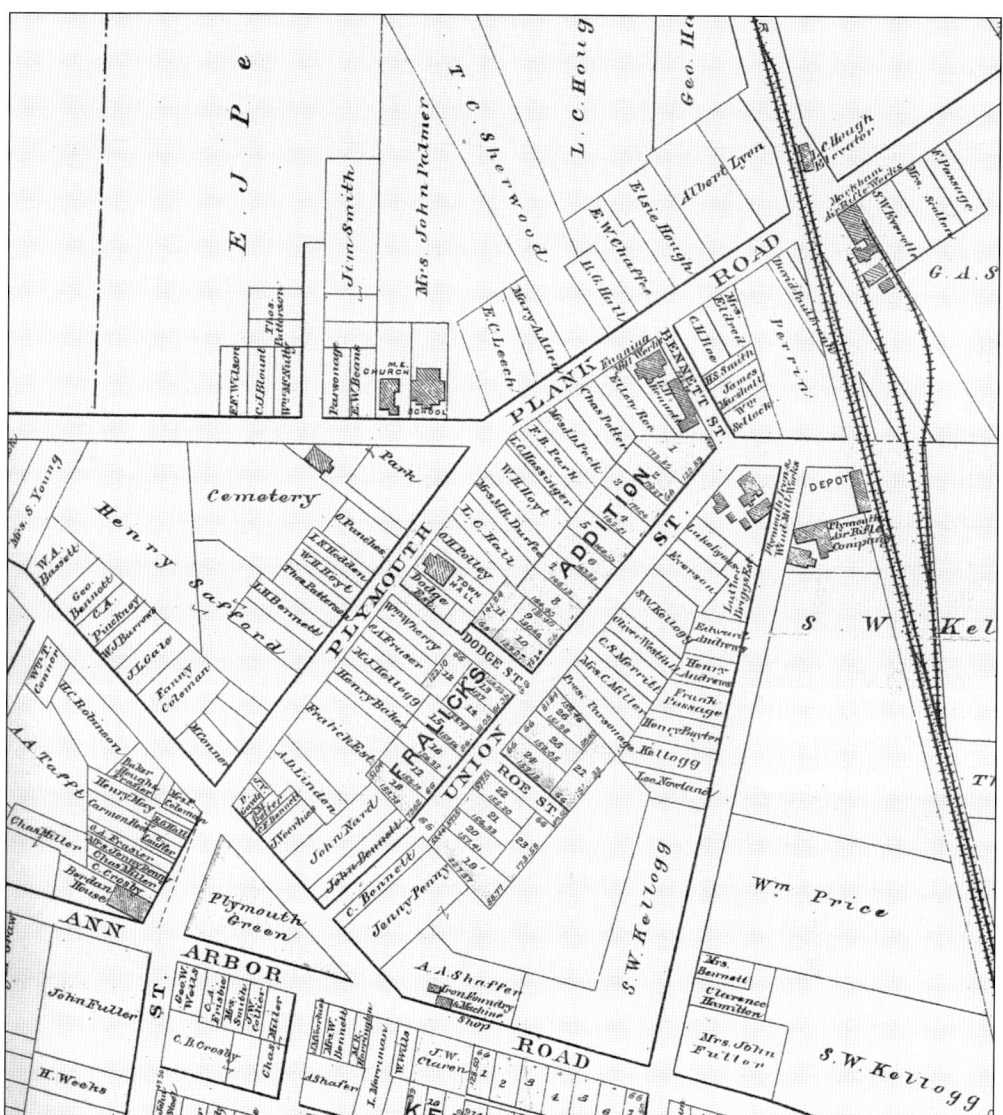

An 1893 map of the village of Plymouth gives a birds-eye view of the layout of the area. In the upper right corner sits the Markham Air Rifle "Works" along the right side of the railroad tracks, while on the left side of the tracks next to the depot sits the "Plymouth Iron & Windmill Works" and the Plymouth Air Rifle Company, separated by Depot Street. Further south on that same street, just north of Ann Arbor Road (now Ann Arbor Trail), is the home of Clarence Hamilton. The main business block of Plymouth is just west of the Plymouth Green (now Kellogg Park). The unnamed diagonal street to the north of the business block is Sutton Street (now Penniman Avenue), where Cyrus Pinckney's house is located. Phil Markham's house at the time was northeast of his factory on Liberty Street (not seen on this map).

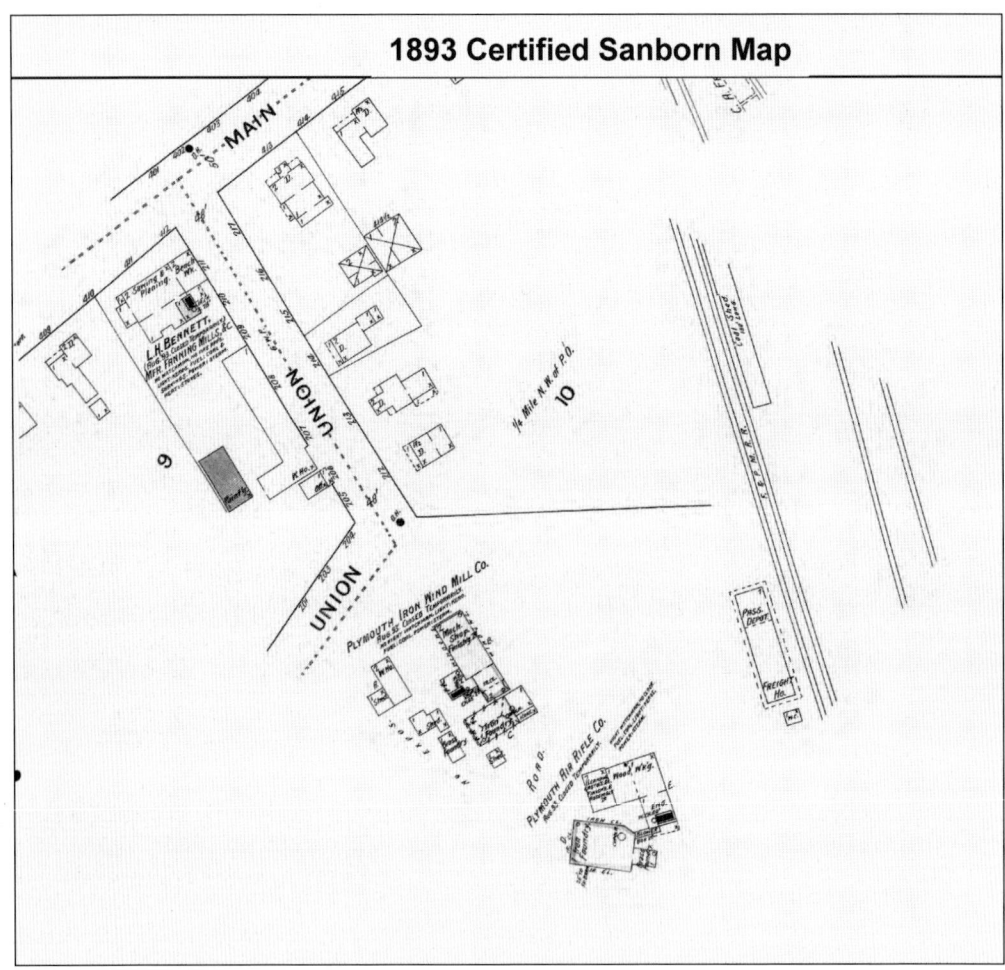

This 1893 Sanborn fire insurance map of Plymouth clearly shows the proximity of the Plymouth Air Rifle Company (PARC) to the Plymouth Iron Windmill Company. The Markham Air Rifle Company was just north of the two factories on the other side of the tracks. The March 30, 1888, *Plymouth Mail* noted, "Pinckney & Hamilton have bought the E.W. Beam shop, near the F. & P.M. [Flint & Pere Marquette] depot to be used as a factory for the Plymouth air rifle. Power, we understand, will be had from the wind mill factory by means of a cable." Apparently that arrangement did not work out because the April 6, 1888, *Plymouth Mail* declared, "Pinckney & Hamilton will not use power from the windmill shops for their gun factory, but have bought an engine." This is the only fire insurance map that PARC appears in since the factory burned in 1894. (Courtesy of Environmental Data Resources.)

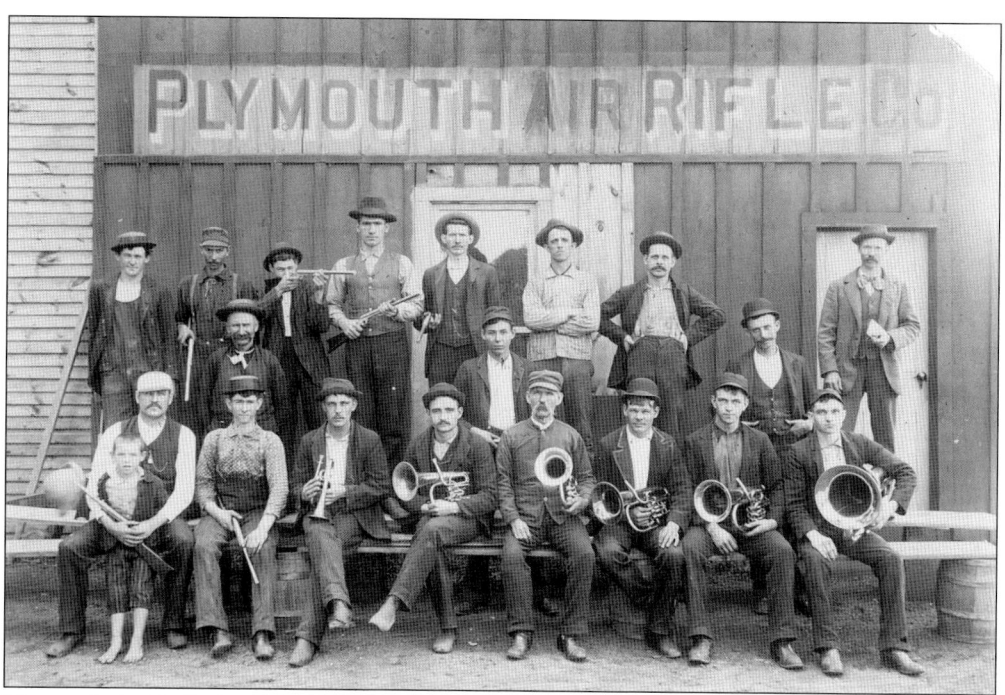

Plymouth Air Rifle Company had its own band made up of employees. Pictured from left to right are (first row) three unidentified, Henry Tanger, Frank Ray, Charles Holloway, Joe Tessman, Henry Sage, unidentified; (second row) Dan Smith, unidentified, Pink Stewart; (third row) unidentified, Lew Fisher, Art Burden, Bert Gunsolly, Jim Cooper, unidentified, band leader George Sage, and W.J. Burrows. Some employees sport Bijou air rifles. This is the only known image of the company.

The Plymouth Air Rifle Company sent this advertising flyer "to the trade" on June 15, 1888, shortly after the start of production of the Plymouth "Breech-Loading Air Rifle." The company was marketing the gun on price, quality, and demand of boys and girls who had just started summer vacation.

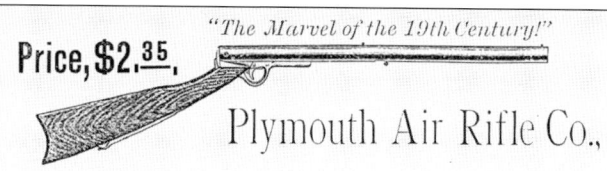

"*The Marvel of the 19th Century!*"

Price, $2.35.

Plymouth Air Rifle Co.,

Plymouth, Michigan, June 15, 1888.

TO THE TRADE—

GENTLEMEN—We respectfully ask your attention to enclosed circular on the merits of our

WONDERFUL ✦ BREECH-LOADING ✦ AIR ✦ RIFLE.

This gun is beyond any comparison in the necessary qualities of perfection and cheapness.

It is not a common wooden gun, but has Blued Iron Barrel, Brass Sights, Fine Oil Finished Walnut, or Antique Oak, Stock and Nickeled Trimmings.

The Plymouth Rifle in fact compares favorably with eight and ten dollar guns and we have fixed the

RETAIL PRICE AT ONLY $2.35!

We shall take pleasure in quoting you a Quantity Price, which will net you a handsome profit.

Though we have just begun the manufacture and have advertised little, the daily inquiries we have received are a surprise to us—indicating clearly that "The Plymouth Air Rifle" meets a popular demand and is destined to have an enormous sale. School vacation is just at hand and we want this Marvelous Lawn and Parlor Rifle put upon your territory to meet the demand of Girls and Boys—old and young—for a new Pastime for the Summer Holidays.

Trusting to hear from you, we are—Very Respectfully,

PLYMOUTH AIR RIFLE COMPANY,

Plymouth, Michigan.

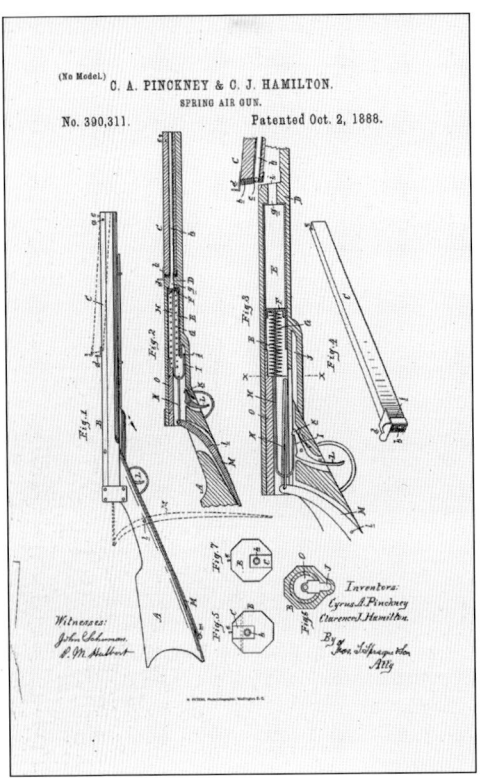

Cyrus Pinckney and Clarence Hamilton applied for their first patent on January 10, 1888. It claimed "certain new and useful Improvements in Spring Air-Guns." The patent was granted no. 390,311 on October 2, 1888. Hamilton applied for a patent for an "Air-Gun" on April 10, 1888, assigning one half of the invention to Pinckney. The patent was granted no. 390,297, also on October 2, 1888.

The Plymouth Air Rifle Company advertised its nickel-plating service to refit old stoves in several issues of the *Plymouth Mail*, including this ad from the September 28, 1888, issue of the newspaper. The company was trying to expand its local offerings to recoup its investment.

A young boy from Honesdale, Pennsylvania, poses with his Plymouth air rifle from the Plymouth Air Rifle Company. (Courtesy of Wesley Powers.)

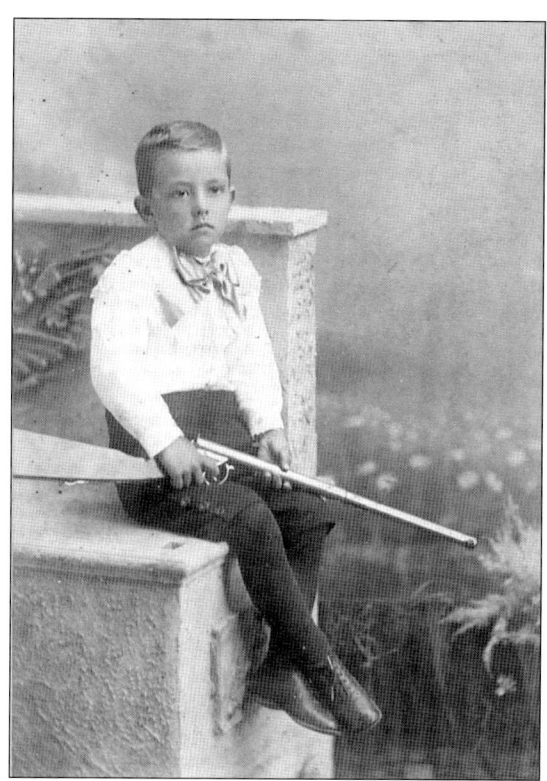

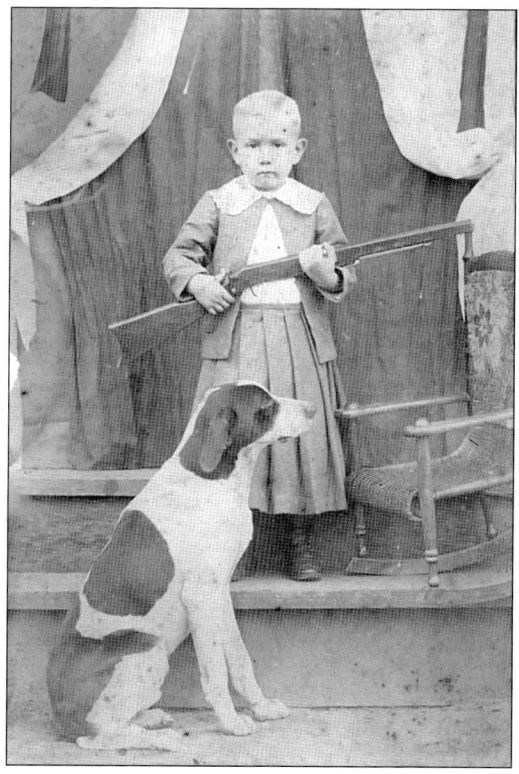

Another young boy poses with his dog and his Plymouth Air Rifle Company Challenge air rifle. (Courtesy of Wesley Powers.)

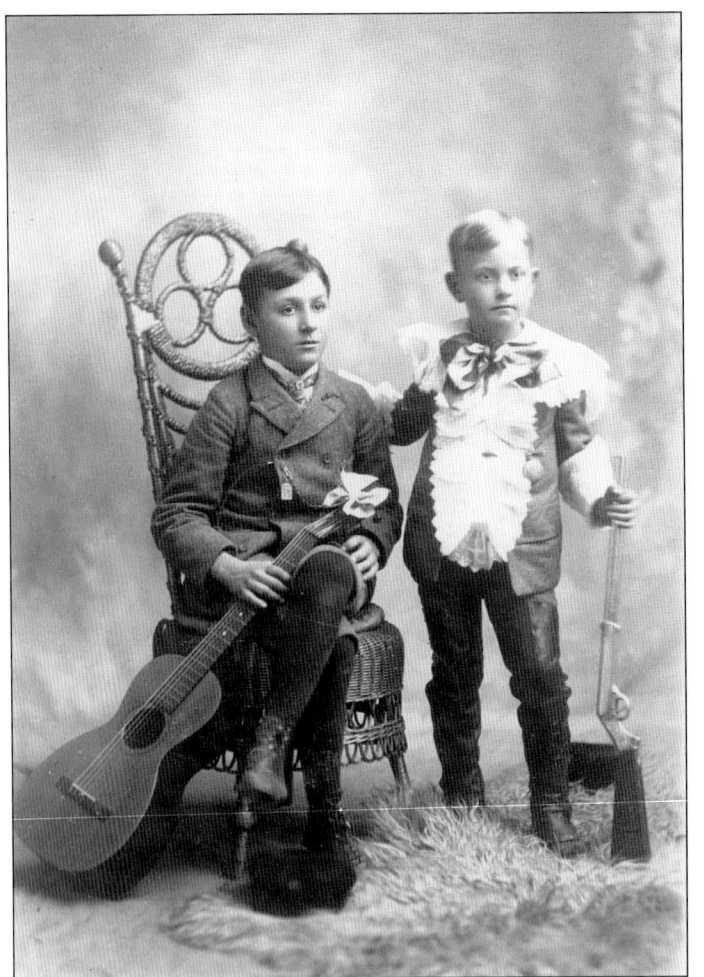

Two young boys, one with a guitar and the other with a Bijou air rifle from the Plymouth Air Rifle Company, pose in this portrait from St. Louis, Missouri. (Courtesy of Wesley Powers.)

This rare Plymouth Air Rifle Company envelope shows illustrations of both the Magic and the Bijou air rifles. The envelope is addressed to the J.A. Dubuar Manufacturing Company in Northville, the town adjacent to Plymouth. Dubuar had begun business as a lumber company but expanded its operations in the 1880s, eventually manufacturing its own air rifles, including the Globe. Daisy purchased the Dubuar Manufacturing Company in 1904. (Courtesy of Michael Pappas.)

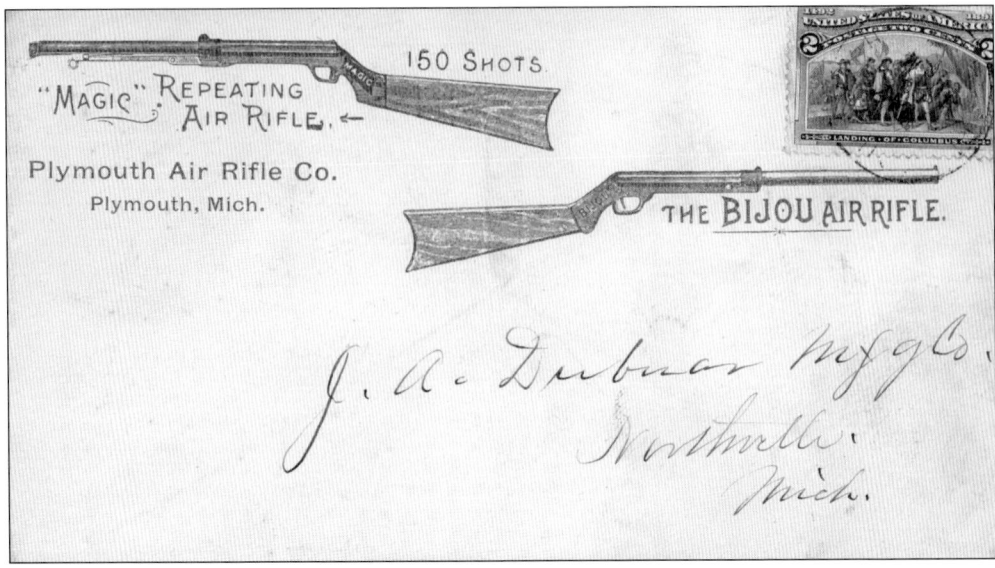

Four
"Boy, That's a Daisy!"

The Plymouth Iron Windmill Company Board of Directors embraced Clarence Hamilton's new, all-metal air rifle, which they dubbed the Daisy. Sales of windmills had remained sluggish, so the stockholders reexamined the state of the company in January 1889. They decided to accept a proposal from Hamilton and Roswell Root for the company to manufacture and sell the Daisy air gun, with Hamilton and Root granting sales rights as long as the company continued to make a profit. If PIWC stopped manufacturing the gun or neglected its sales, the rights would revert to the inventors. Production began in earnest in April 1889. It was the same year that the company reported earnings rather than a loss, with sales tripling from the previous year. Charles H. Bennett was hired by the company in January 1891 as a salesman. He traveled to Chicago and showed the gun to Hibbard, Spencer, Bartlett & Company, and the company wanted an exclusive agreement in Chicago for the purchase of 10,000 guns. According to *Daisy's Diary: 80 Years of Progress*, Bennett nearly fainted and "to stall for time to find out if the factory could produce that many, told the Hibbard buyer Daisy's main office would have to pass on the 'exclusivity' requirement. [He] wired the factory, [and the] Board of Directors met and decided they could make [them] if given six months to do so." Earnings and sales continued to grow, and the company was able to offer dividends in cash for the first time in 1893. PIWC disposed of its windmill assets in 1894, moving forward with its future in the air rifle business. At the January 26, 1895, board meeting, the name of the company was officially changed to Daisy Manufacturing Company.

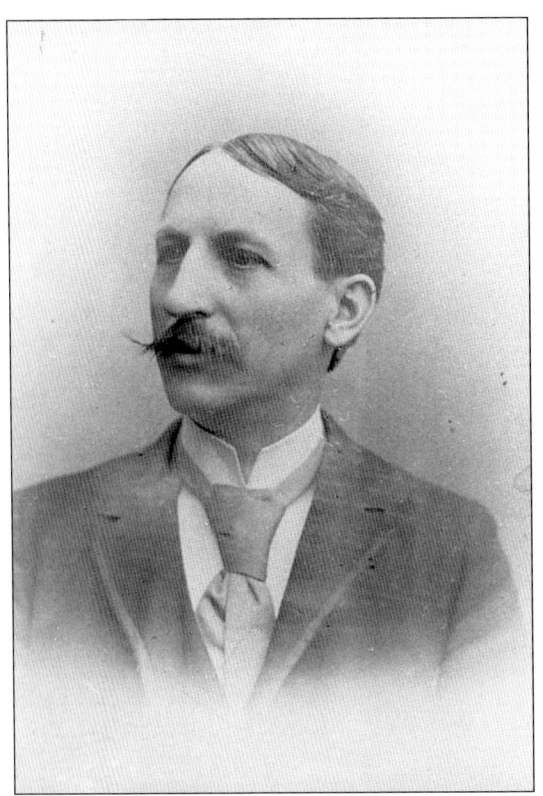

Lewis Cass Hough (1846–1902) was the general manager of the Plymouth Iron Windmill Company when Clarence Hamilton introduced his new, all-metal air rifle invention to the board of directors. He is credited with saying, "Boy, that's a Daisy!" after test-firing the air rifle. Hough also served as a Michigan state senator, supervisor of Plymouth Township, president of the village, and vice president of the Plymouth Savings Bank. He began the Hough dynasty at Daisy Manufacturing.

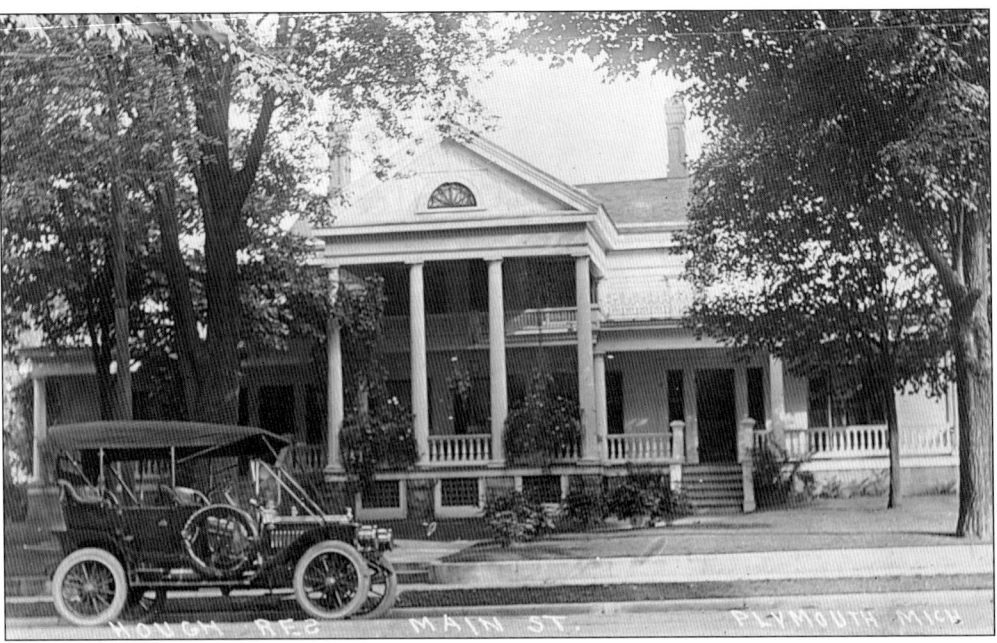

Lewis C. Hough built his home at 243 North Main Street in Plymouth about 1885. At the time, Hough owned the L.C. Hough Elevator Company, which was directly across the street from where Phil Markham built his factory. After Hough's death in 1902, his son Edward C. moved into the home with his family. The house burned down in January 1963.

Roswell L. Root (1841–1903) believed in Clarence Hamilton's inventions so much that he was one of the founders of the Plymouth Iron Windmill Company. Root had rented space to Hamilton in his store on Main Street until Hamilton became superintendent at PIWC. Root served in Company C, 24th Michigan Infantry during the Civil War, ran his business in Plymouth, and served as a trustee on the Plymouth Village Common Council.

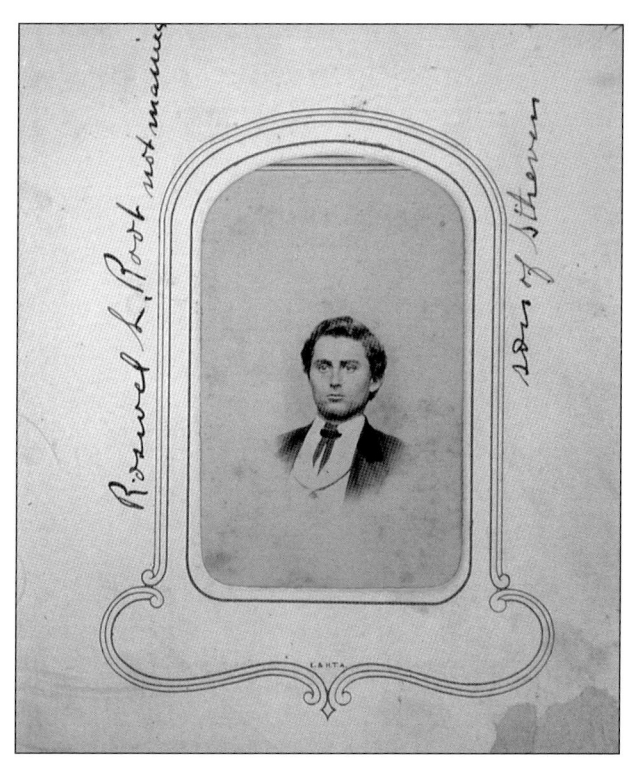

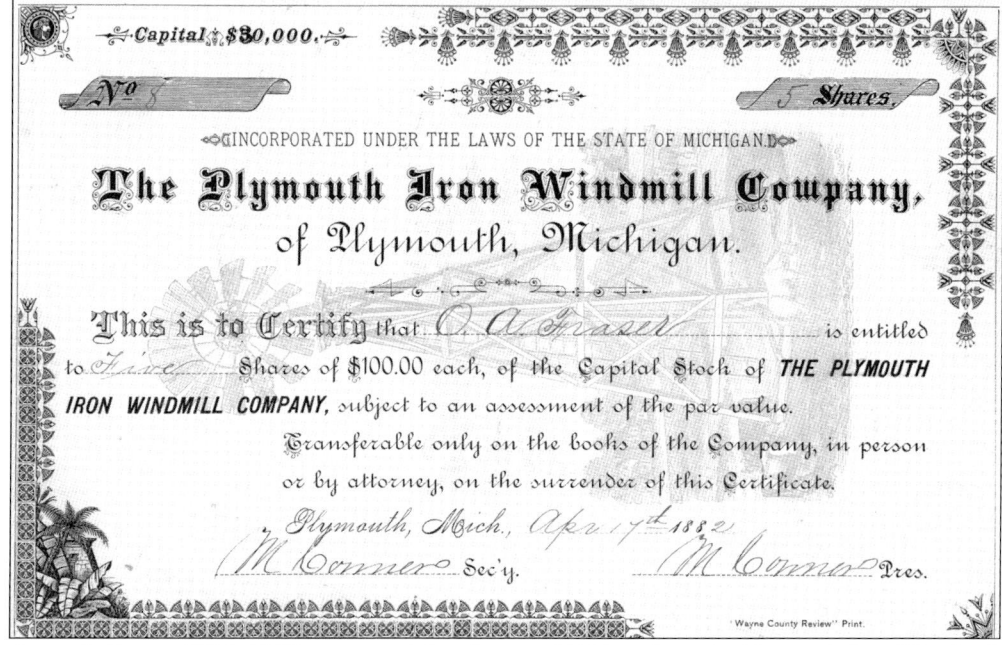

Oscar A. Fraser (1829–1912) was issued five shares of $100 each in the Plymouth Iron Windmill Company on April 17, 1882, three months after he attended the initial stockholder's meeting for the company. Fraser served as the second president of the company from 1884 to 1885. He was also in the mercantile business, was a cashier of the First National Bank, and later a director of the Plymouth Savings Bank.

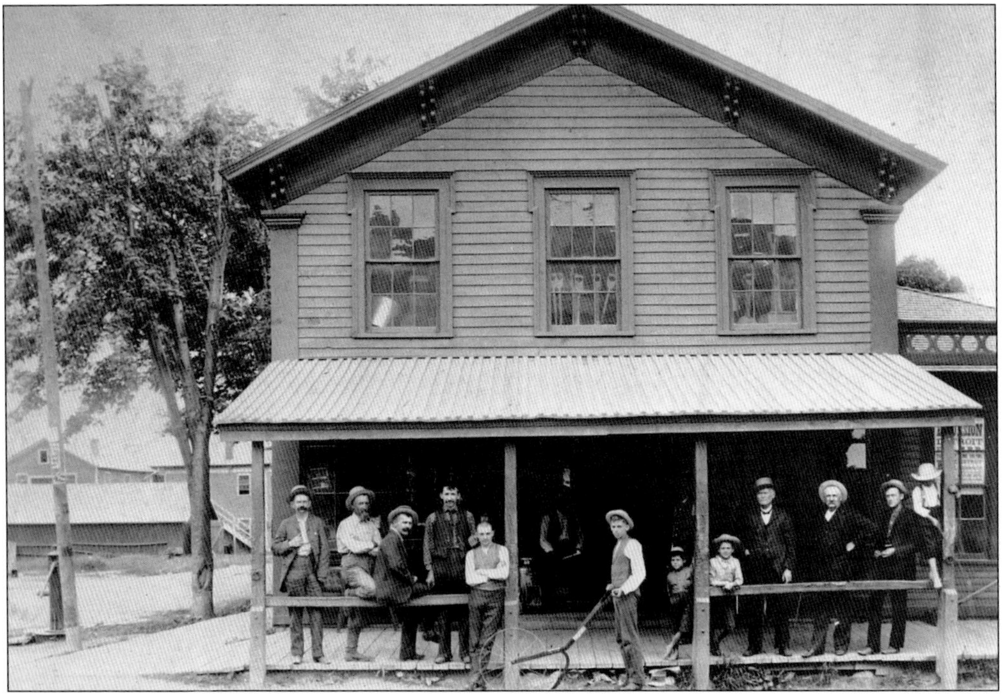

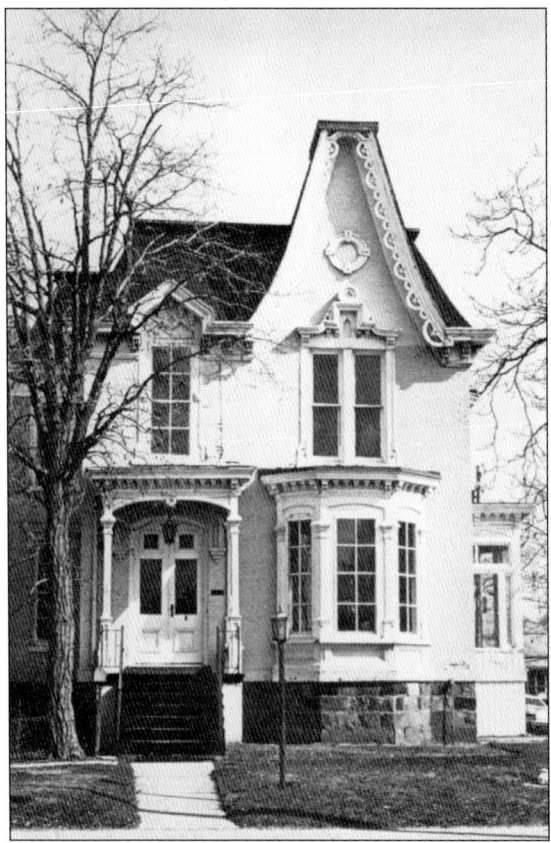

Michael Conner (1829–1895) was the first and fifth president of PIWC, serving from 1882 to 1883 and 1889 to 1892. He owned Conner Hardware Store (pictured) at the corner of Main and Sutton Streets from 1857 until his death, was a musician in the Plymouth Community Band, and served as village president 10 times. Conner is the third man from the right, and Henry Baker stands to the right of Conner. This building was replaced in 1893 after a fire.

Henry W. Baker (1833–1919) built this Second Empire–style house on South Main Street in 1875. The home is located in what was then considered the fashionable residential section of town. Baker was a founder of the Plymouth Iron Windmill Company and served as president from 1887 to 1888 and then president of Daisy from 1895 to 1919. The house still stands and is in the National Register of Historic Places. (Courtesy of Plymouth Community Arts Council.)

Calvin B. Crosby (1829–1909) was the third president of PIWC in 1886, the same year he served as Plymouth village president for the second time (he was also president in 1871). During the Civil War, Crosby formed Company C of the 24th Michigan Infantry Regiment and served briefly as its captain. He was a Plymouth merchant for many years and served as a Michigan state senator from 1887 to 1888. (Courtesy of Michigan State Archives.)

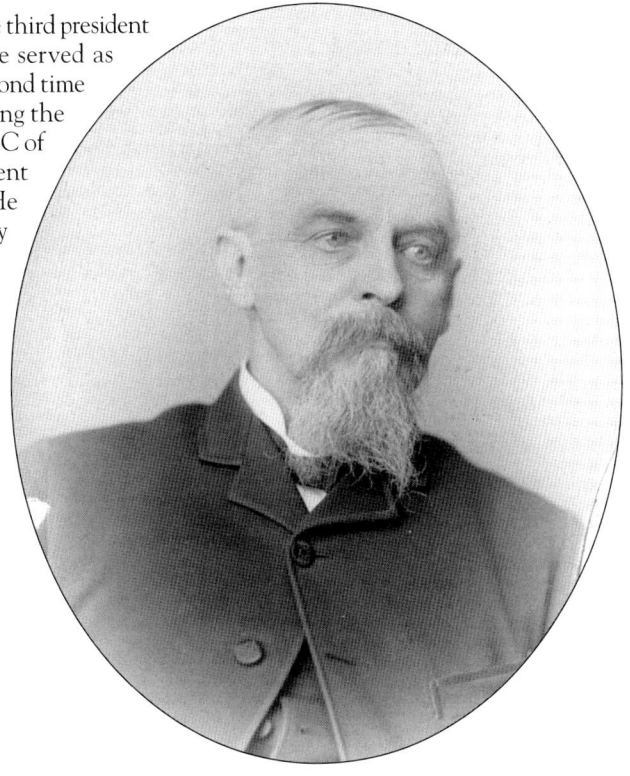

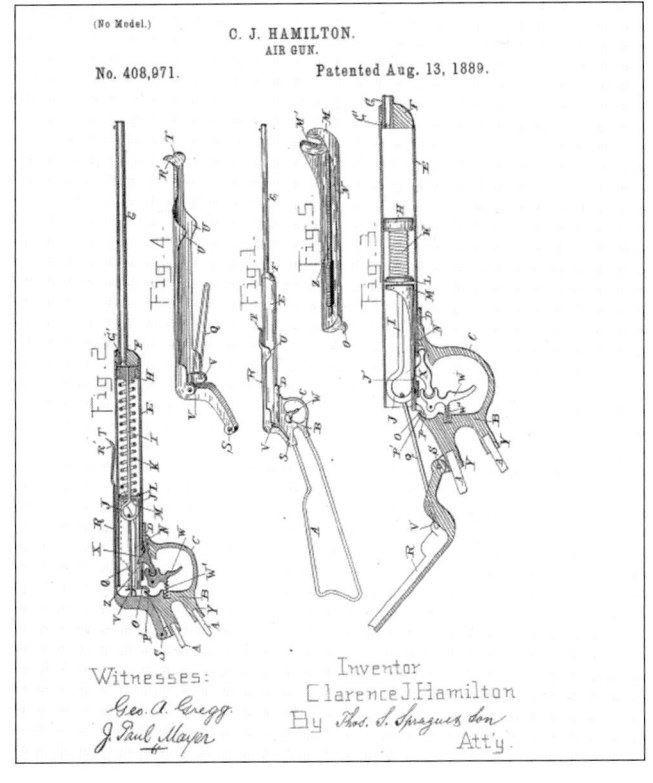

According to *Daisy, It All Starts Here*, "On March 6, 1888, [Clarence] Hamilton approached the windmill company with an all-metal air gun of his own design. He chose to take it to the windmill company because it had blast furnaces and it was equipped to mold and stamp the metal parts necessary to build his gun." Hamilton received patent no. 408,971 on August 13, 1889, assigning half to Roswell Root.

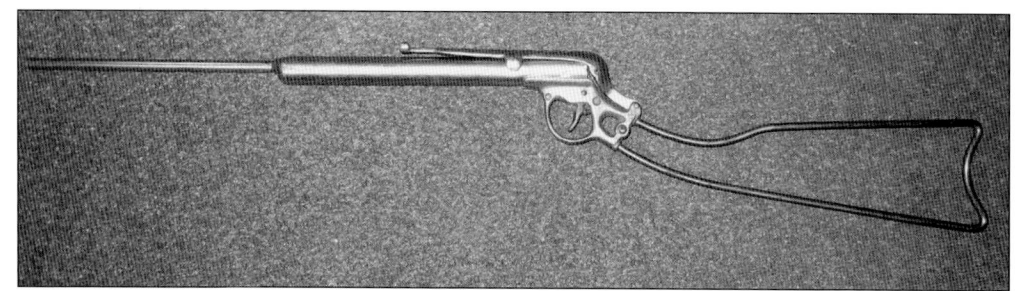

PIWC began production of its air gun around April 1889, according to the *Plymouth Mail*. The First Model Daisy, pictured above, is considered variation four because it includes the patent date and uses block lettering with a serif. There were five variations of the First Model, and all but the first variation have a brass frame; the first variation has a cast-iron frame. All variations have a wire skeleton stock. According to *An Encyclopedia of Daisy Plymouth Guns*, "Starting with the very first guns, all of the company's air rifles had the word 'DAISY' printed on them." This First Model Daisy is on permanent exhibit at the Plymouth Historical Museum. Seen below is the nameplate on top of the First Model Daisy, variation four.

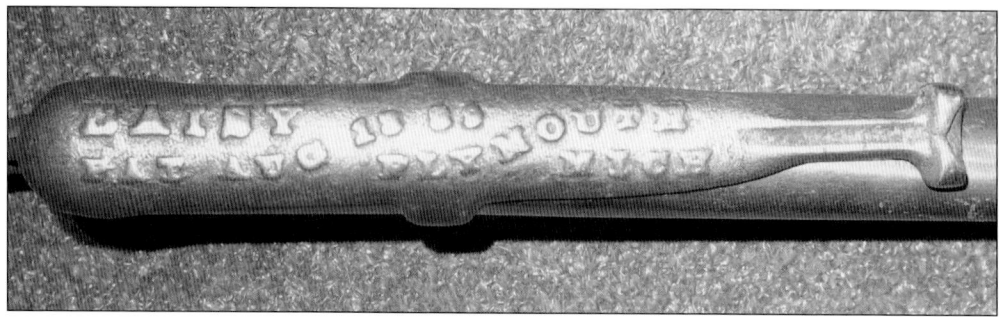

Two boys from Gozad, Nebraska, show off their prize possessions. The younger boy on the left is holding a First Model Daisy, while the older boy is holding a Hopkins & Allen .22-caliber rifle.

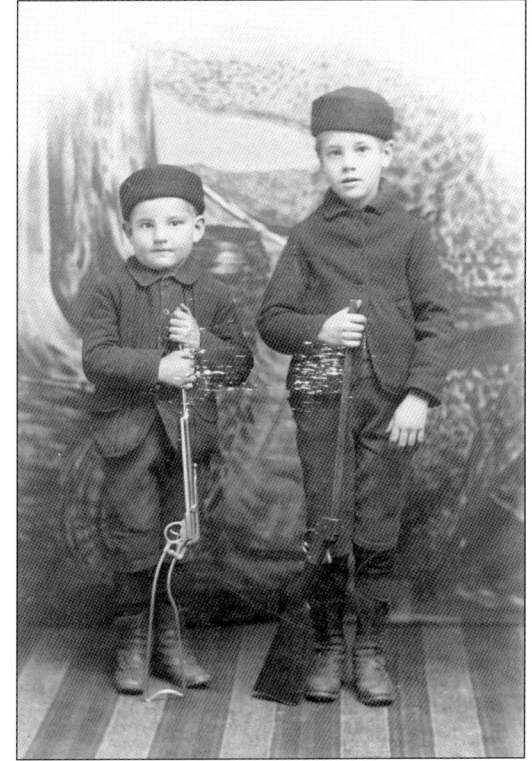

Employees of the Plymouth Iron Windmill Company stand in front of the first brick factory building in Plymouth in 1889, the year that the company was nearly shut down because of a decrease in windmill sales. The side of the building with the company name faced Union Street.

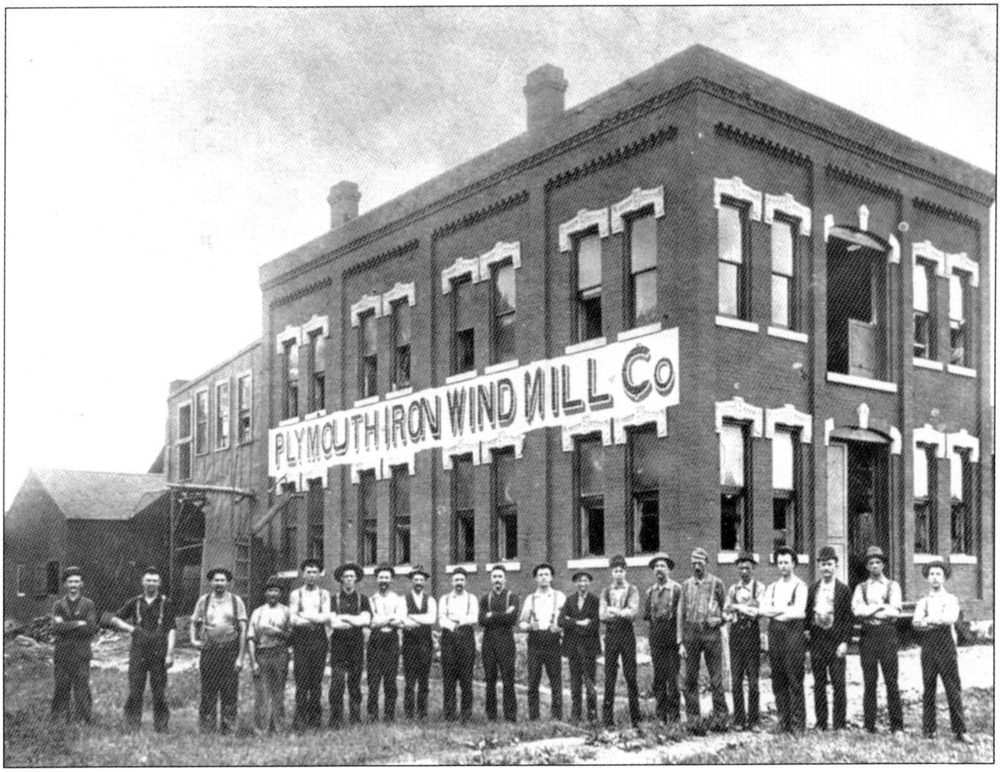

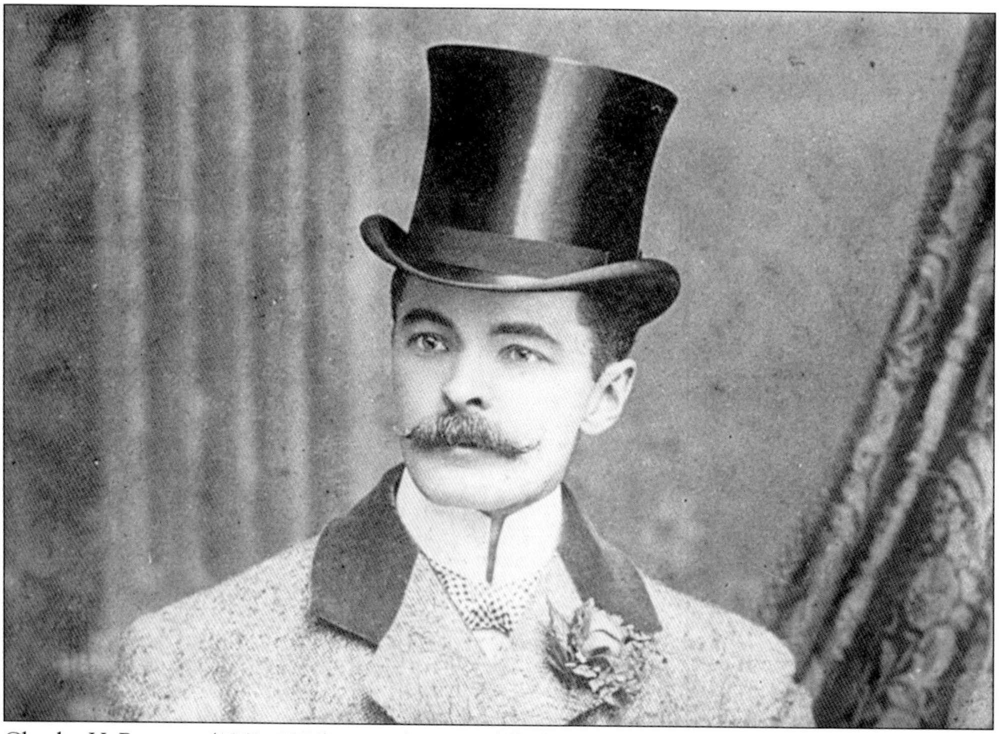

Charles H. Bennett (1863–1956), seen above, peddled fanning mills for the L.H. Bennett Fanning Mill Company owned by his father, Lewis H. Bennett, in the late 1880s. According to Charles, "This delightful occupation consisted of driving about the dirt roads of southern Michigan with a pair, or span . . . of horses hitched to a specially built long wagon upon which was loaded four fanning mills." In 1889, he purchased about a dozen First Model Daisys and sold them to farmers along his route. His success led to a sales job at PIWC in January 1891. The fanning mill company, pictured below around 1870, was the first factory built in Plymouth (1850). Charles is the child wearing the derby hat in the foreground, and the company at that time was owned by his uncle Charles Bennett. One fanning mill is on the ground in front of the door, while others are loaded on the one-horse dray.

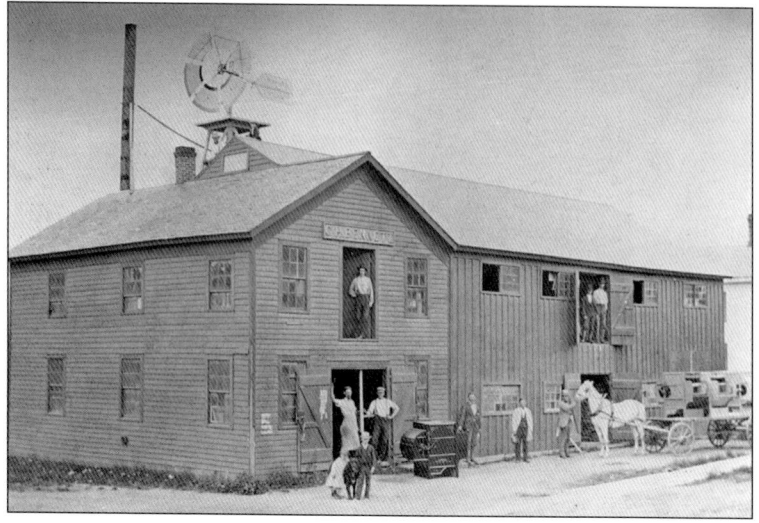

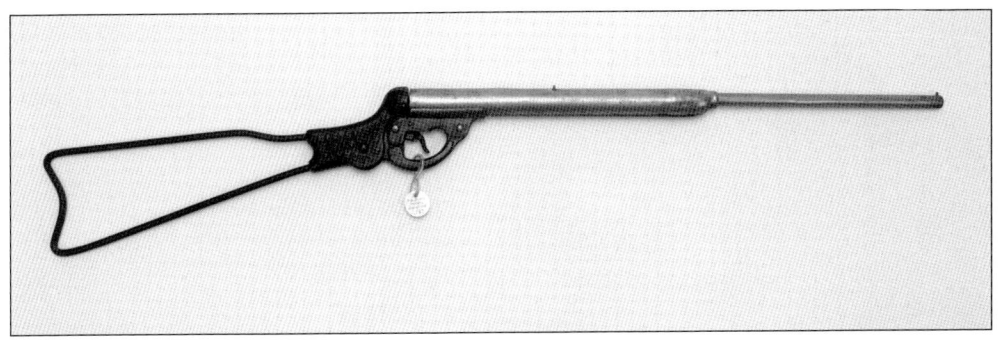

The Second Model Daisy (above) was introduced in 1890 and is considered a cast-iron, break-action gun. This is the last Daisy to indicate on the grip that it was manufactured by the Plymouth Iron Windmill Company (below). The gun used zinc for the barrel and air chamber. It was only manufactured until 1891, when the company introduced the Third Model. Because of the short production run of this model, surviving specimens are rare. (Both courtesy of Dr. Robert Beeman.)

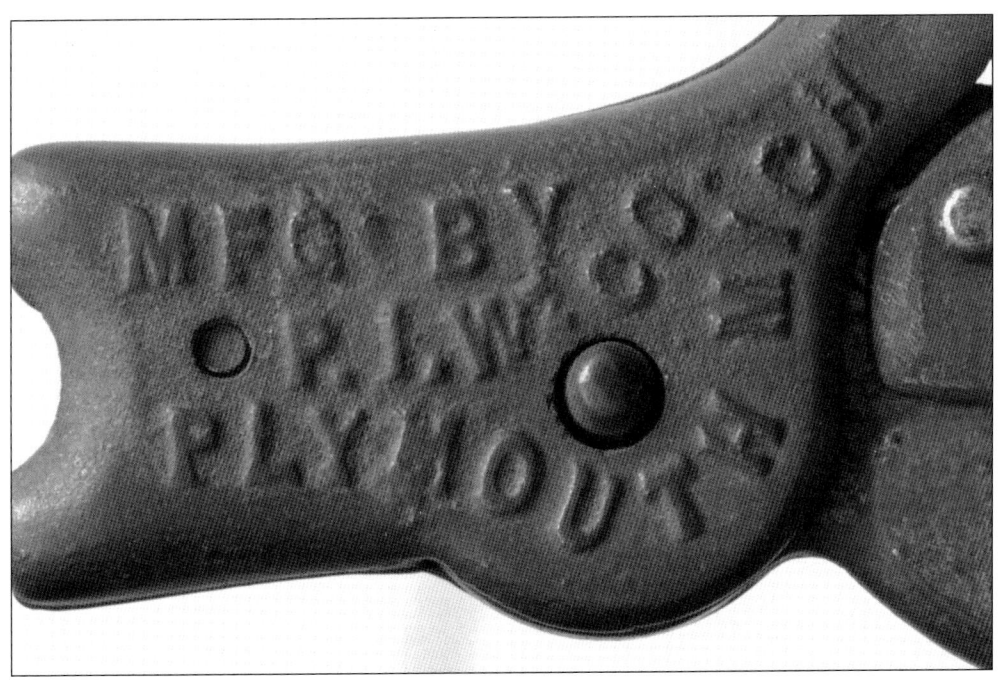

Edward Cass Hough (1872–1959) was hired as a bookkeeper for the Plymouth Iron Windmill Company in January 1893. He was the son of Lewis Cass Hough, who was president of the company at that time. Edward worked for PIWC and then Daisy Manufacturing Company for the rest of his life, a span of 66 years. On the board, he first served as secretary before becoming treasurer in 1901, vice president in 1915, and president in 1956.

On January 26, 1895, the directors of PIWC voted unanimously to change its name to Daisy Manufacturing Company. The resolution was offered by Director T.C. Sherwood and recorded by E.C. Hough, the secretary of the board of directors. The January 8, 1897, issue of the *Plymouth Mail* noted, "The windmill shop was shut down last week. They are getting ready to commence work on 100,000 walnut gun stocks for the Daisy Co."

Five

PLYMOUTH'S VIEW OF DAISY

The village of Plymouth was very supportive of its growing air rifle industry. The three gun factories provided steady work for many residents in Plymouth and the surrounding communities. Daisy Manufacturing Company made its first advertising appropriation of $2,000 for an in-store poster (shown on page 88). In December 1897, an agreement was signed by competing air gun manufacturers Daisy, Markham, J.A. Dubuar of Northville, and the Crescent Gun Company of Saginaw, Michigan, agreeing to price controls. Daisy purchased Dubuar in 1904, and Crescent went out of business about the same time. Daisy's sales climbed as new guns were introduced. The year 1900 became a milestone for the company, as its advertising budget was increased to $20,000, and sales for the year were $130,513—the first year the company topped $100,000 in sales. The growth in sales required additions to Daisy's factory complex, beginning in 1897, when a warehouse was added. Charles Bennett became the general manager of Daisy in 1902 after the death of Louis C. Hough. In 1907, Bennett made a trip around the world drumming up business for the company. A stop in China sparked a popular tale, as related in the *Daisy's Diary*: "While there [Bennett] permitted a powerful mandarin to shoot him in the seat of his pants repeatedly (to prove Daisy was safe for sale). Mr. Bennett later said he ate the next several meals standing up!" And, while the company looked for sales internationally, the local economy benefitted from the construction work and the other tangible signs of a prosperous establishment. Through the 76 years that the Plymouth Iron Windmill Company and Daisy Manufacturing Company were viable contributors to the Plymouth community, many families went through the cycle of life as employees and beneficiaries of the company. In 1954, Daisy executives decided not to build a much-needed new plant in Michigan, but rather to search elsewhere for its new home. In 1957, the decision was made to relocate to Rogers, Arkansas, and ground was broken on the company's new facility. Daisy stopped production in Plymouth in May 1958.

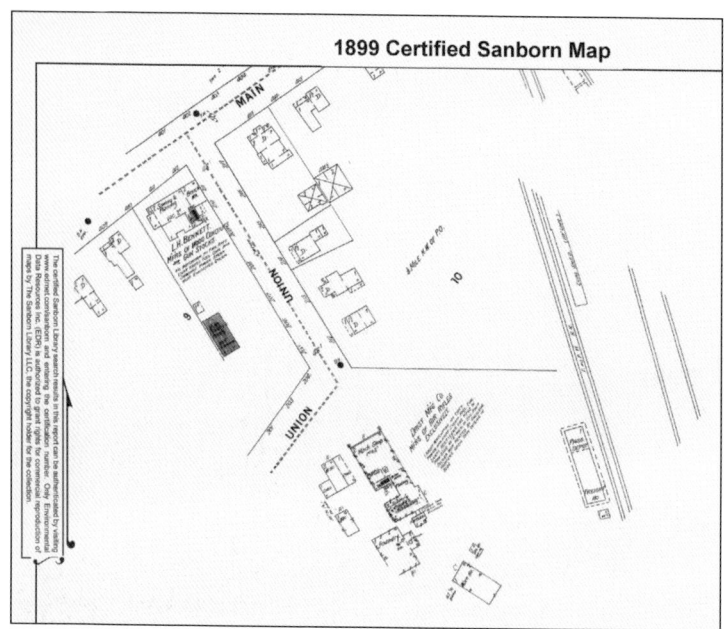

In early 1897, Daisy built a warehouse where the Plymouth Air Rifle Company had been located across Depot Street. In May of that year, the brass foundry shop burned, and a new brick foundry was built. Note the L.H. Bennett Company up Union Street from Daisy. Charles Bennett's father's company had been manufacturing fanning mills but by 1899 was making wood conduits and gun stocks for Daisy. (Courtesy of Environmental Data Resources.)

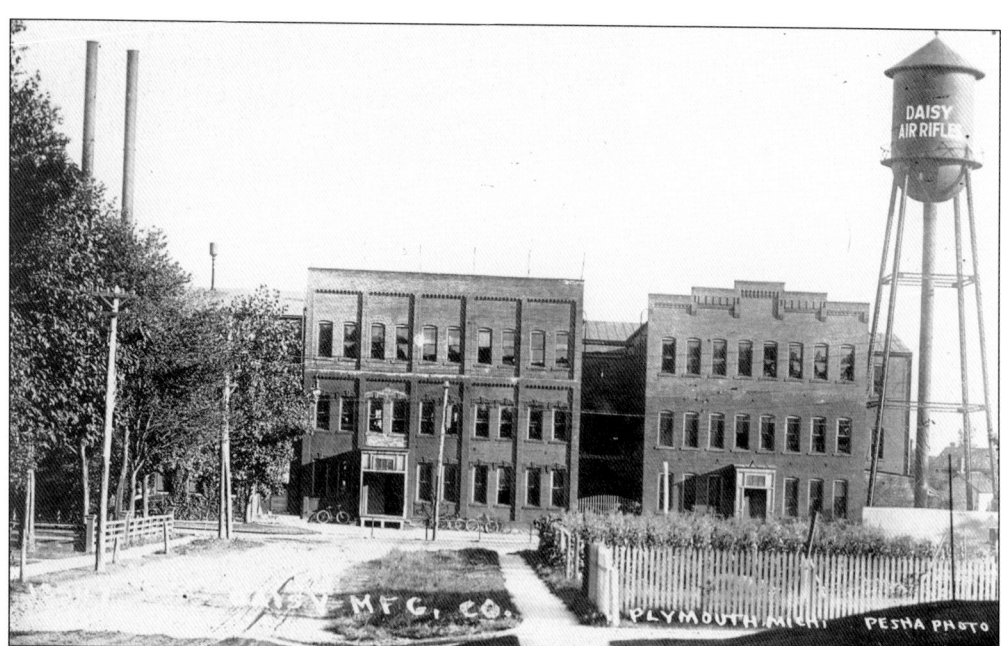

Daisy's business expanded rapidly in the early 1900s, requiring the company to add more buildings to its complex. This 1907 image shows two of the key additions: a third floor was added to the original factory for assembling (center), and the factory on the right was built for woodworking and finishing.

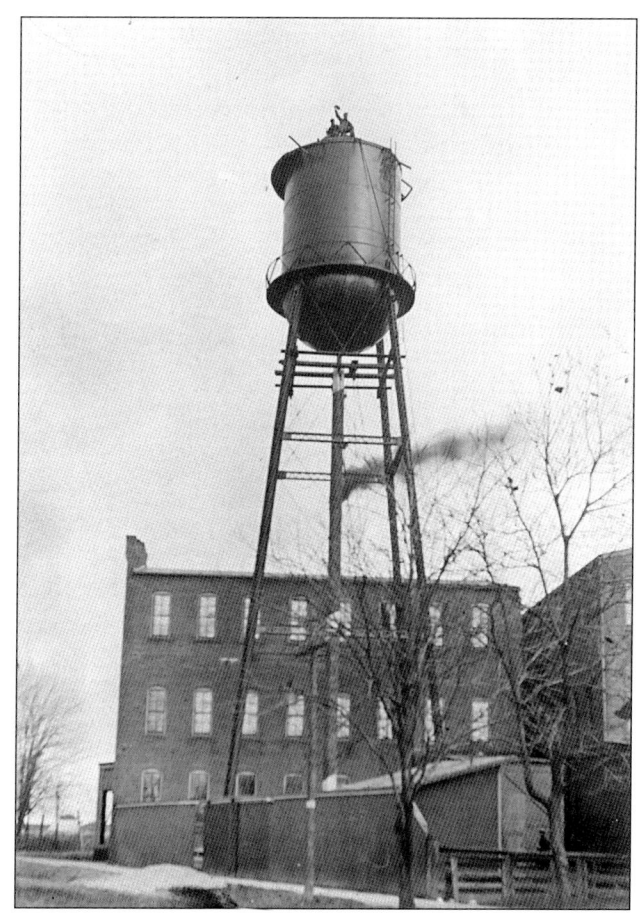

These two real-photograph postcards were shot on the same day in 1908. Shown at right is a street-level view of the factory addition from 1907 and the water tower, with two men standing on top. Below, the men on top of the water tower took this view of Plymouth looking east. A train is approaching the Flint & Pere Marquette depot from the east. The houses on the east-west street (near the approaching train) front Ann Arbor Road (now Ann Arbor Trail). The buildings on the left are part of the Lloyd L. Lewis Hardwood Lumber Plant on Mill Street. Downtown Plymouth is out of the image to the right. (Both courtesy of Michael Pappas.)

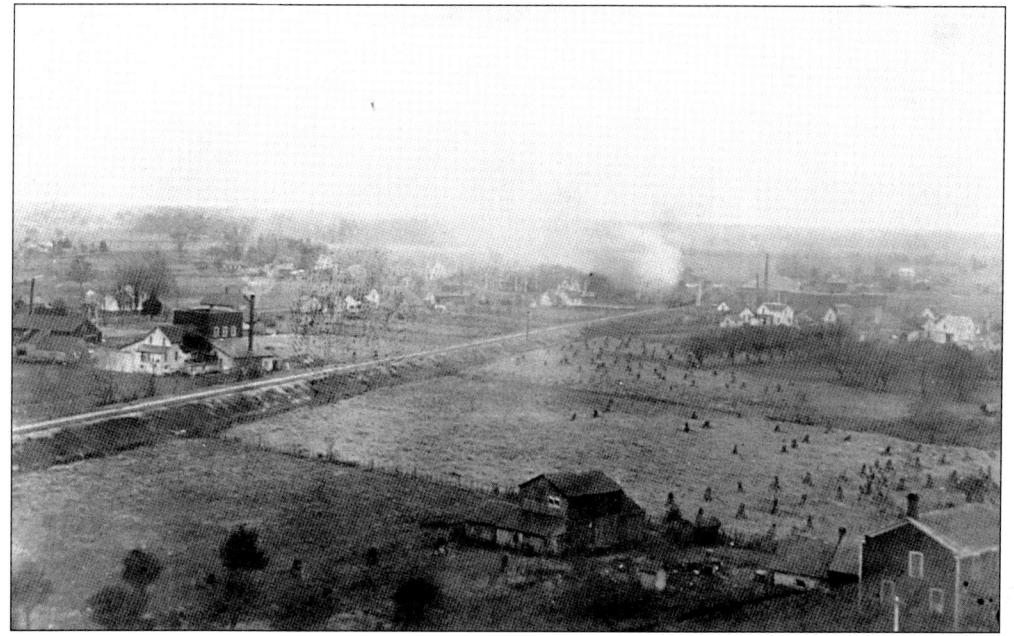

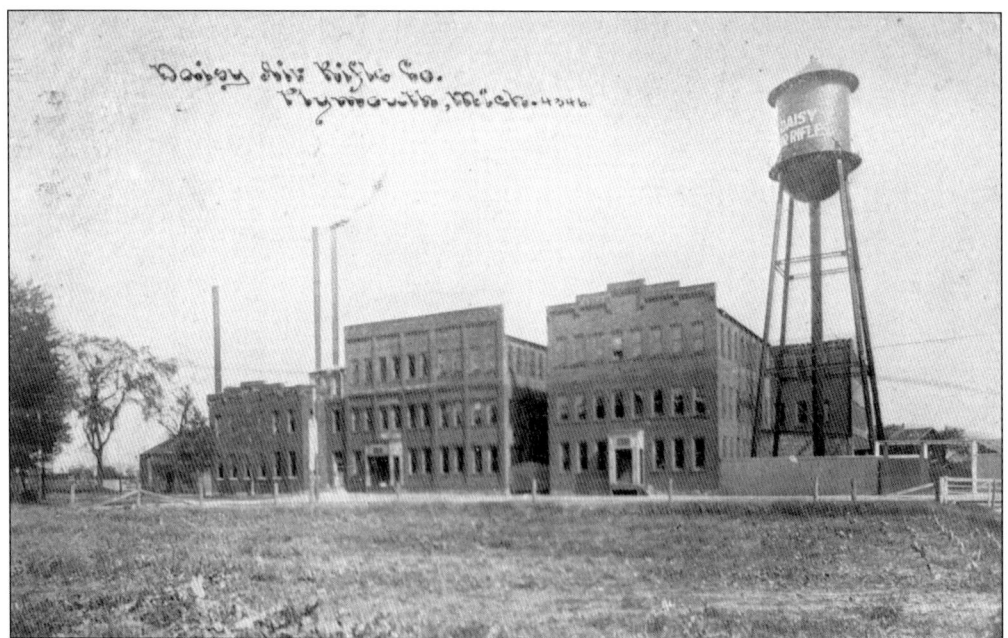

This 1910 image shows the other major addition on the far left: a two-story office building erected in 1901. According to the November 22, 1901, *Plymouth Mail*, Daisy executives were embarrassed to have visiting buyers meet with them in the dingy, small office space they used in the original factory building. The new office was designed with visitors in mind and was more spacious and elegant.

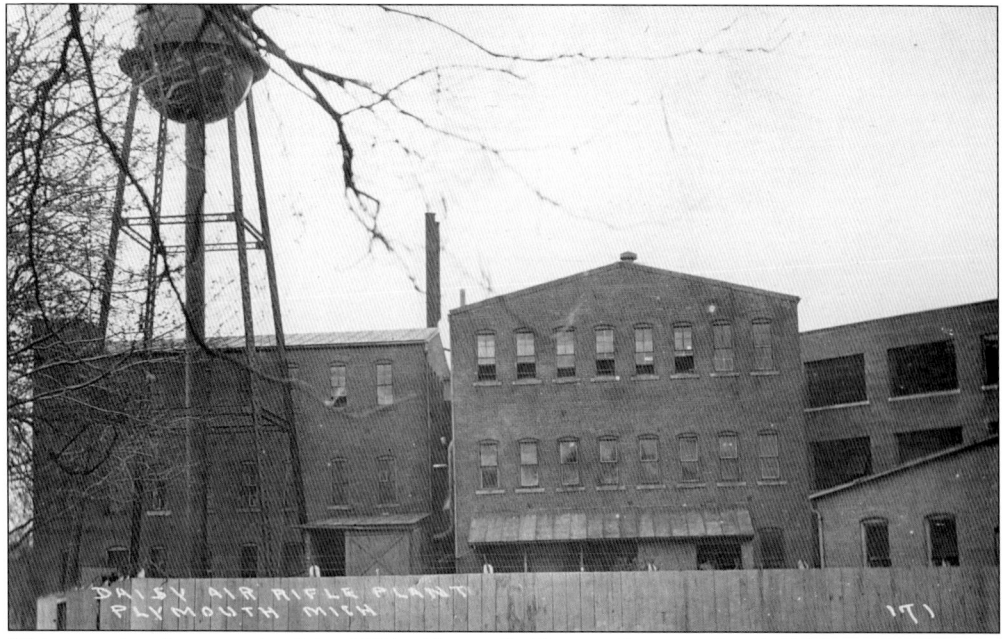

This is a view from south of the 1907 addition (left), as well as another building erected before 1909 used for storage on the first floor, soldering on the second floor, and packing on the third floor. (Courtesy of Wesley Powers.)

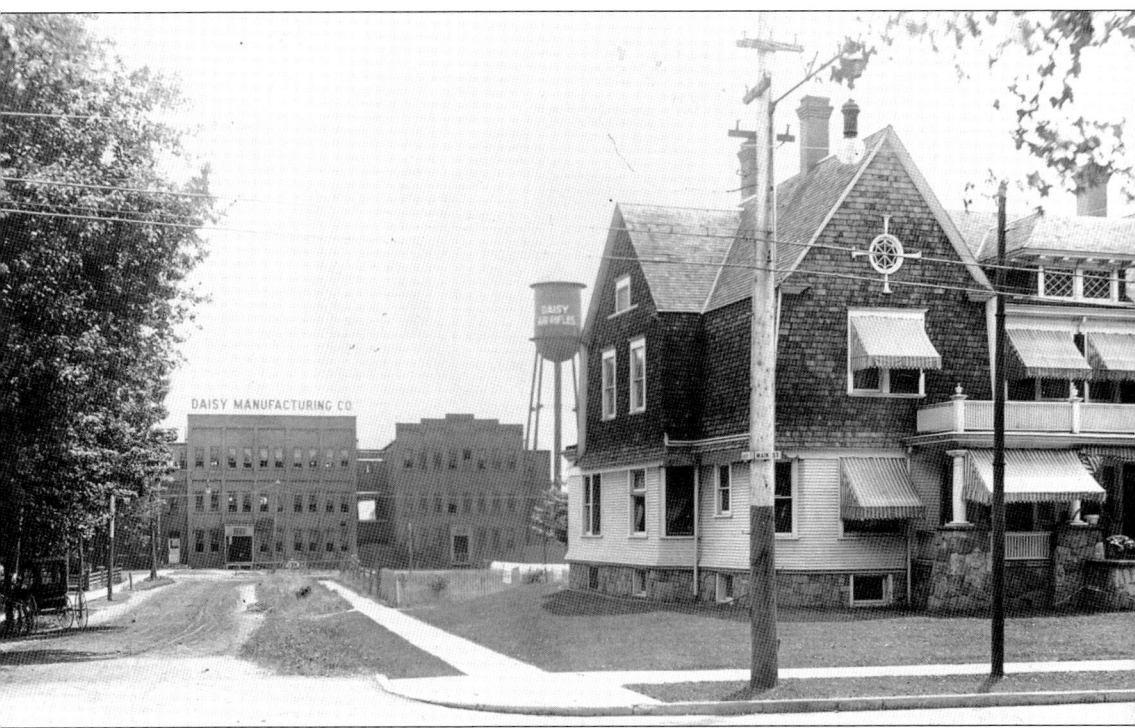

This 1912 view of Union Street includes the double home belonging to Charles and Fred Bennett. The brothers purchased the property from their father, Lewis, in the early 1900s, tore down the fanning mill factory, and built this home at 188 North Main Street, where Lewis and Fred and their families lived; Charles lived just down the street at 134 North Main. Note the Daisy company name added to the top of the original building.

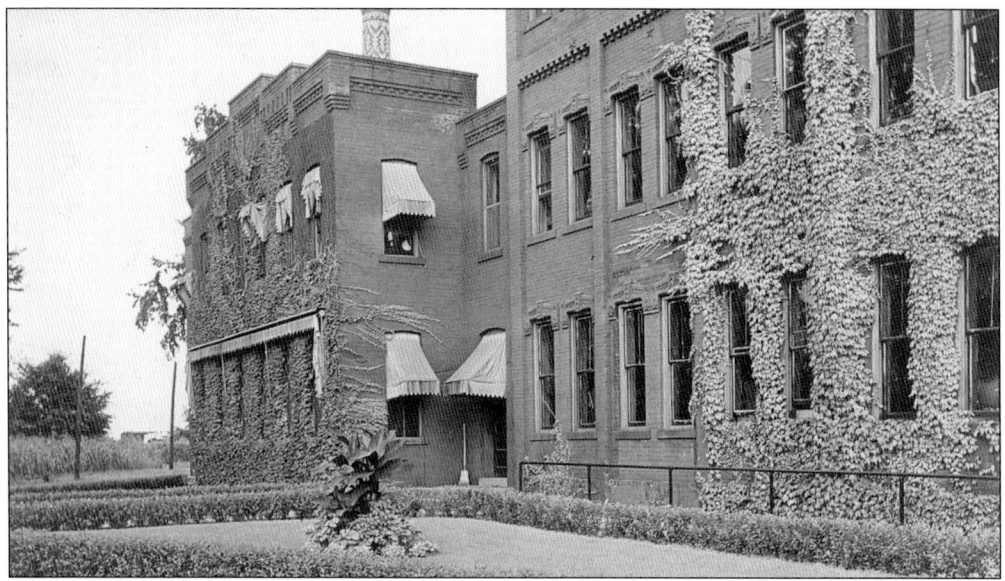

Here is a close-up view of the original building (right) and the two-story office building added in 1901. The offices were on the first floor, while testing was conducted on the second floor. Ivy covered the buildings in the summertime. By the time of this photograph, the entrance to the company had been moved from the original building to the section linking the two buildings. The bricked-up entrance and new windows are left of the ivy.

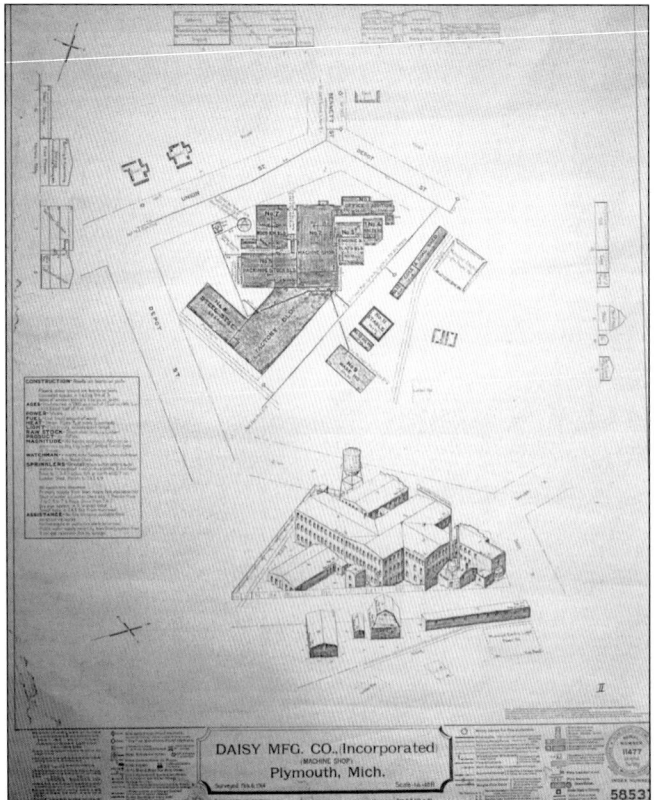

Daisy Manufacturing Company commissioned this survey of the complex in 1914 for insurance purposes. It is particularly interesting because it not only includes a 3D drawing of the buildings, but it also contains elevations showing the purpose of each floor of each building along the outer edges. At this time, the office building was still two stories.

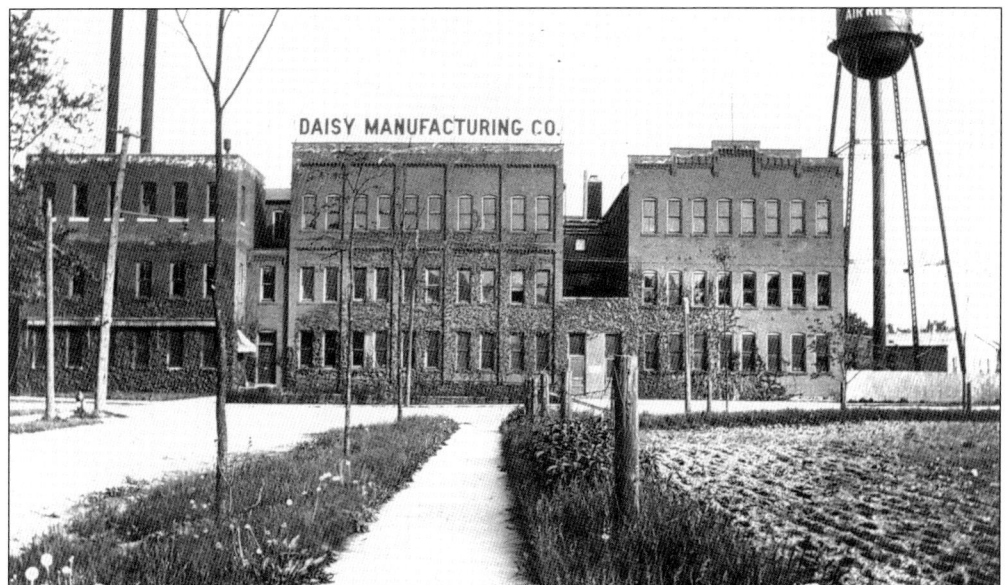

The image above was taken shortly after the third floor was added to the office building on the left, between 1914 and 1918. The 1918 Sanborn fire insurance map shows a third floor on the office building and a recessed company entrance between that building and the original building in the middle. The photograph below was taken probably in the 1920s, based on the automobiles and the new entryway that was added after 1918, but before the 1927 Sanborn fire insurance map was drawn. Note the water tower is dark with white painted lettering.

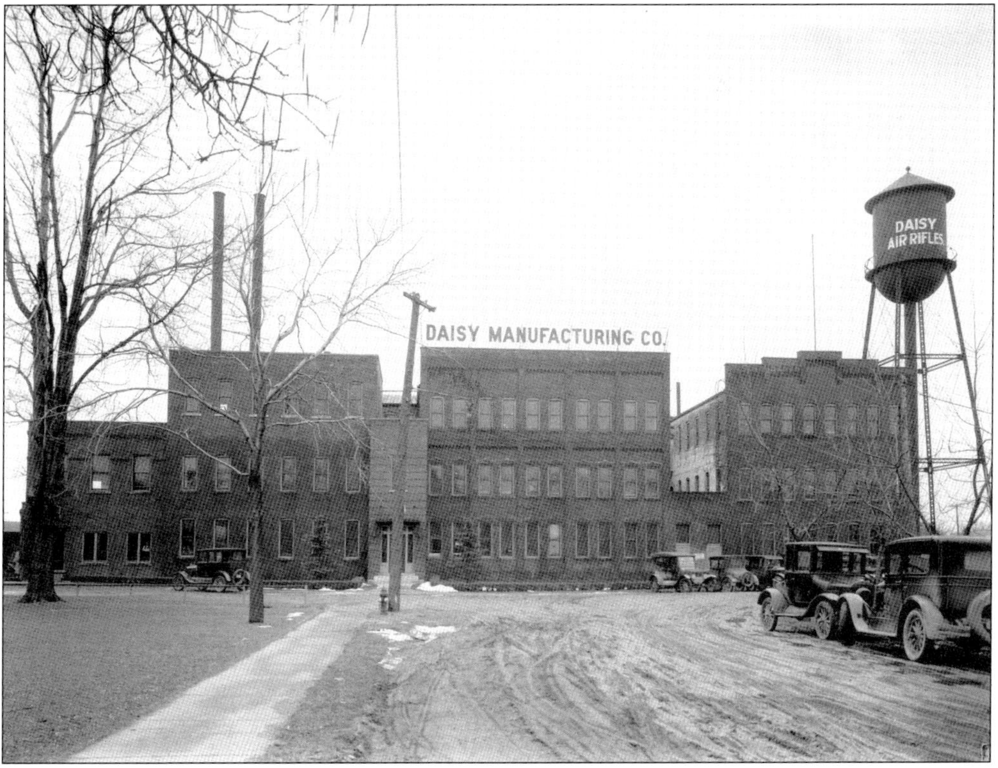

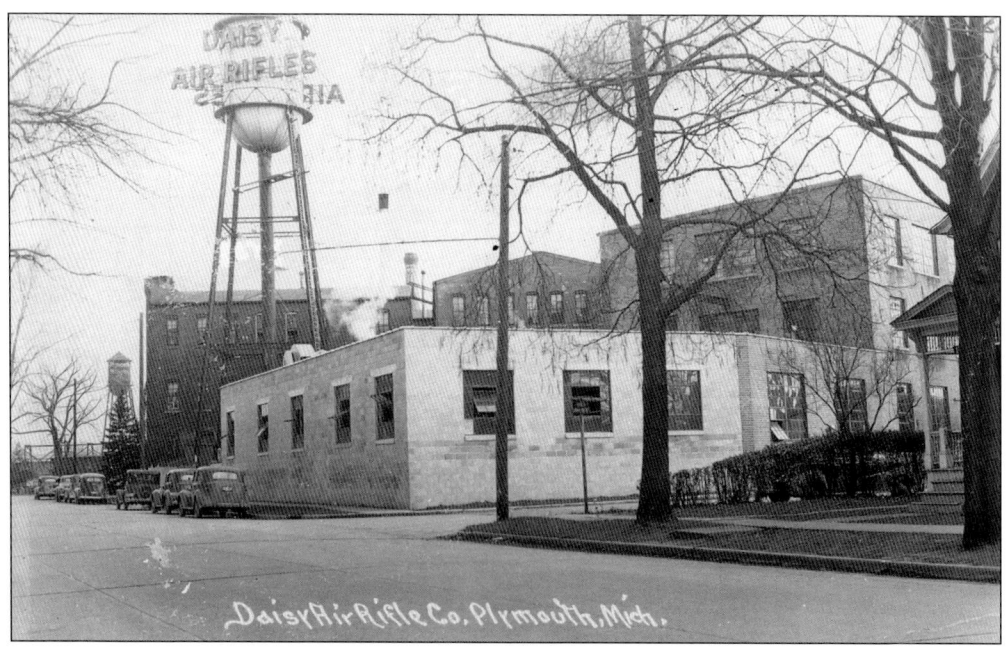

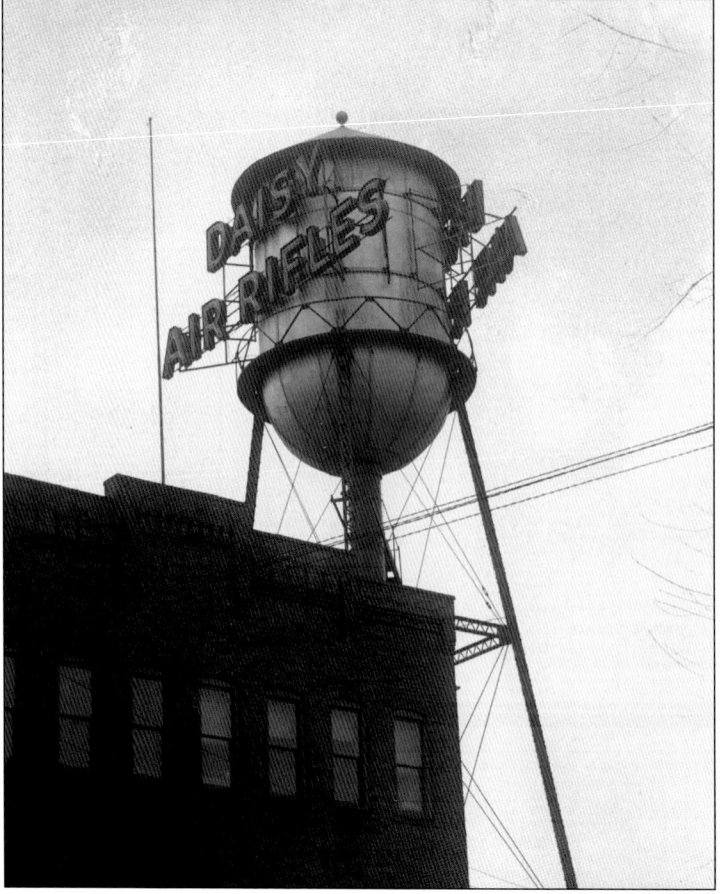

At some point in the late 1920s or early 1930s, the company upgraded the 35,000-gallon water tower with three-dimensional neon lettering "Daisy Air Rifles" and lightened its color, seen above. The one-story building in the foreground was part of the factory complex added around 1939; it contained the steel-shot department. The street in front of this new building is Depot Street, which had been rerouted between 1914 and 1918. The street was later renamed Hamilton Street. The image at left shows a nice close-up view of the updated water tower.

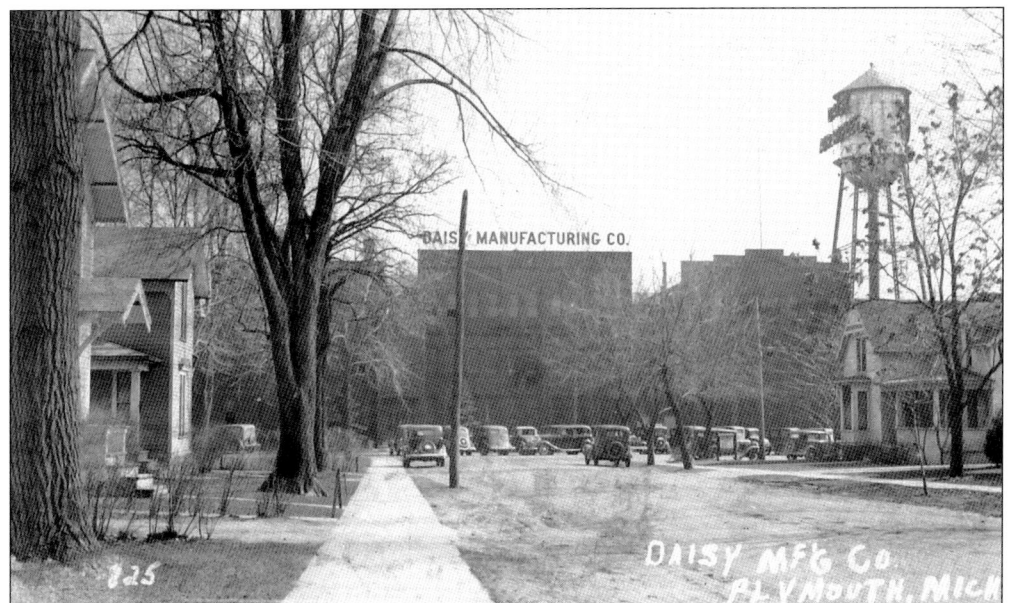

This 1930s view of Union Street and Daisy shows some of the residences that had been added over the years. (Courtesy of Michael Pappas.)

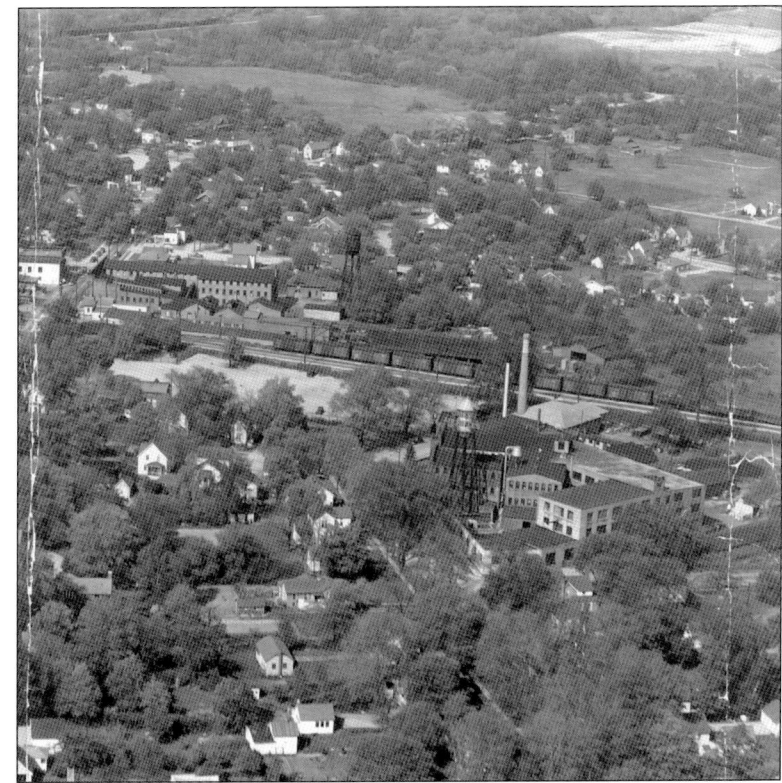

Cass S. Hough, son of Edward and grandson of Lewis, was an aviator. He took this aerial view of the Markham/King complex (upper left) and the Daisy complex (middle right) in 1938. By this time, Daisy had moved the manufacturing of King air rifles to its own factories, and the King complex was not being used.

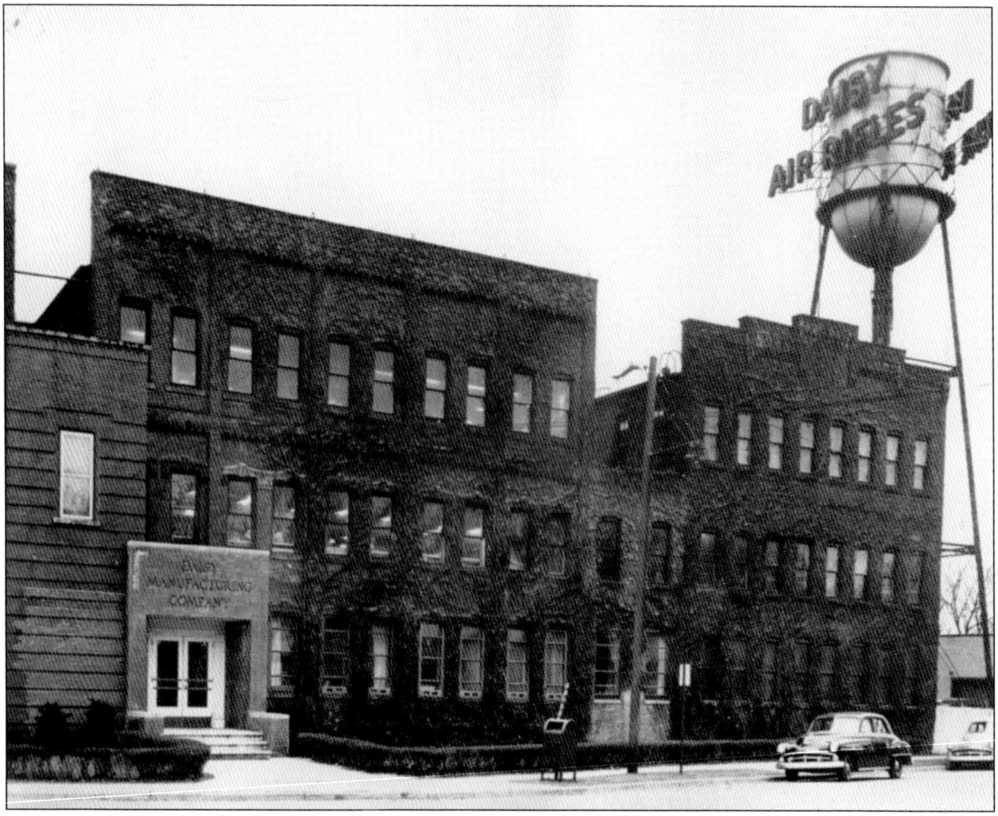

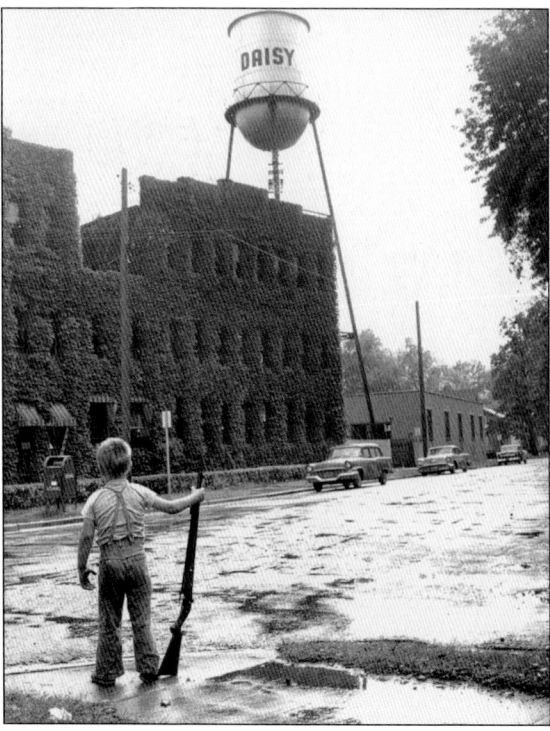

This 1947 view of Daisy shows another change to the entryway of the company. The company's name was removed from the top of the original building and added to the remodeled entryway. The bricked-up former entrance is obvious on the left.

By September 1956, Daisy had once again changed the appearance of the water tower, removing the 3D neon lettering and replacing it with the painted word "Daisy." The little boy in the foreground holds a Daisy No. 25 pump air rifle.

Production of air rifles shut down on May 1, 1958, as Daisy prepared to move its operations to Rogers, Arkansas. The next day, a fire swept through the eastern end of a steel warehouse building that housed mostly air rifles, many of which were specially ordered by Sears and Montgomery Ward. The warehouse was situated between the main Daisy factory buildings and the railroad tracks. While there was no sign of arson, the damage was estimated at just under $200,000, according to the May 8, 1958, *Plymouth Mail*. Cass Hough, Daisy's executive vice president at the time, indicated that the loss was only about five percent of the company's warehouse supply. During the fire, employees had let local boys walk off with large quantities of air rifles. The *Mail* reported two weeks later that city commissioners were considering an air rifle ordinance because of the proliferation of "misguided BB firing."

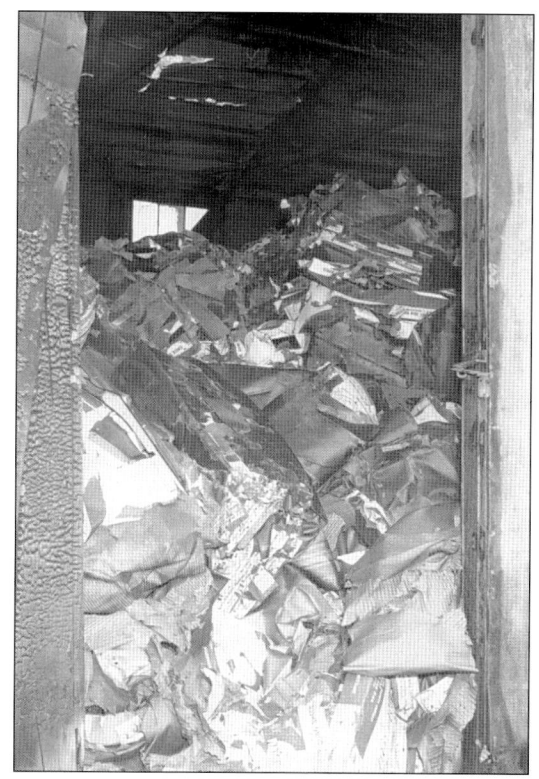

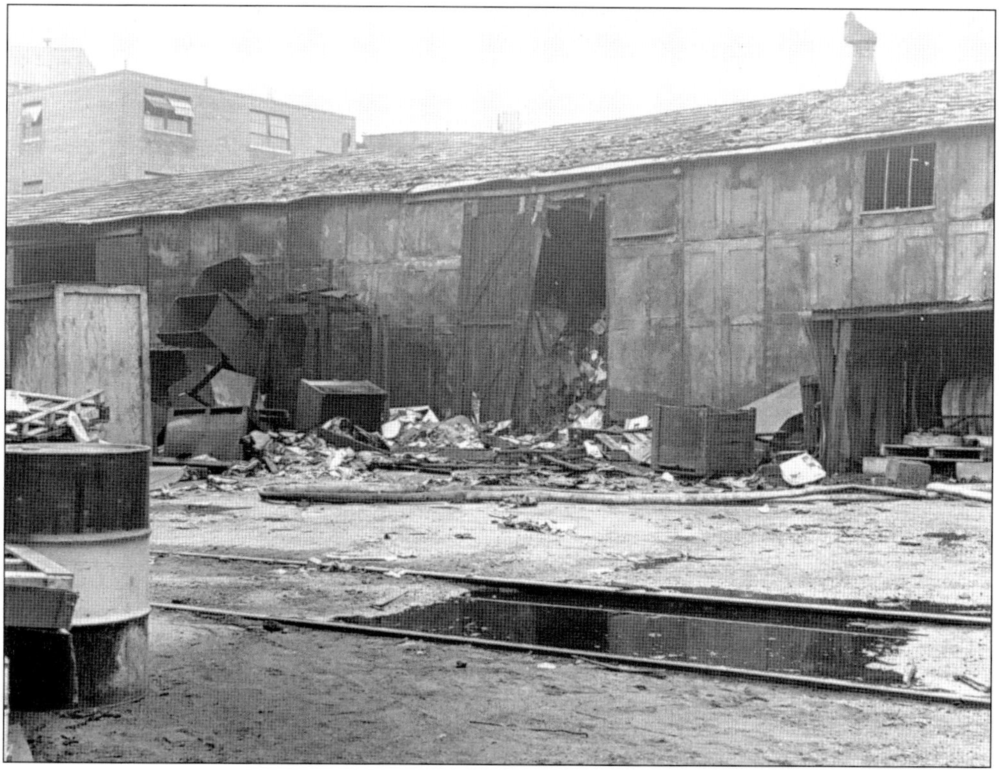

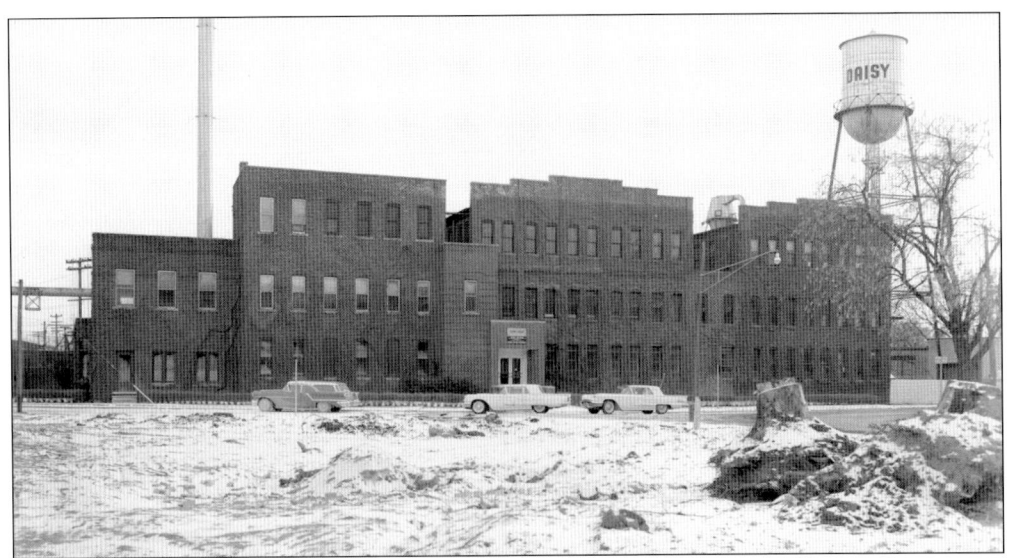

Daisy Manufacturing Company moved to Rogers, Arkansas, in 1958. By 1961, the Daisy complex was on the market, with a "For Sale" sign prominently displayed where the bronze-lettered company name had been added a decade before. The lettering was removed and is now in the Daisy Museum in Rogers, Arkansas. The building was purchased in 1964 by DSI Corporation, which later changed its name to Adistra Corporation.

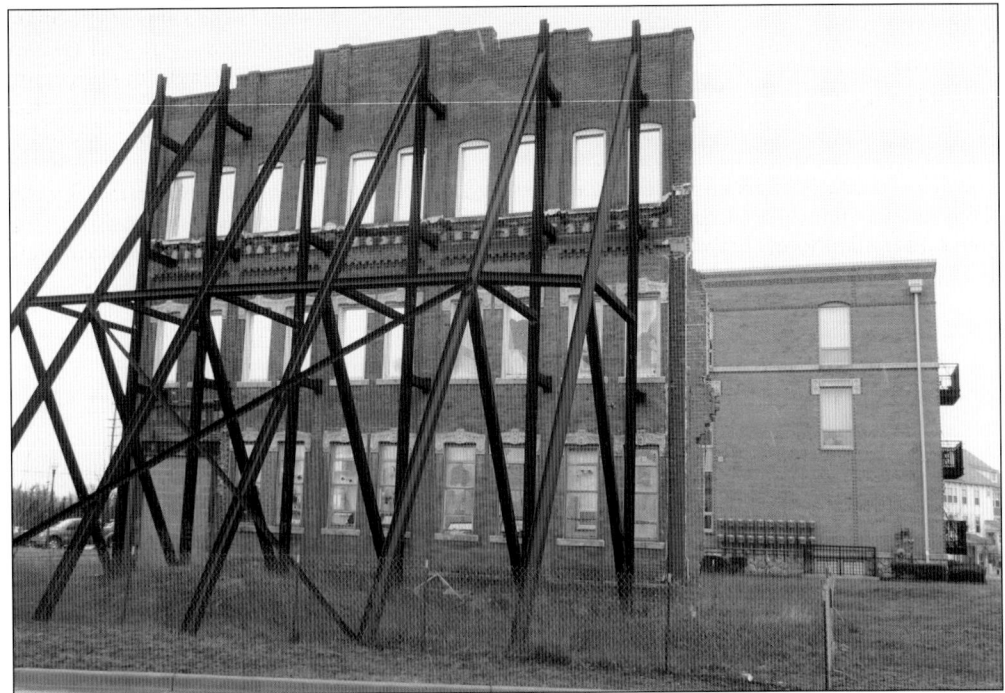

In late 2003, the former Daisy complex was demolished with the exception of this wall of the 1882 Plymouth Iron Windmill factory. The wall was saved to be included in the Daisy Square Condominium Project. As of April 2013, the wall stands alone, supported by steel beams and not incorporated into the project. Windows are broken, the brick and mortar are deteriorating, and the wall's future remains unknown.

Six

DAISY'S INNER STRENGTH

Any company is only as good as its employees, and Daisy Manufacturing Company was fortunate to have a long-tenured, dedicated workforce, starting with the executives and working down to those who got their hands dirty. The Plymouth Iron Windmill Company began by offering stock, but control of the company for the bulk of the 76-year Plymouth period rested with a handful of people and nine presidents (only seven people, as two served as president twice). Charles H. Bennett was president of Daisy for 36 years (1920–1956), and he was preceded by Henry W. Baker (1895–1919; his first term was 1887–1888). Daisy management had a track record of looking out for the welfare of its employees. In a letter dated November 16, 1974, Cass S. Hough relayed the following story: "A little known fact, and one that attests to Dad's [Edward Hough] almost incredible loyalty to the employees at Daisy, was the fact that when all the banks closed in Michigan in early 1933, and practically all companies were either unable to pay their employees or paying them in script, Dad and I went to Montreal; Dad borrowed American funds on his own personal Sun Life Insurance policies; we brought the money back to Plymouth, and Daisy employees never missed a payday in hard cash because of this." And, in a metropolitan area known for its fierce loyalty to labor unions, the employees at Daisy voted repeatedly not to become unionized. Shortly following the close of World War II, Daisy signed an agreement of trust for employee profit sharing and a retirement fund. When the company left Plymouth for Rogers, Arkansas, approximately 12 percent of the employees moved also, uprooting their families and their lives. Most of those who moved were supervisors or staff. Others were interested in moving but had to compete for jobs with the workforce in Arkansas. According to the *Plymouth Mail* of May 1, 1958, "For many, Daisy Manufacturing has been their entire life's work and some families have had two or three generations at work in the plant."

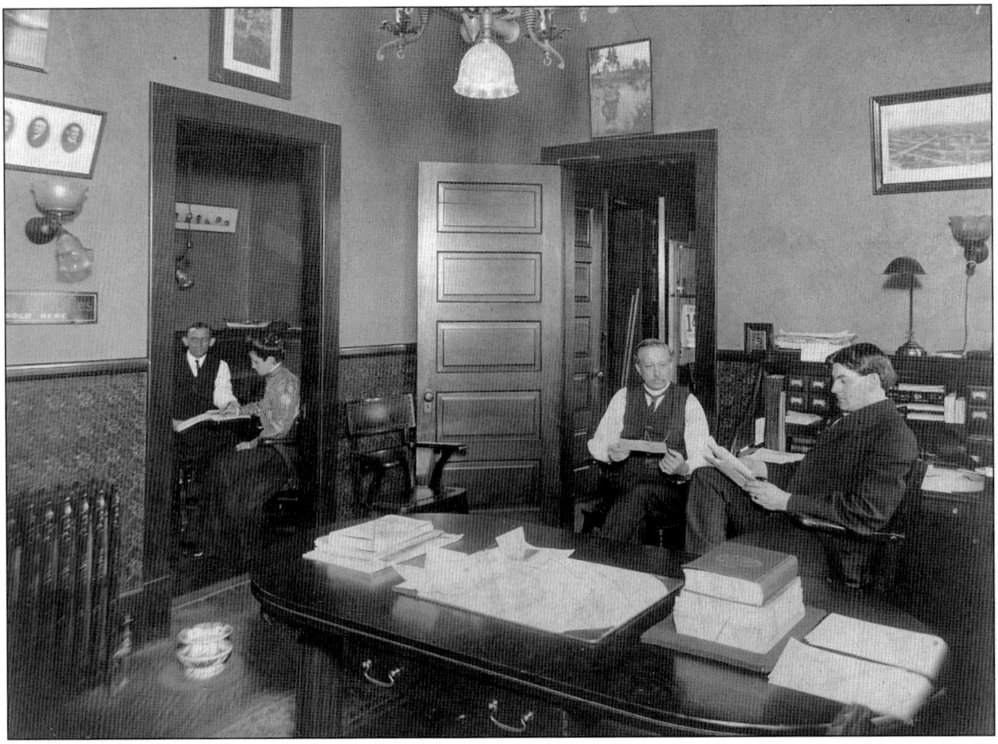

Daisy's office building addition in 1901 was a major improvement over the small, dingy area previously used. Company executives were proud to show off their new digs: the walls were plaster with a four-foot wainscoting, and the woodwork was quarter-sawed white oak with a piano finish. The calendar in the back room in this image indicates the date was Monday, March 14, 1910.

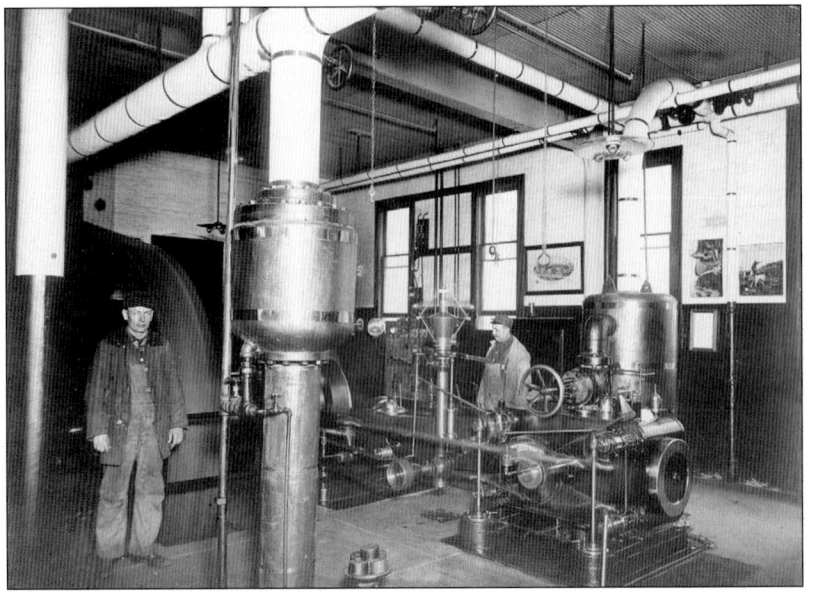

Here is a view of the Daisy boiler room around 1910. The boilers provided steam heat and power to the buildings. They were housed in a building just behind the 1901 office; both structures were probably built at the same time.

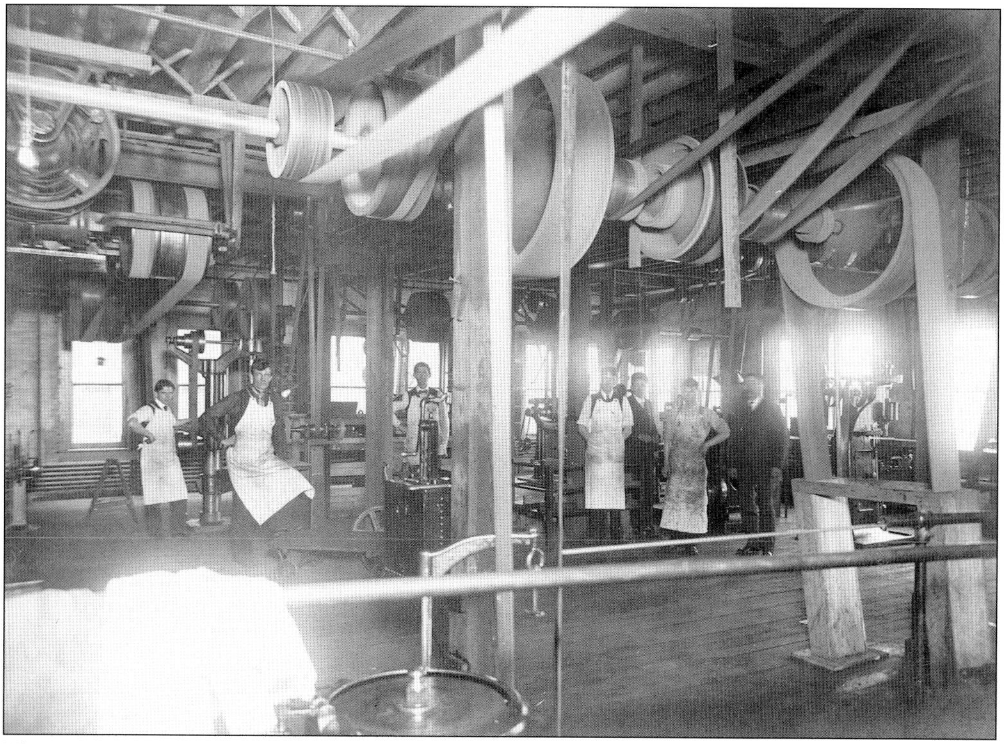

The pressroom at Daisy housed the stamping machines, where air rifle parts were "pressed" from thin sheet metal. The pressroom was located on the first floor of the machine shop in the original plant building. These photographs were taken around 1910.

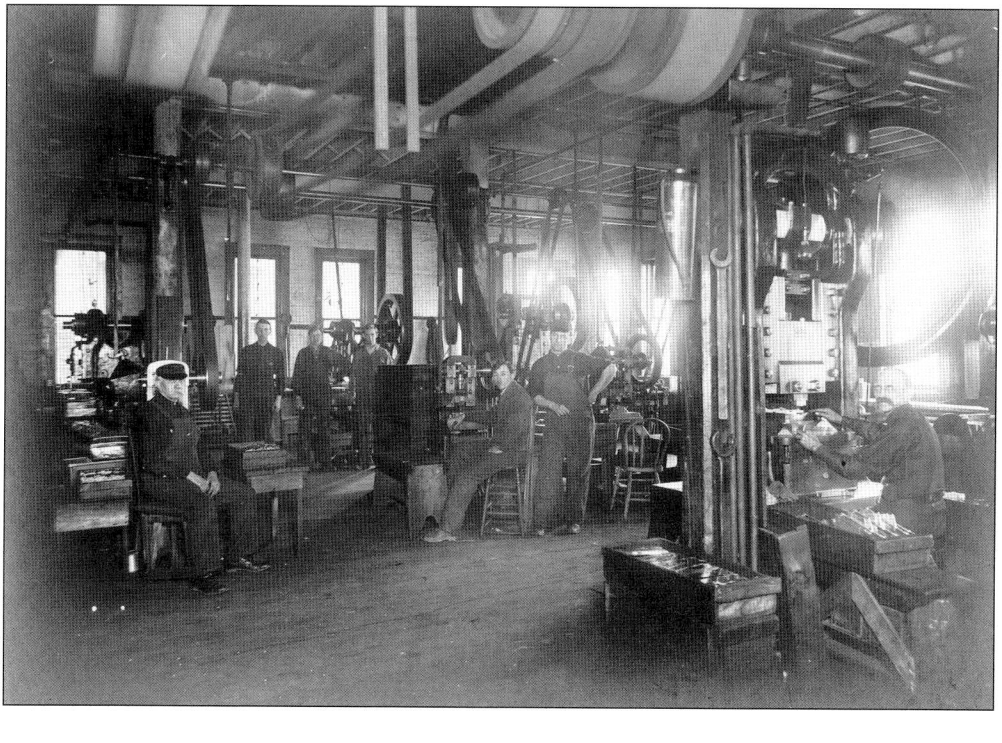

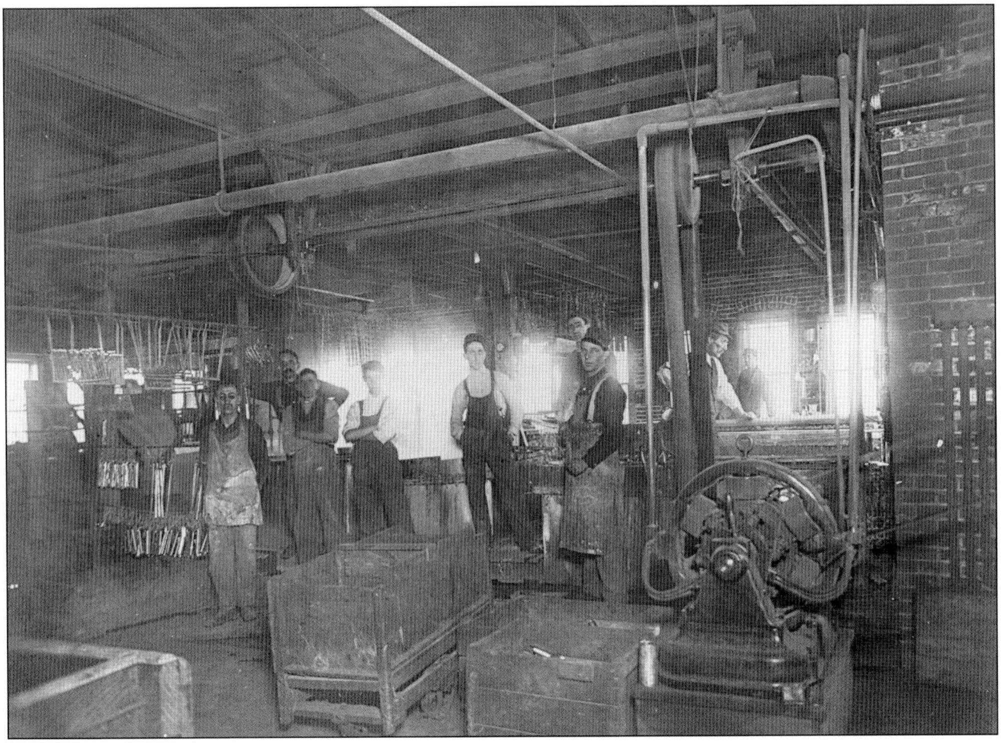

Daisy's assembly room is where the parts made in other locations of the plant were brought together and assembled into working air rifles. Before the third floor was added to the original building in 1905, assembling was done in the rear of the building, along with soldering and polishing. Once the third floor became available, the assembly room moved there in the front of the building, and polishing was done on the same floor in the rear of the building. These photographs are from 1909 or 1910, based on the advertising on a hanging lamp in the image below that reads, "Take home a Little Daisy Pop Gun," which began being manufactured in 1908.

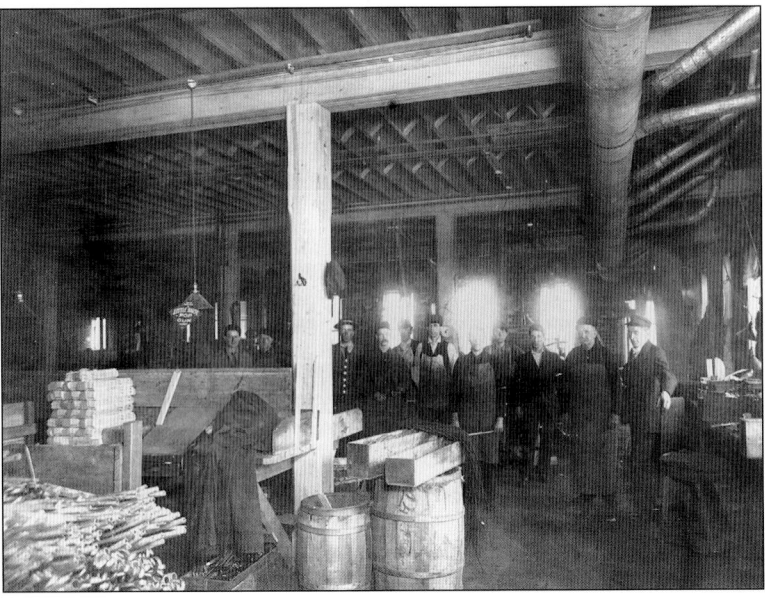

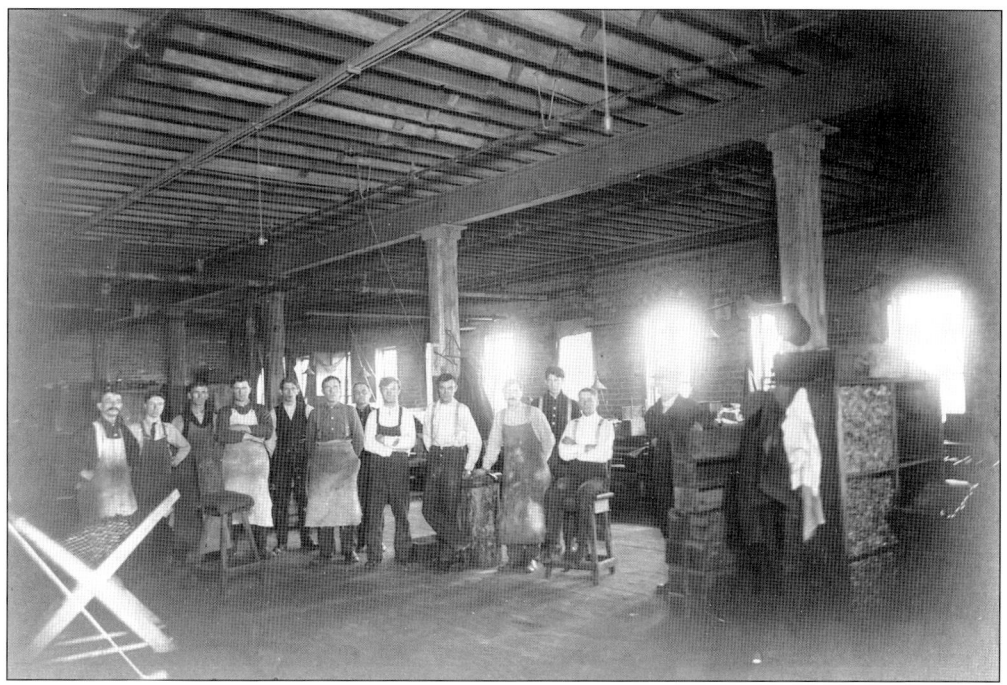

Pictured around 1910, the stock room at Daisy was located in the factory addition of 1907, where woodworking was performed on the first and second floors and rubbing and varnishing was done on the third floor. This is where the wooden stocks for the guns were crafted.

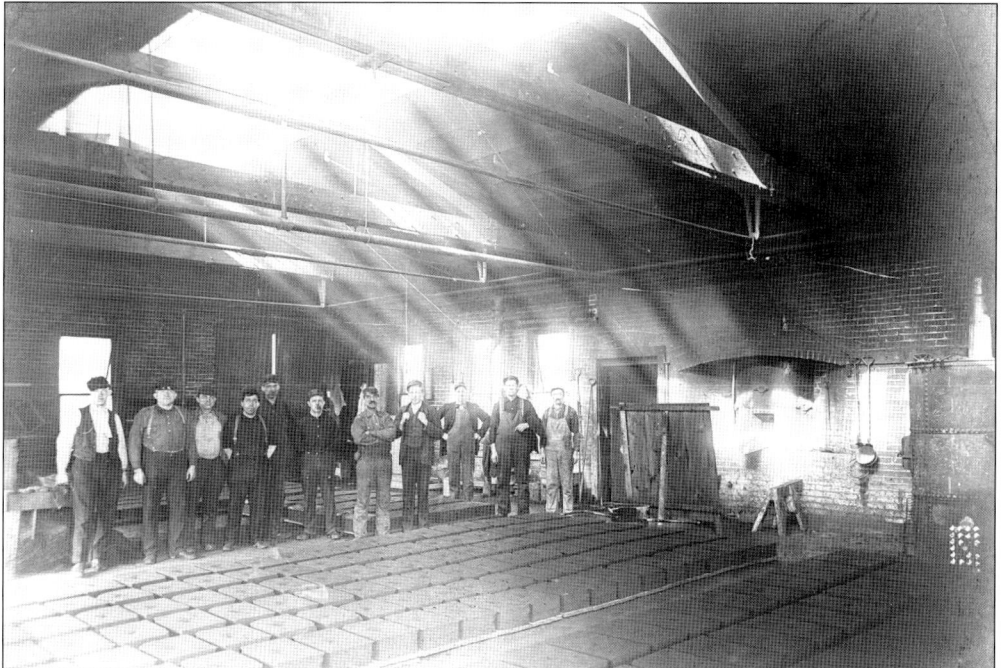

Daisy's shot department was where the company repackaged the shot that it bought in bulk. The lead shot was received in barrels and poured into tubes with the imprinted Daisy logo. In 1910, Daisy sold large quantities of its rebranded shot tubes.

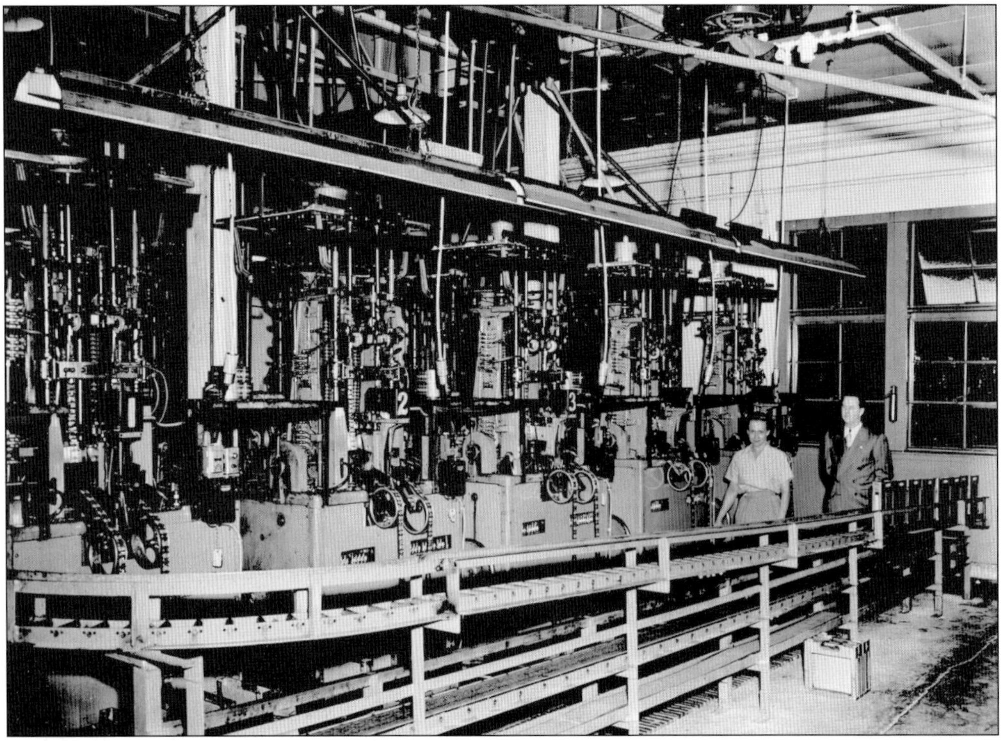

In 1928, Daisy entered into the shot business when it became a partner and the sole sales agent for the American Ball Company of Minneapolis, Minnesota. In 1939, Daisy jumped into the shot business with both feet by buying the American Ball Company and moving all of its shot-making equipment to the Daisy plant in Plymouth. Both of these views show the shot-packing department in December 1949.

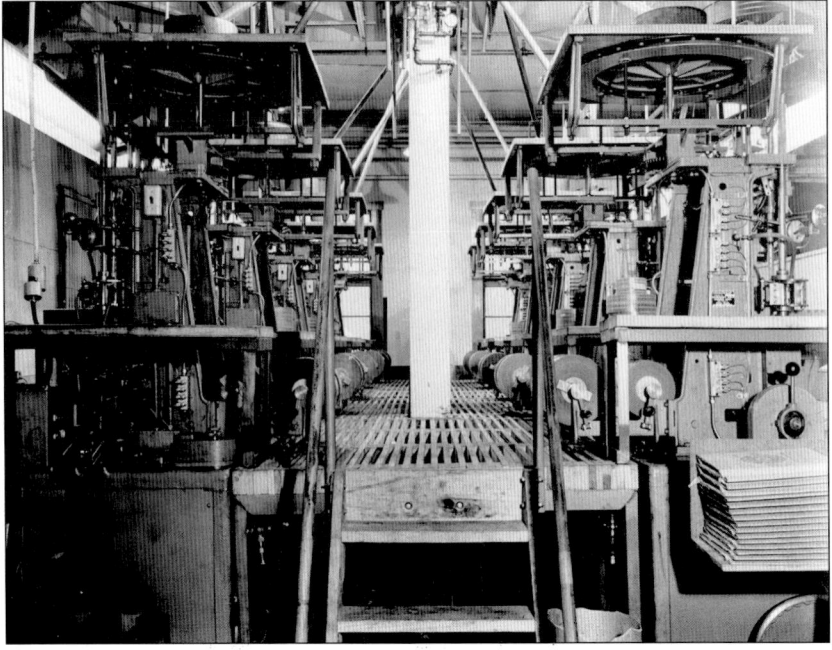

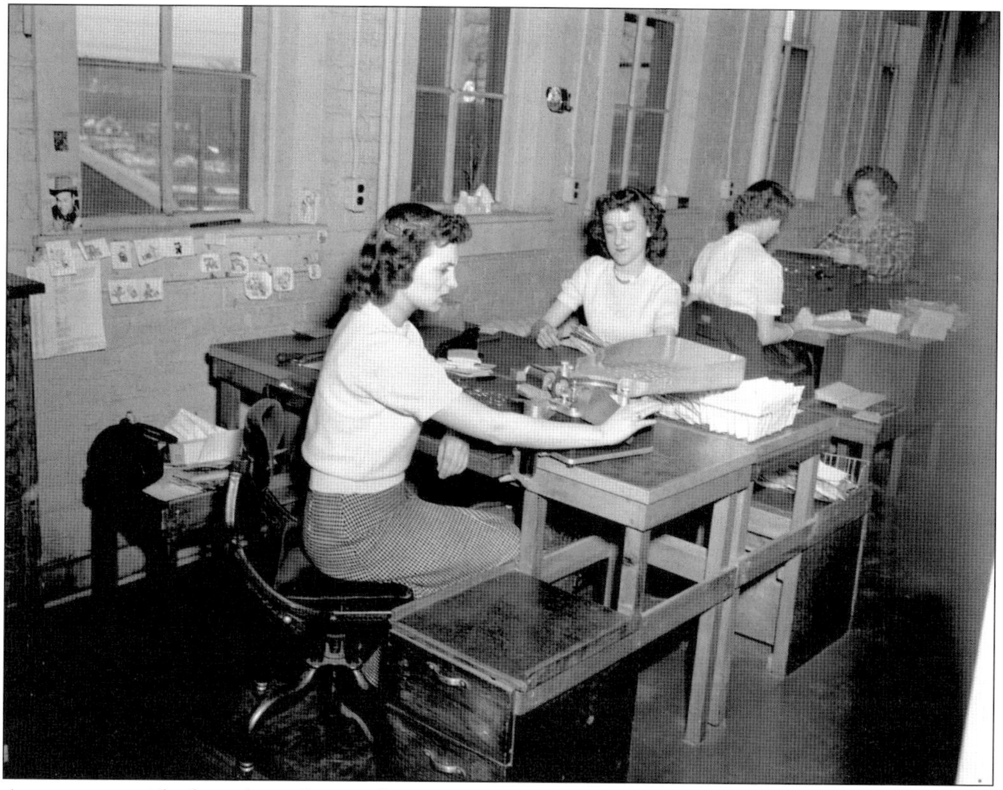

A company with the sales volume of Daisy in 1950 had a busy mail-room staff accepting orders, answering mail, and routing correspondence to the various departments and individuals within the company. The mailing department also handled all outgoing promotional mail, including sending handbooks and special and general mailings, stuffing enclosures in envelopes, and mimeographing. Clara Simonetti (at left above and in background at right) and Irene Dely (second from left above and foreground at right) counted and packaged coins after letters were opened. They also ensured that each piece of mail was pigeonholed for routing.

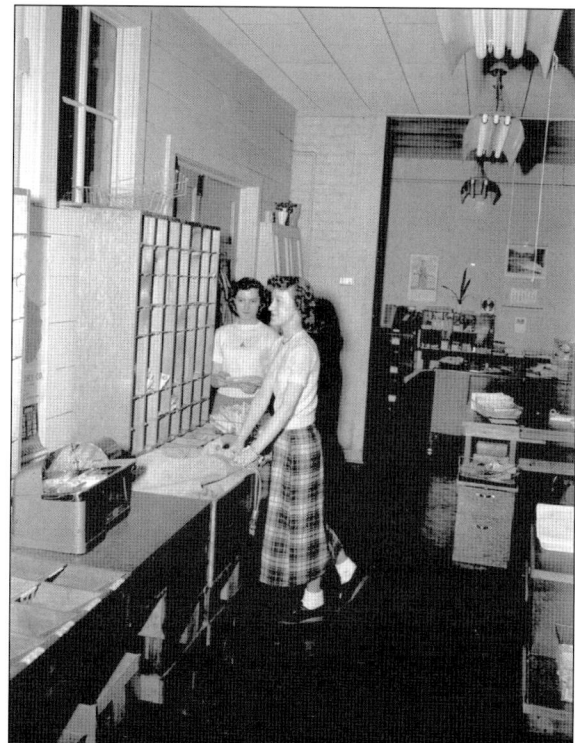

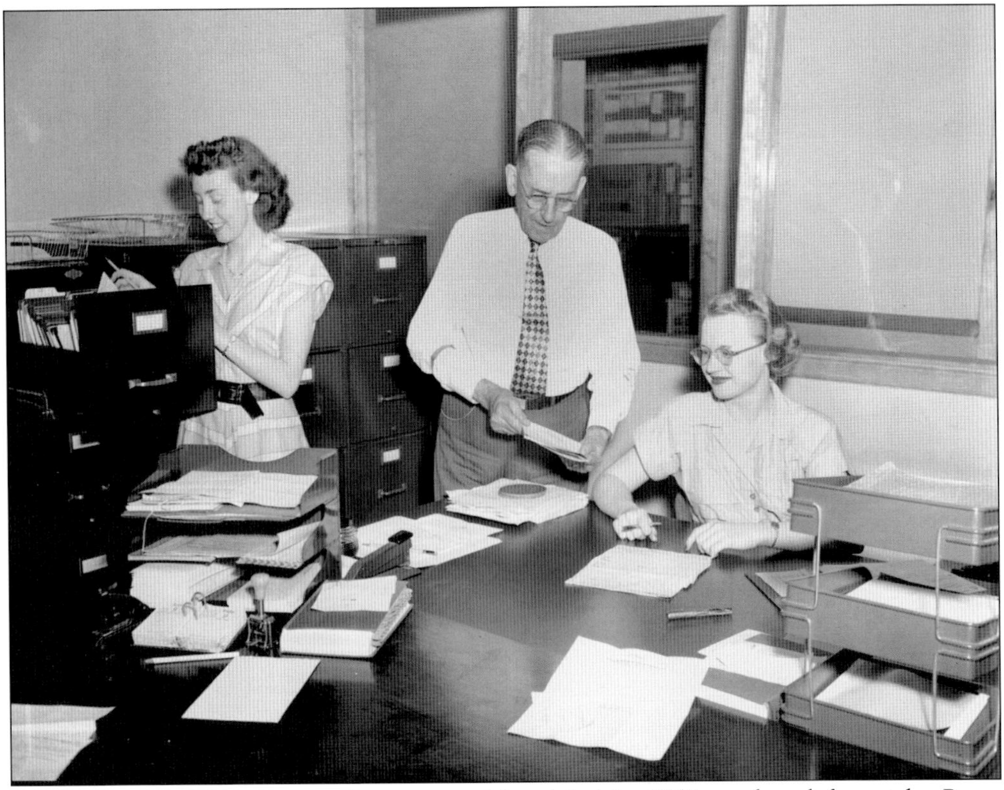

Employees in the Daisy Service Department (above) in May 1950 are, from left to right, Peggy Plummer, Chauncey H. Rauch, and Mabel Vickstrom. In late 1914, Rauch was a Daisy salesman who saw the need for a special department for the repair of broken guns when he observed many broken guns getting dusty at the Daisy plant and at dealers' shops waiting for repair. Rauch convinced Charles Bennett and Edward Hough to set up the service department. The Daisy Testing and Inspection Department (below), a part of the service department, was where men repaired and tested guns. The employees are, from left to right, Vito Sambrone, James Pinion, Raymond Bailey, Edgar Burden, and Harry Micol.

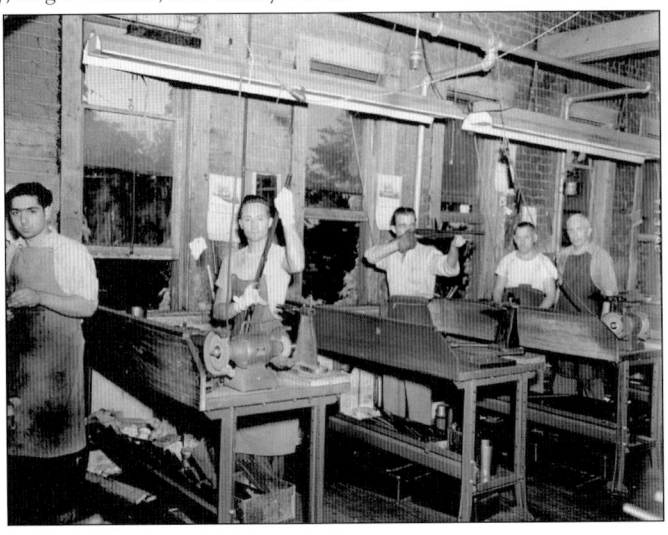

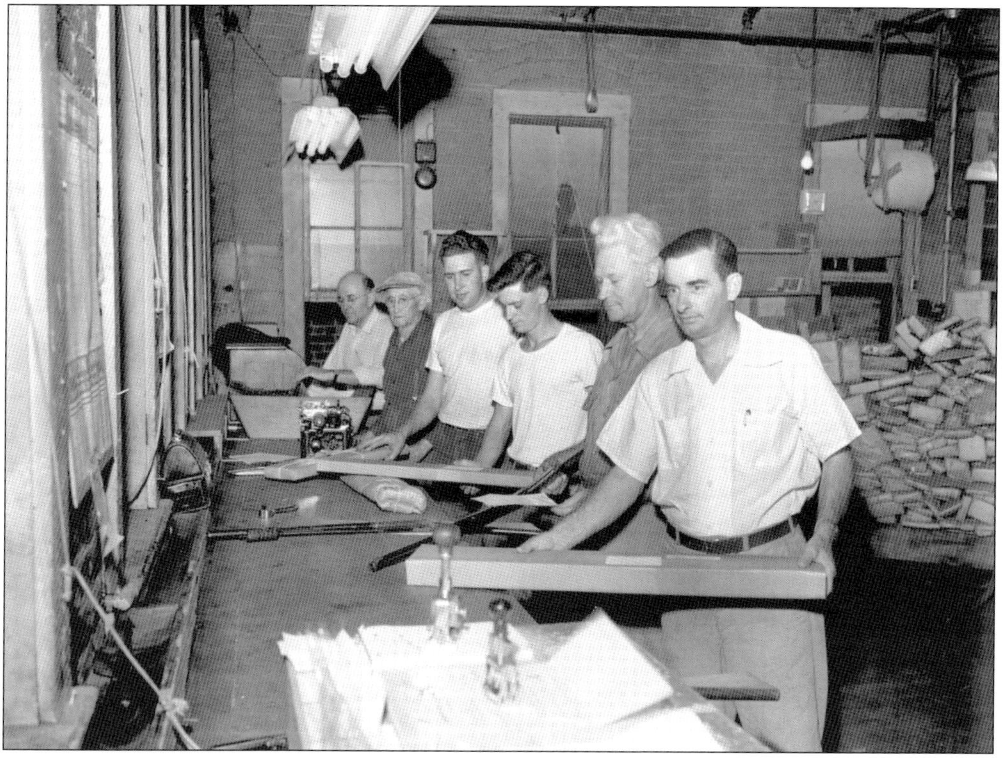

Employees of the receiving and shipping section of the service department prepare to open boxes of guns returned for repair. Pictured from left to right are George Gottschalk, Art Burden, Gerald King, Wayne Greening, Art Locke, and David Baker.

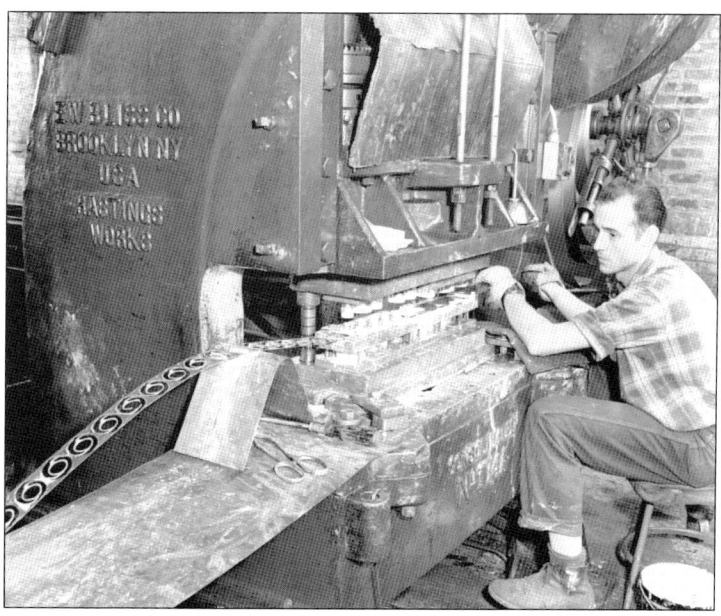

A Daisy Manufacturing Company employee stamps out parts for Daisy air rifles.

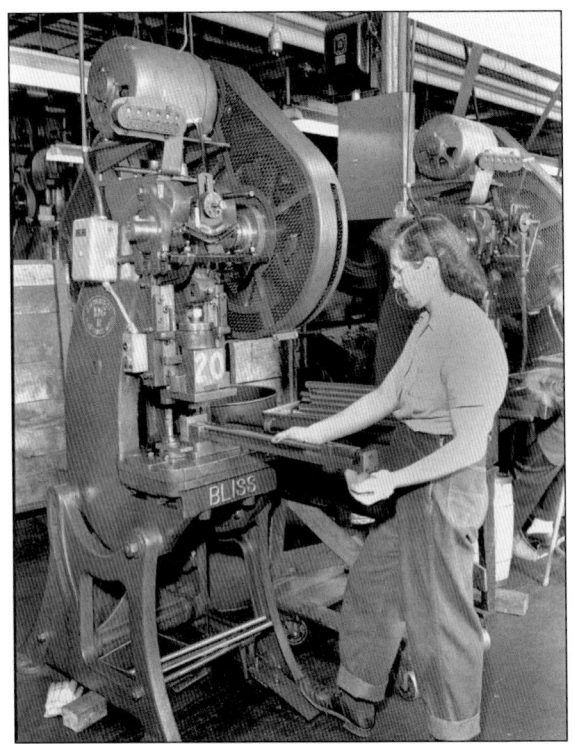

Women were an integral part of the Daisy workforce since the company's early days. In both images here, women operate stamping machines making parts for Daisy air rifles. They were taken in December 1949.

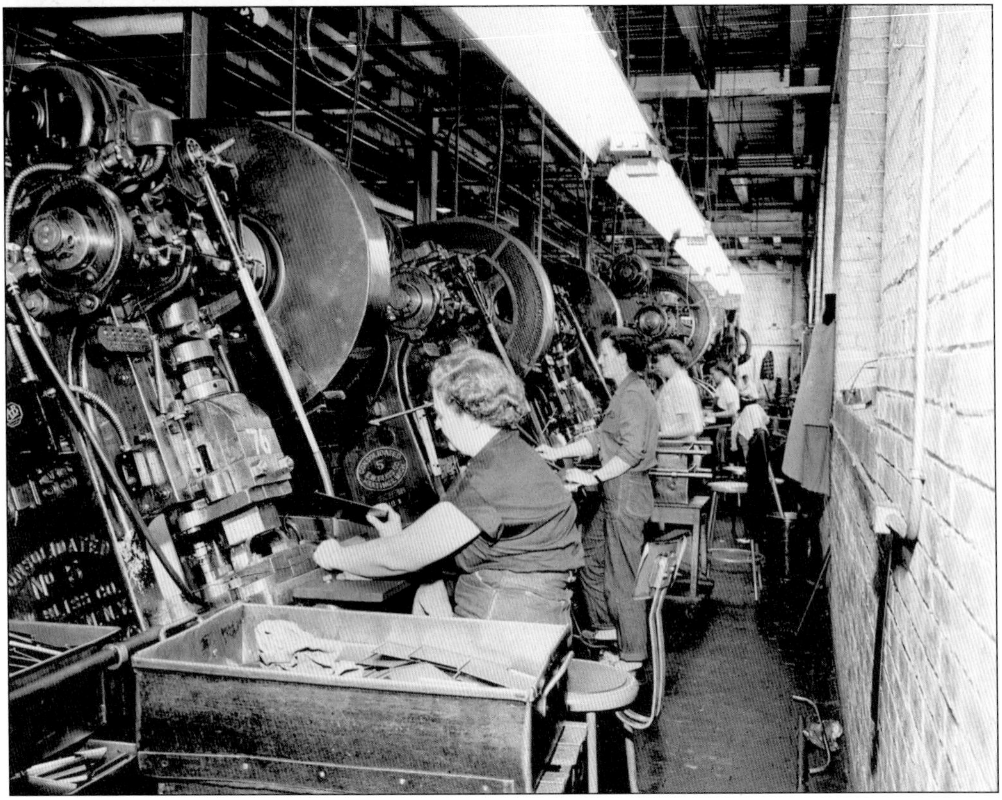

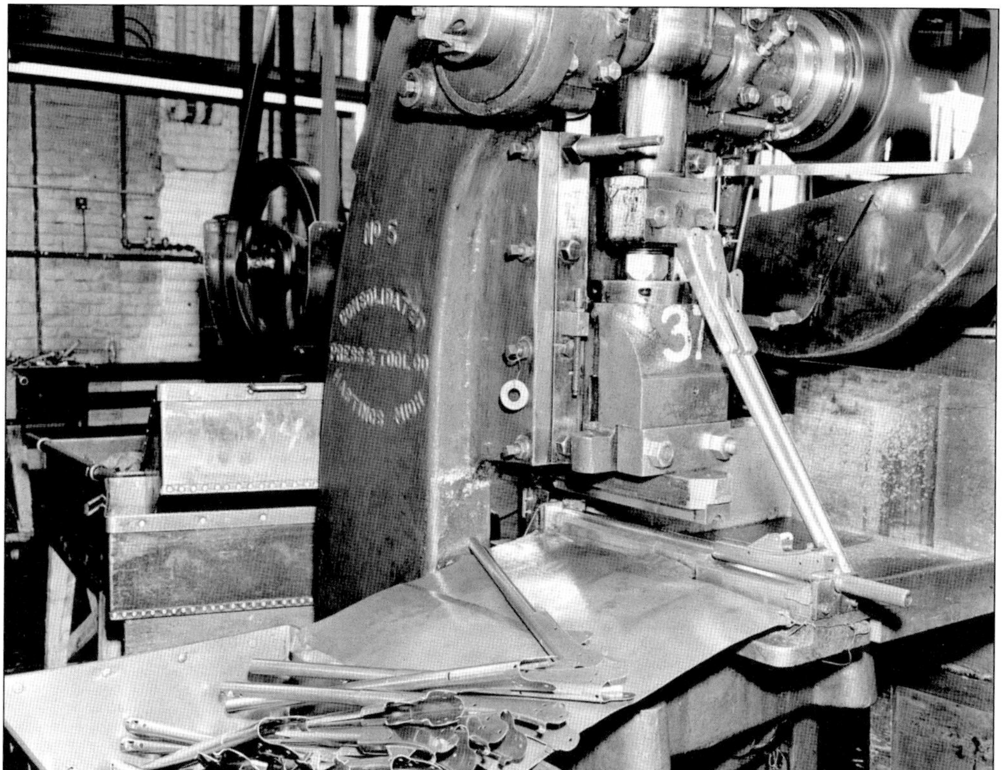

Thin sheet metal was used to form gun barrel shrouds with this stamping press.

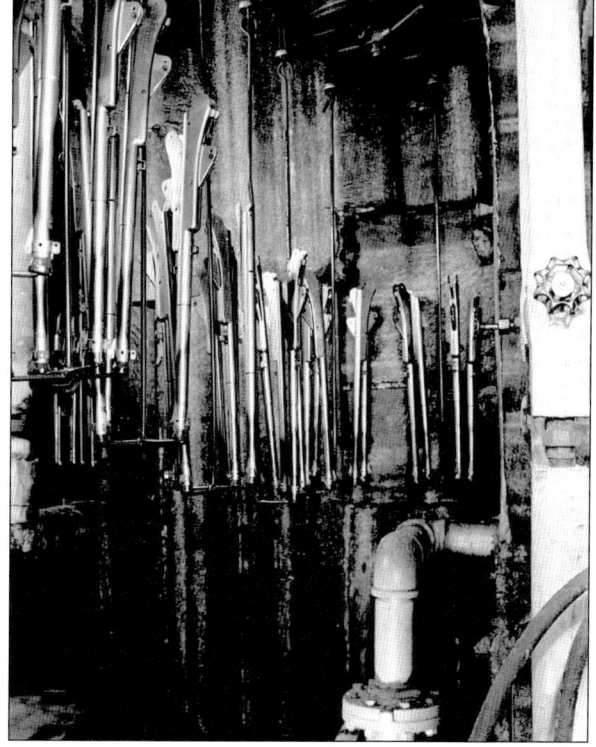

Gun barrel shrouds hang from hooks during the finishing process.

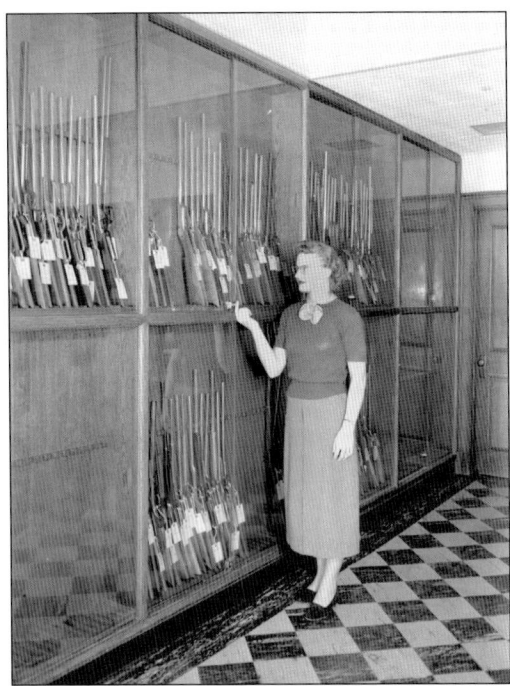

During the Great Depression, Daisy offered a trade-in program allowing kids to turn in old guns to receive new models for a small fee. The program was very successful, as more than 100,000 older guns were turned in. While some were of no value, many were early models that became part of the company's archive of guns. The guns were displayed in the Daisy lobby in Plymouth and are now at the Daisy Museum in Rogers, Arkansas.

"Old 766" sat on the railroad spur behind the Daisy plant in 1949, serving as an auxiliary source of heat while workmen changed the old coal-fired boilers to oil. The project included the installation of two oil burners, as well as sinking a 20,000-gallon storage tank in the ground. Shavings and sawdust from the woodworking department would be burned in an incinerator built into the base of the old lighting plant's brick chimney.

Everyone was asked to pitch in to help the company save on costs. This poster encouraged employees to pick up scrap from the floor to recycle because it meant money in their pockets. Daisy instituted profit sharing in 1946; this photograph was shot in June 1949.

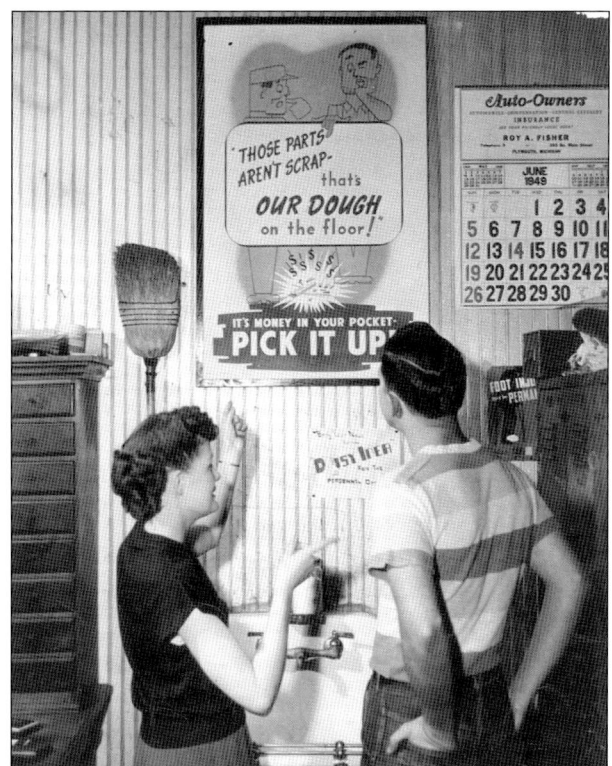

Daisy employees relax on the company lawn during their lunch break in the late 1940s.

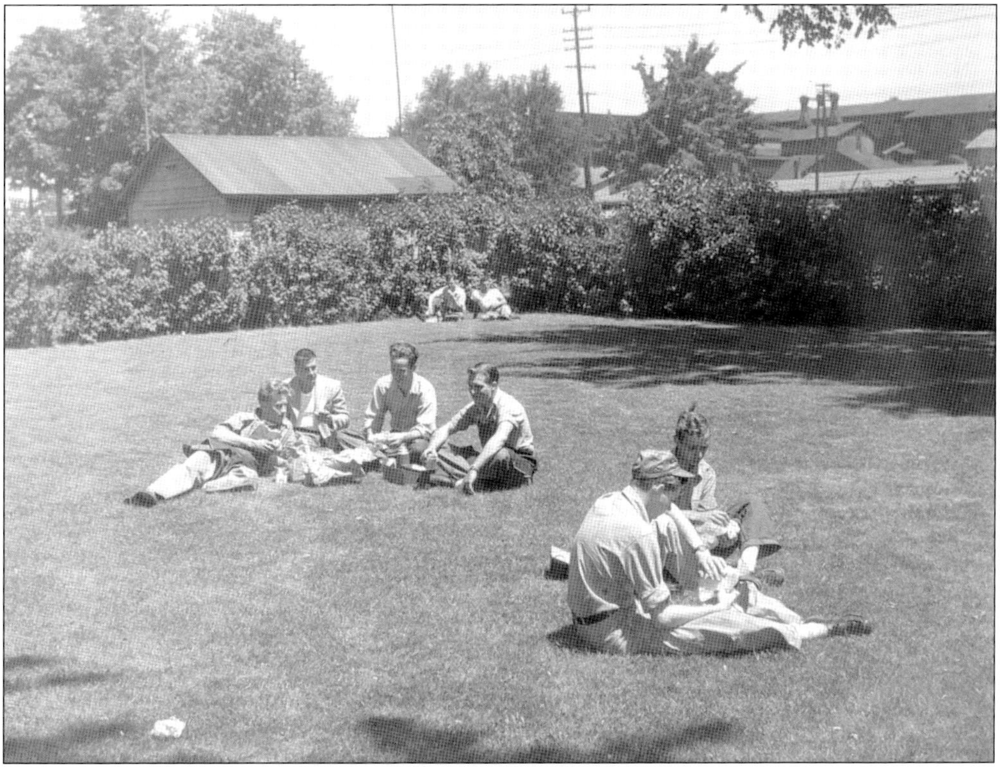

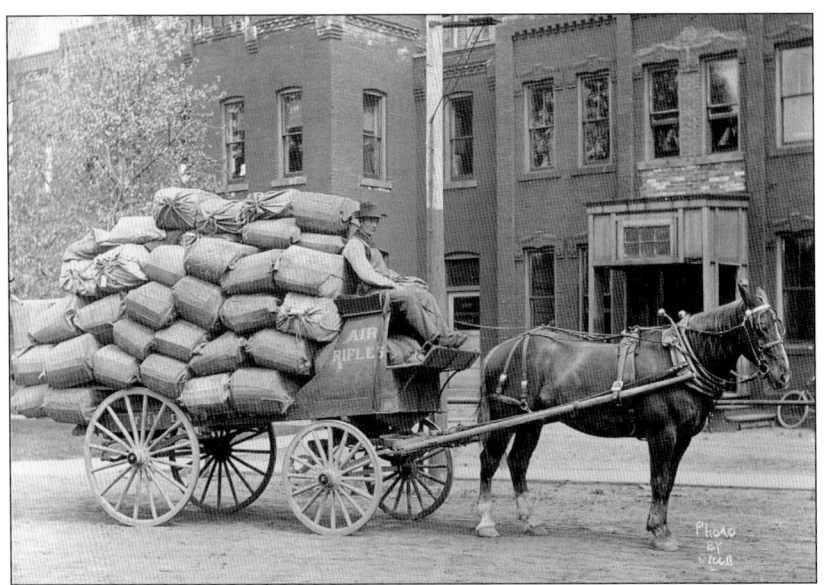

Edward C. Hough sits atop a dray in 1906 preparing to deliver air rifles for Daisy.

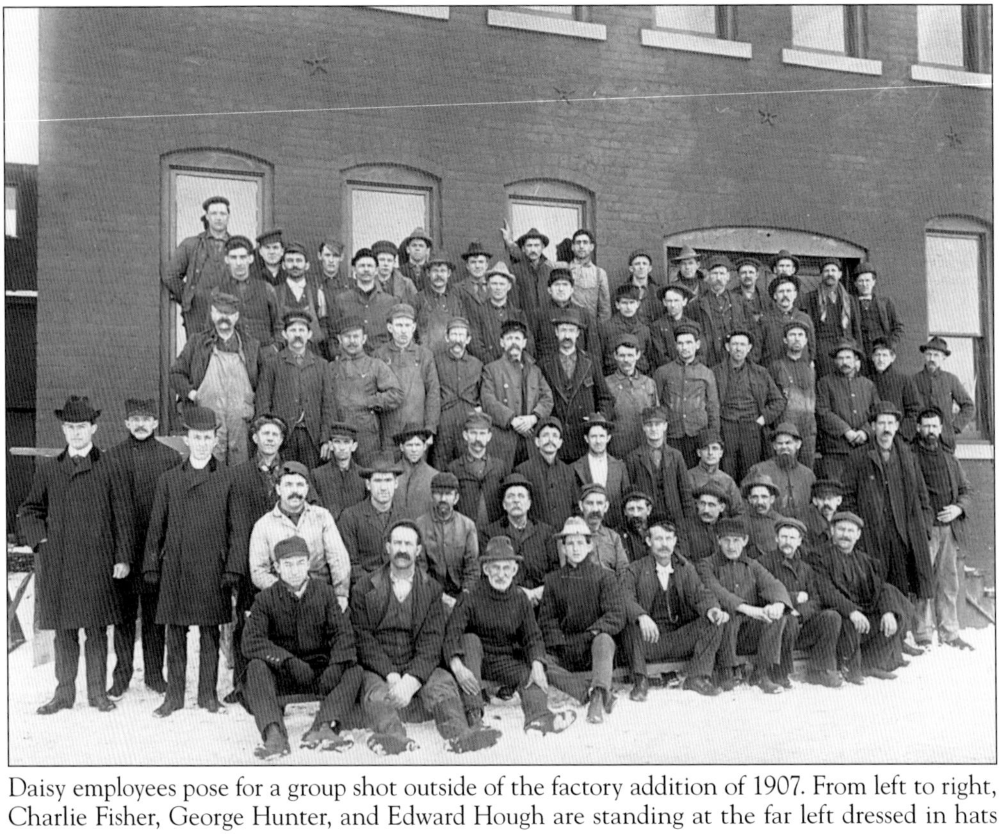

Daisy employees pose for a group shot outside of the factory addition of 1907. From left to right, Charlie Fisher, George Hunter, and Edward Hough are standing at the far left dressed in hats and overcoats.

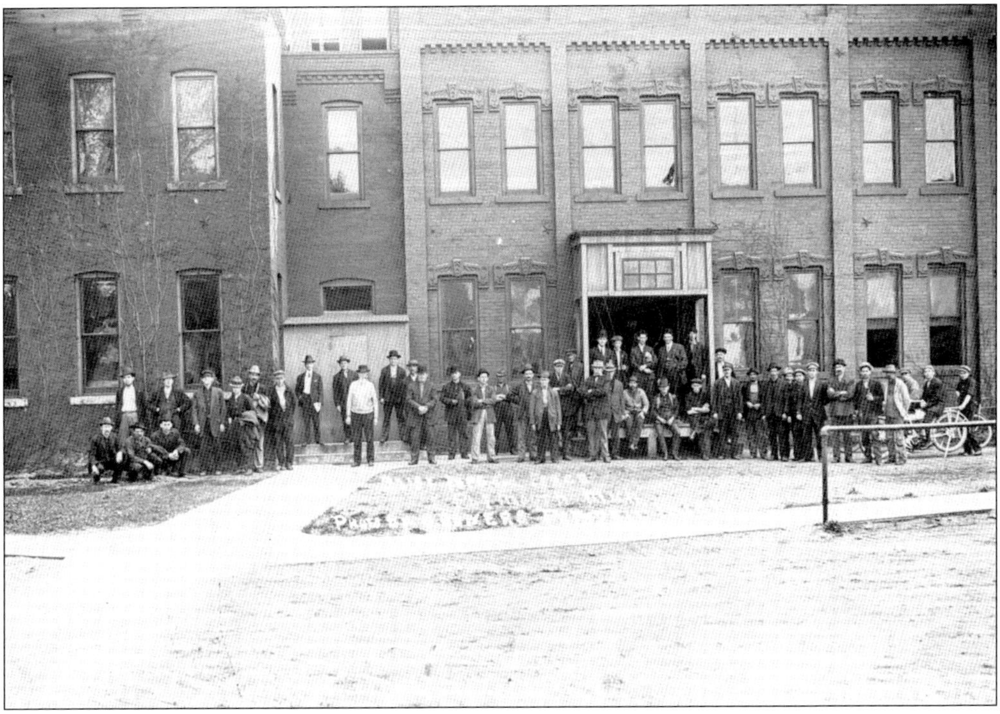

Above, employees pose for a company photograph in front of the original Daisy factory building around 1910. Note that the company entrance is still part of the original building. Another company photograph is seen below, but this one was shot in 1916 in front of the original factory. By this time, the entrance to the company had been moved from the original building to the section that joined the old building with the office addition of 1901. The second set of windows from the left replaced the old entrance.

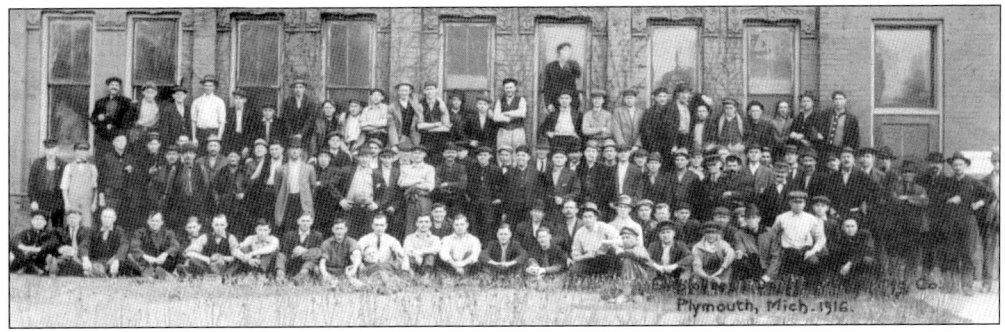

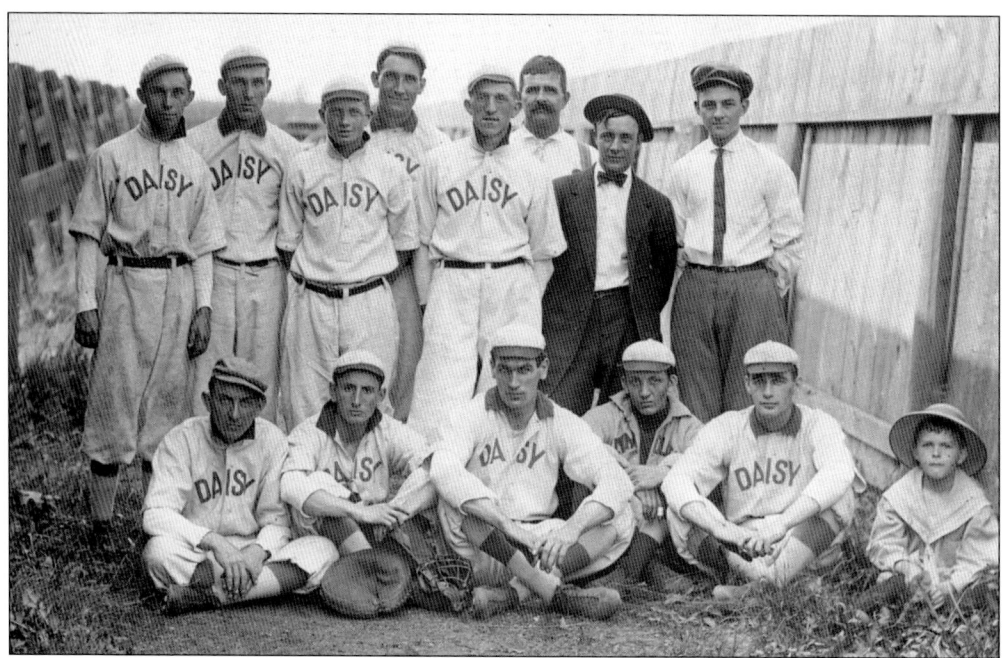

Daisy fielded a baseball team for many years, beginning as early as 1910 when this photograph was taken. The team participated in the local league, playing against the Plymouth team as well as other local teams. Two players in this photograph are identified: William Taylor is standing on the far left, and Claude Williams is seated second from the left.

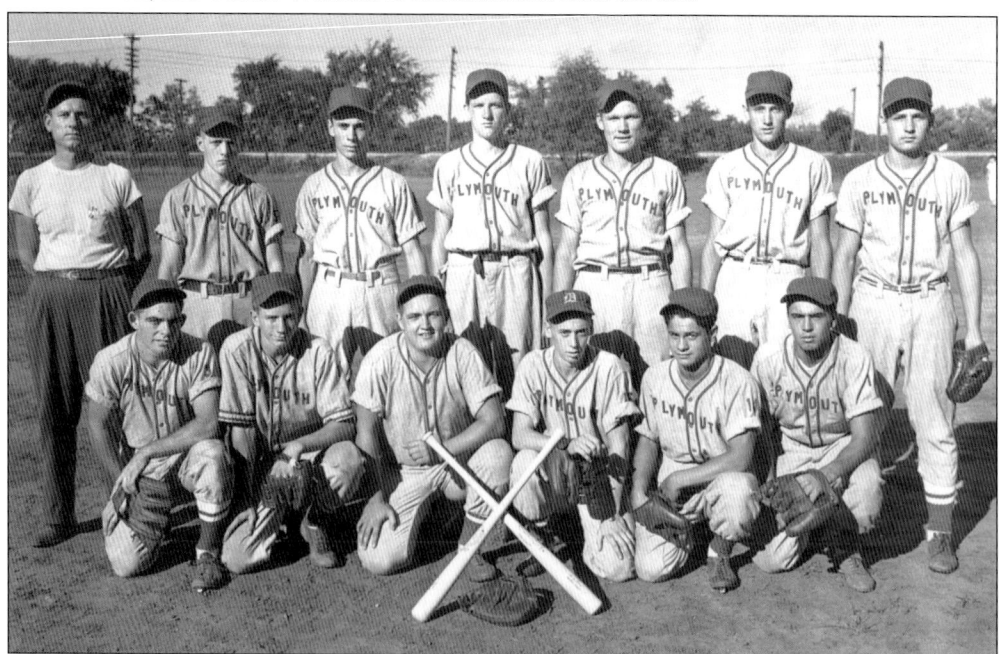

The Daisy-sponsored boys' baseball team in 1949 was considered the best Class D team in the state. From left to right are (first row) William Newstead, Richard Fenton, Robert Gow, E. David Reitzel, Ariston Luzod, and Thomas Fairbanks; (second row) manager Walter Dzurus, Richard Gray, Mickey Brown, Wally Dzurus Jr., Harold Campbell, Ed Groves, and Ron Bouldin.

The Daisy-sponsored girls' basketball team won the Inter-City League championship in March 1950. The squad's record for the season was 12–2. Manager Floyd Fleming holds the traveling trophy that the team kept as long as it retained the championship.

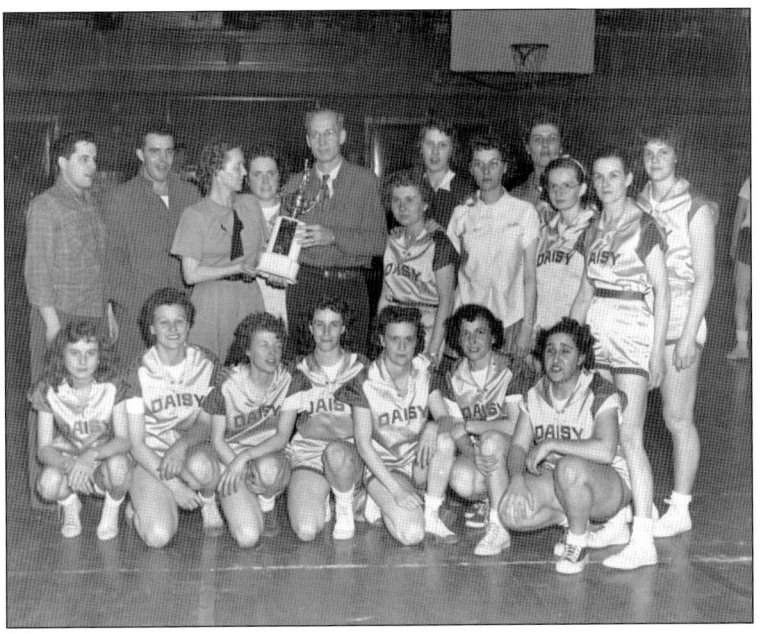

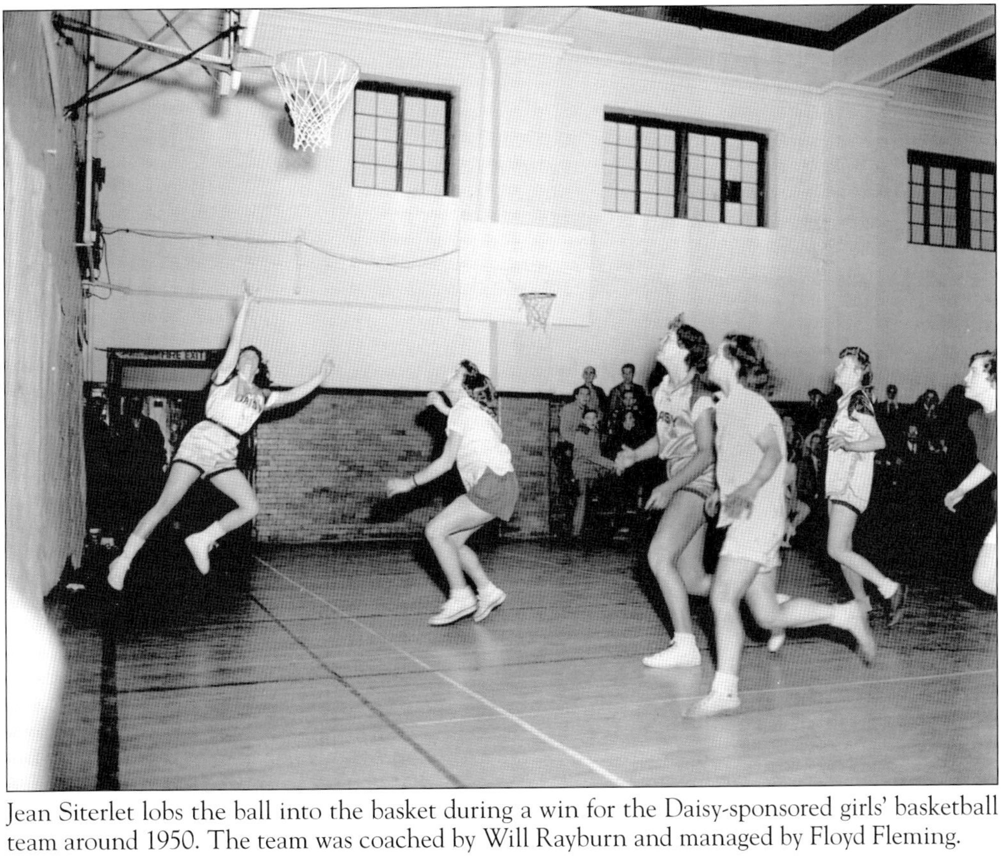

Jean Siterlet lobs the ball into the basket during a win for the Daisy-sponsored girls' basketball team around 1950. The team was coached by Will Rayburn and managed by Floyd Fleming.

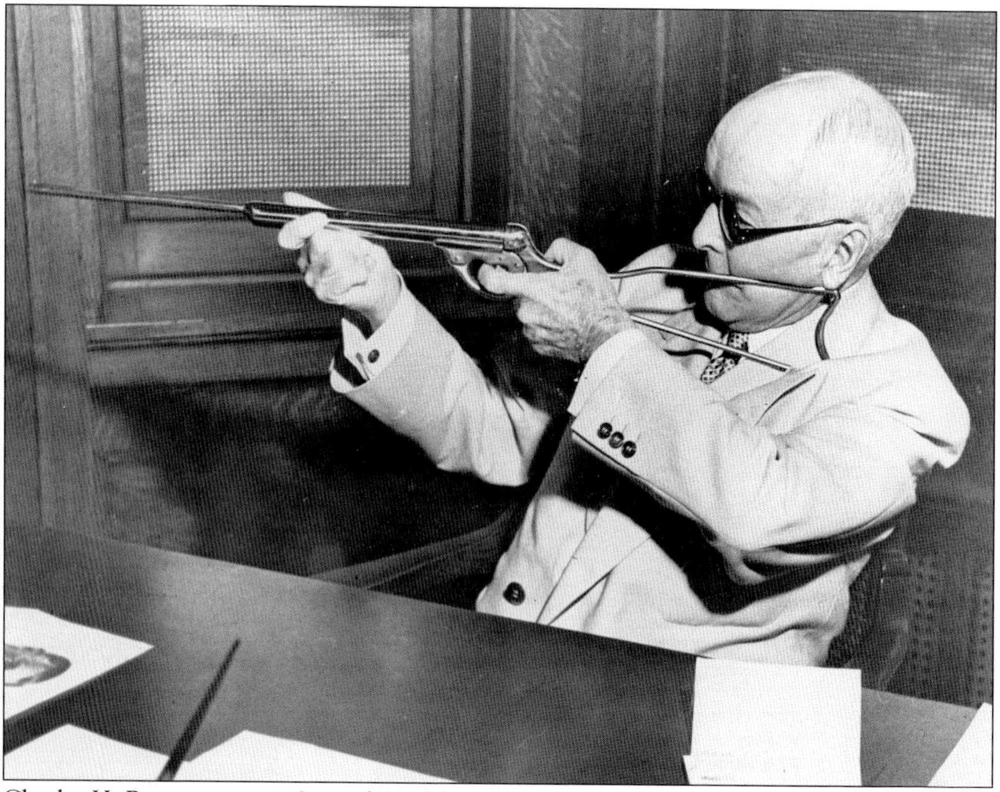

Charles H. Bennett aims a Second Model Daisy, reminiscing about his many hours spent on the road in the early 1890s as a traveling salesman for the Plymouth Iron Windmill Company. According to historian Wesley Powers, this gun is believed to have a prototype receiver, not a production receiver, as there are no markings. The air chamber and barrel are from a First Model Daisy. This air rifle is on exhibit at the Daisy Museum.

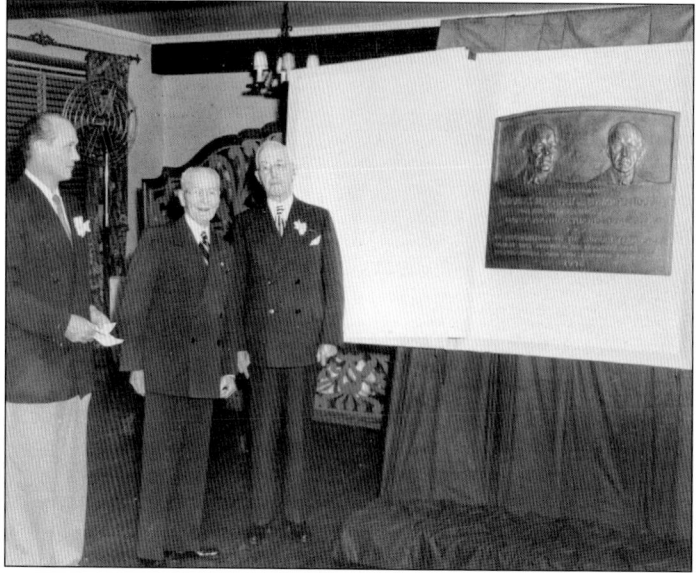

Cass Hough (left) dedicates a 60-year plaque in 1948 to Charles Bennett (center), and Ed Hough for their teamwork and leadership of the Daisy Manufacturing Company.

Cass Sheffield Hough (1904–1990) graduated from Culver Military Academy in 1921 and the University of Michigan in 1925. In 1926, he performed his first solo flight in a Hisso Jenny biplane and held pilot's license no. 1 in Michigan. Cass joined his father, Edward, at Daisy in 1926. Cass was a visionary who guided Daisy in new directions over the next 50 years.

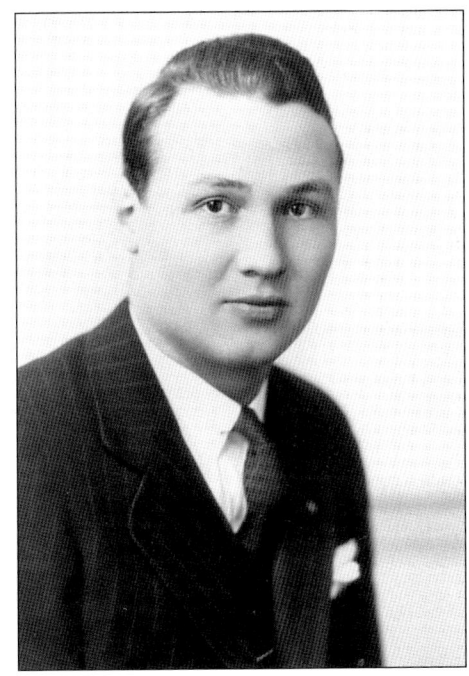

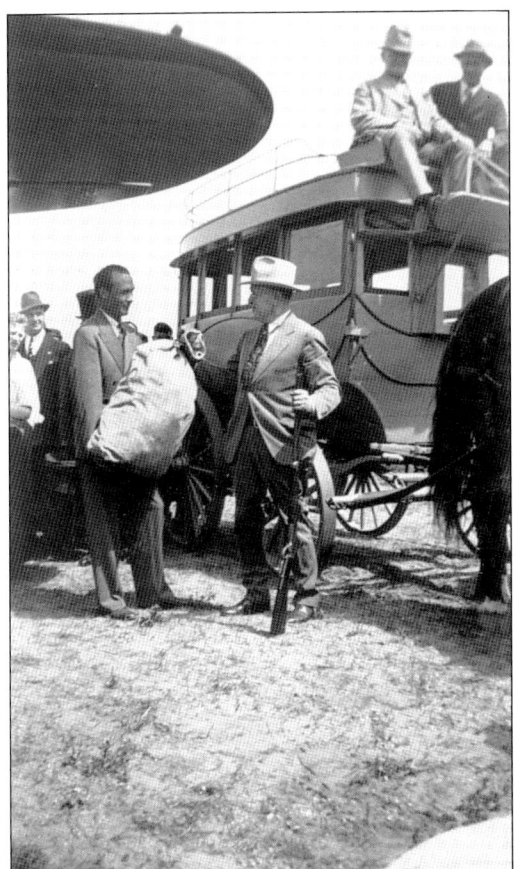

In May 1938, the United States observed Airmail Week, celebrating the 20th anniversary of the inauguration of airmail service. Henry Ford sent an old stagecoach and horse team from Dearborn to Plymouth, driven by Plymouthite Harry Robinson, with Elmer Perrin, a mail carrier of Northville, riding shotgun. Harry Lee (right) handed Cass Hough the first shipment of airmail, destined to be sent directly from Plymouth. Hough flew the mail to its destination.

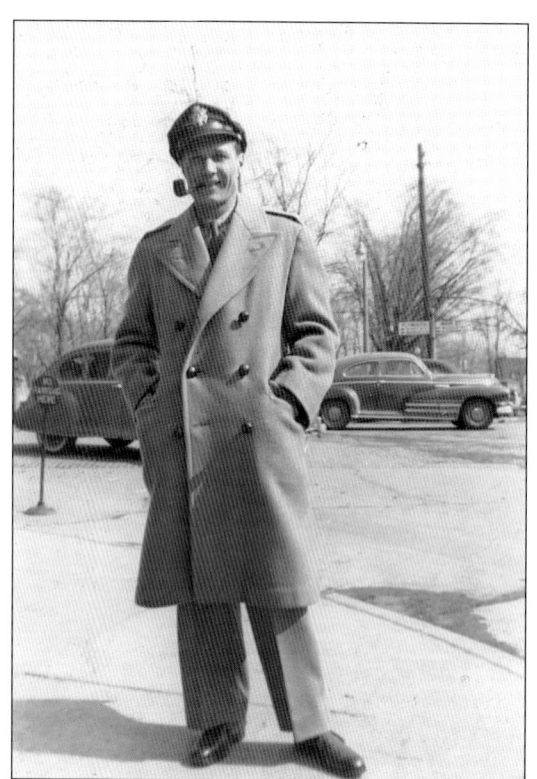

Cass Hough was commissioned into the US Army Air Corps Reserve in 1938 and was assigned to Selfridge Field in Harrison Township, Michigan. He was called to active duty in 1941 before Pearl Harbor and flew a P-38 to England. He received acclaim for his problem-solving skills and flying ability. In this 1943 image, Hough is a lieutenant colonel. He was released from active duty in 1945 as a colonel and returned to Daisy.

Cass Hough served in many positions during his extensive career at Daisy, including director, sales and advertising manager, executive vice president, and president. He was elected president on January 29, 1959, five days after his father died. Hough was instrumental in the relocation of Daisy to Rogers, Arkansas, a move that his father opposed. This portrait was taken in Hough's office at Daisy in Plymouth in 1950 when he was elected mayor of the city.

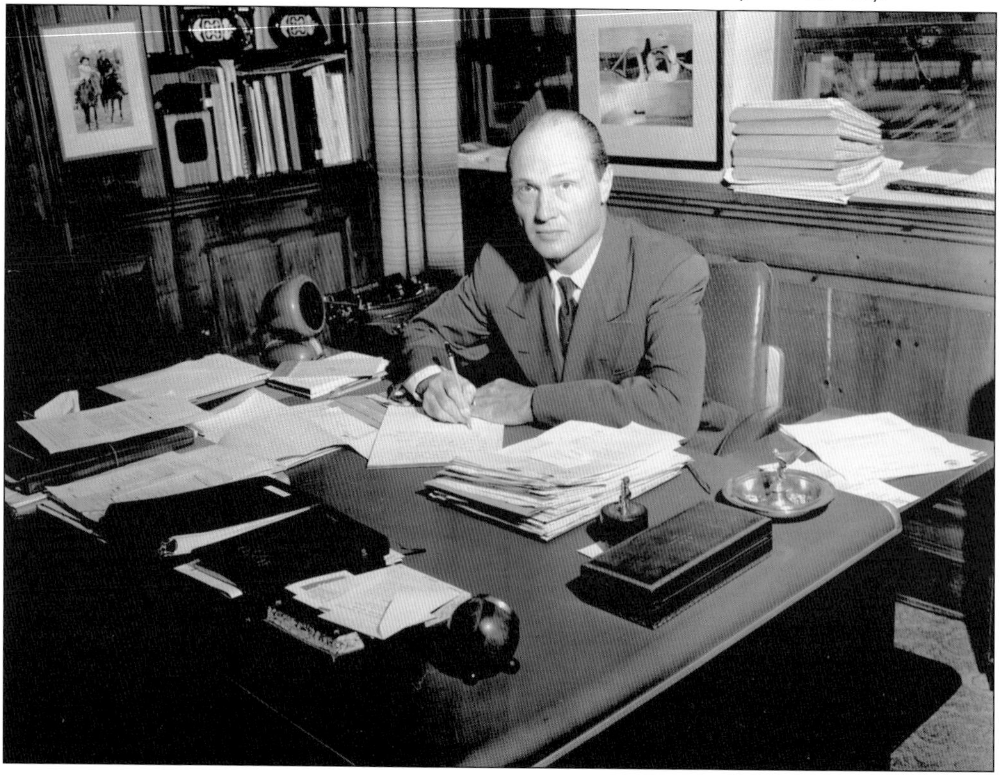

Seven

THE ESSENCE OF DAISY

Daisy began its unique marketing strategy in 1895, printing and distributing a poster that showed a train loaded with Daisy air guns traveling around the world. That was just the beginning of Daisy's aggressive approach to advertising both its brand and its products, aiming to become the dominant air gun manufacturer. The company has always shown a willingness to experiment with innovations while keeping down expenses by reusing patterns and equipment from earlier models. Cass S. Hough, grandson of Louis Cass Hough, joined the Daisy team in 1926, bringing along an unexpected natural marketing ability. Cass left his astronomy-teaching job at the University of Michigan to join his father, Edward Cass Hough, in the "family business." Cass was sent over to work at Daisy-owned Markham Air Rifle Company in 1928 as secretary and treasurer. By 1931, he was named Daisy sales and advertising manager and never looked back. At a time when the United States was suffering from the Great Depression, Daisy's strategy was to keep introducing new products with unique features. Cass even took to barnstorming as a relief pilot to promote the new Buck Rogers line in 1934 and 1935. All of this marketing and advertising created an insatiable demand for Daisy products—until World War II began. Like other manufacturers that used steel in their products, Daisy had to retool during the war years to help with the war effort. The company was able to produce some wooden guns during the lean war years, but its primary focus was making 37-millimeter canisters and assorted other war materials. Even after the war ended, the company had difficulty returning to its pre-war footing because of the lack of available steel. According to *Daisy's Diary*, in 1947 "customers [were] pleading for BB guns and shot—telling us to 'name our prices.' " About the time that Daisy was catching up with customer demand, the Korean War broke out and production was again curtailed because of the lack of steel. By 1953, the company was back on track, introducing 10 new guns in one year.

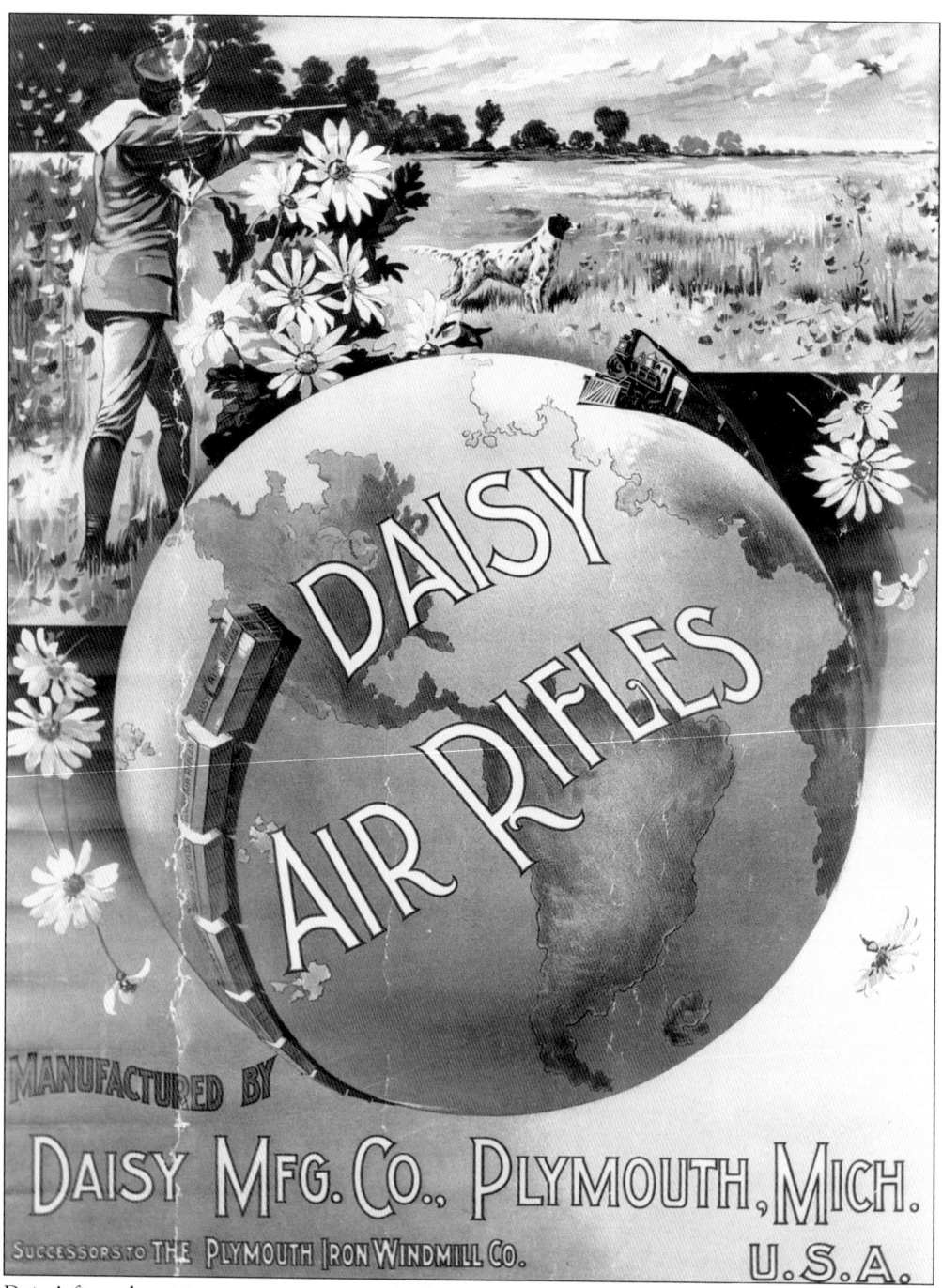

Daisy's first advertising appropriation was for the in-store poster seen here. The creation of the poster in 1895 depleted the advertising budget of $2,000 but initiated an aggressive marketing campaign of appealing to America's youth. The advertising budget for the company increased each year, and by 1958, the year Daisy left Plymouth, it was nearly $250,000. Note that the ad indicates that Daisy Manufacturing Company was "Successors to the Plymouth Iron Windmill Company."

At right, a little boy in Chicago is pleased to pose with his Third Model Daisy air rifle. The Third Model was produced between 1891 and 1899. It is unclear which variation of the Third Model this gun is, but the raised-letter variation one, manufactured in 1895, was the first Daisy gun to have the new company name on the grip. Below, a boy from Jamaica in Queens, New York, poses with his tent, flag, and stacked air rifles. The air rifles on the left and right are Third Model Daisies, while the one in the center was made by James A. Dubuar Manufacturing of Northville and is a Globe. Daisy purchased Dubuar in 1904 and marketed the Globe and Warrior models through 1906. (Both courtesy of Wesley Powers.)

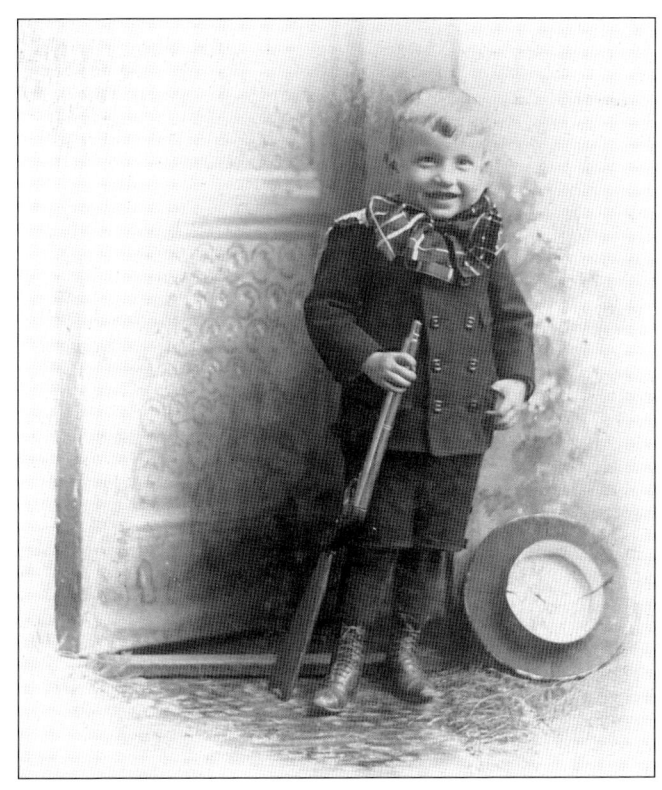

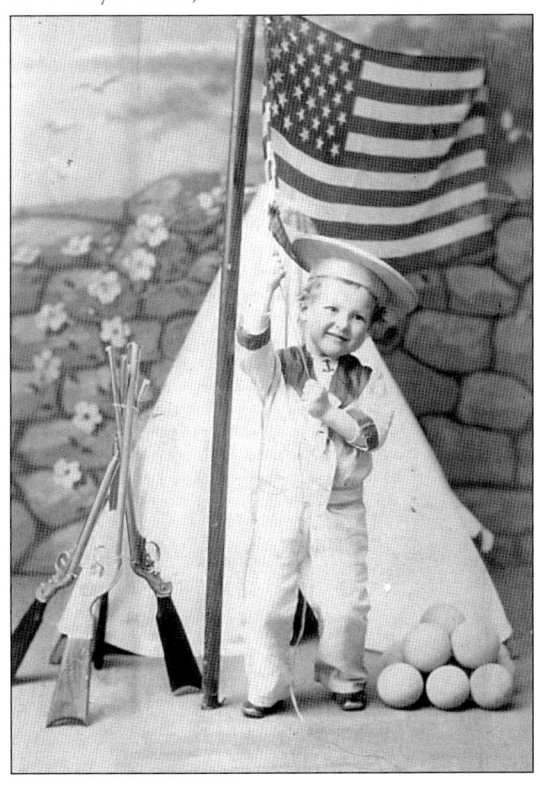

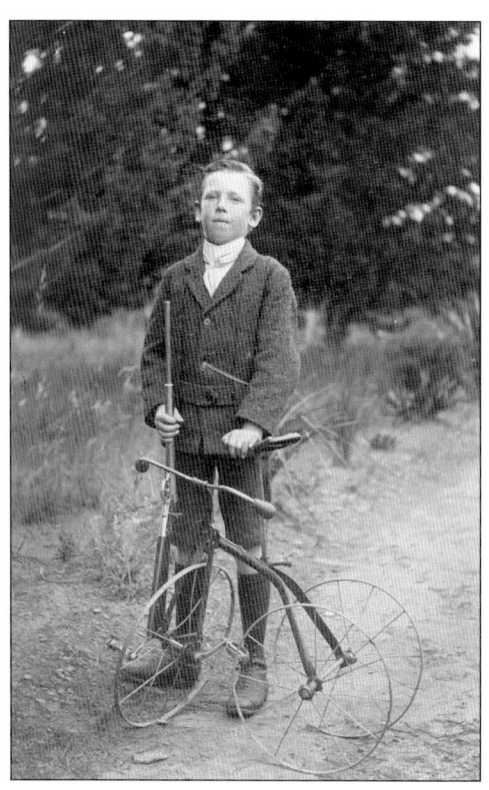

At left, a boy with his tricycle holds a 20th-Century Model Daisy. Below, a barefoot boy in overalls and straw hat also holds a 20th-Century Model Daisy. Written on the back of the photograph is "Gleen Godin." Daisy marketed the new 20th-Century Daisy in 1898 as being "so arranged that the shooting barrel can be instantly removed and either darts or BB shot used." (Both courtesy of Wesley Powers.)

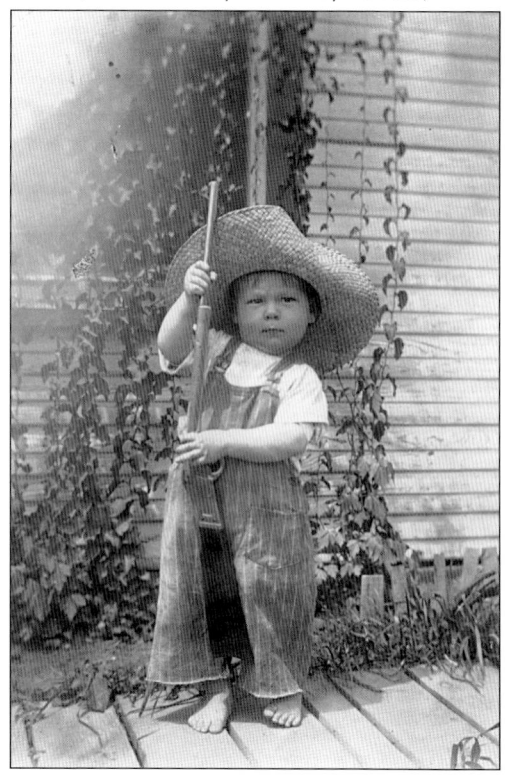

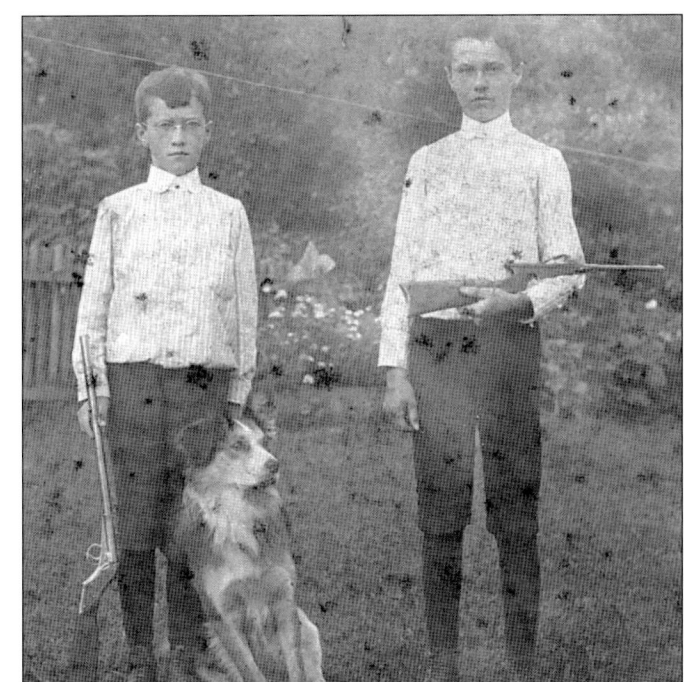

These boys, possibly "Scotch and Carbon Black" from what is written on the back of the image, display two different Plymouth guns. The boy on the left has a Daisy Sentinel, while the boy on the right has a Hamilton No. 15. Daisy first offered the Sentinel in 1899–1900. It was designed by Alfred W. Chaffee, a disgruntled defector from Markham Manufacturing Company. The photograph was probably taken about 1901, as the Hamilton No. 15 became available that year. (Courtesy of Wesley Powers.)

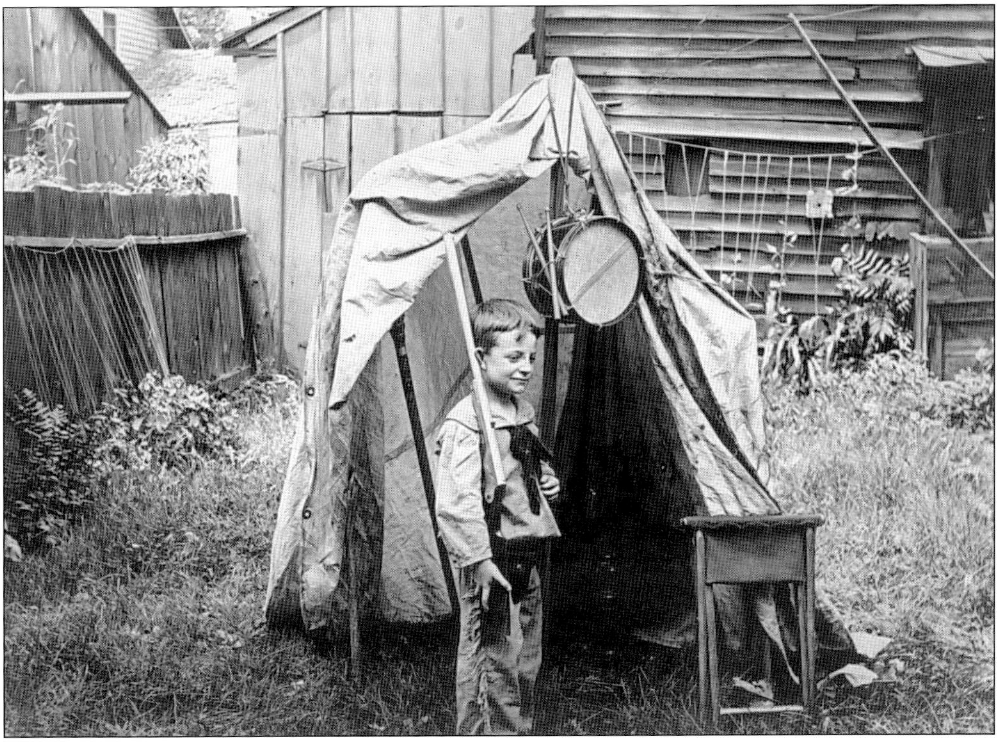

This little boy appears to be ready for any eventuality with his tent, folding chair, drum, and a Bennett Model Daisy. This model, also known as No. 3, was possibly named for the first patent holder for this gun, Frederick F. Bennett, not Frederick's older brother Charles H. Bennett. The gun was manufactured between 1903 and 1909. (Courtesy of Wesley Powers.)

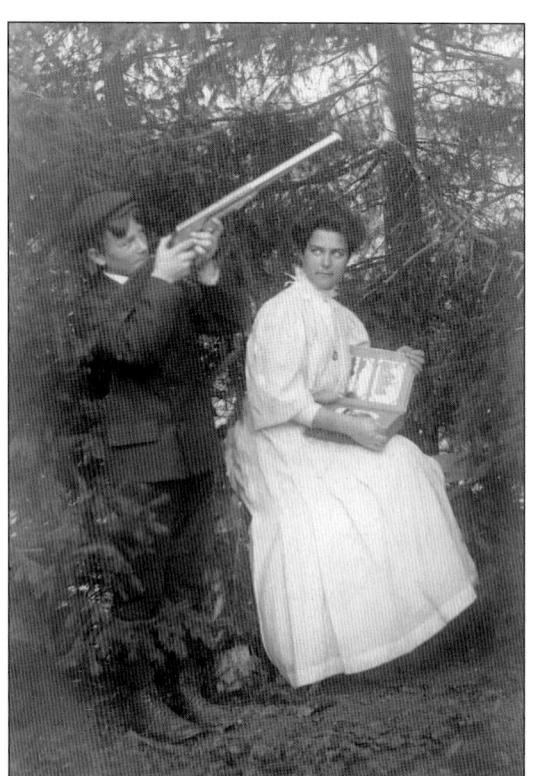

A young man takes aim with his Bennett Model Daisy, while a woman holding a photograph album watches warily. According to historian Gary Garber, "The No. 3 Bennett looked more like a real rifle than any gun Daisy had previously made." (Courtesy of Wesley Powers.)

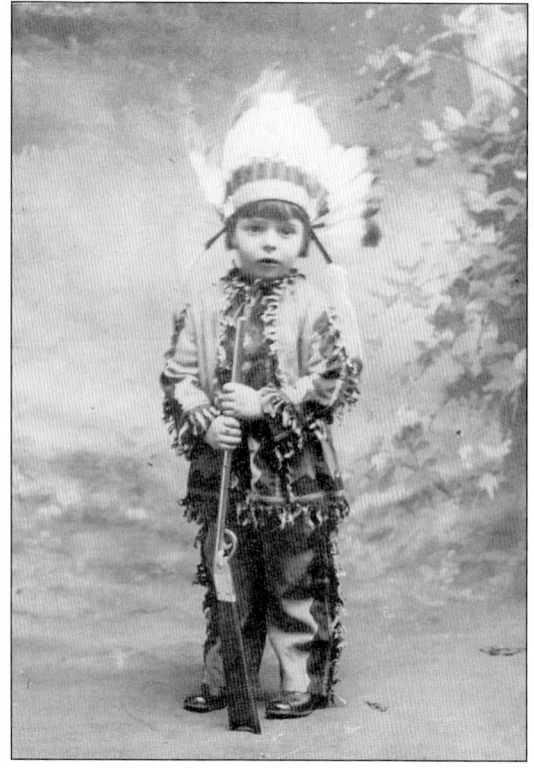

A boy dressed in a Native American costume holds a No. 20 Little Daisy Single-Shot air rifle. The boy was from West Hoboken, New Jersey. Daisy began manufacturing this gun in 1909 in a variety of configurations before ceasing production in 1942. It was the least expensive gun during its era according to historian Gary Garber. (Courtesy of Wesley Powers.)

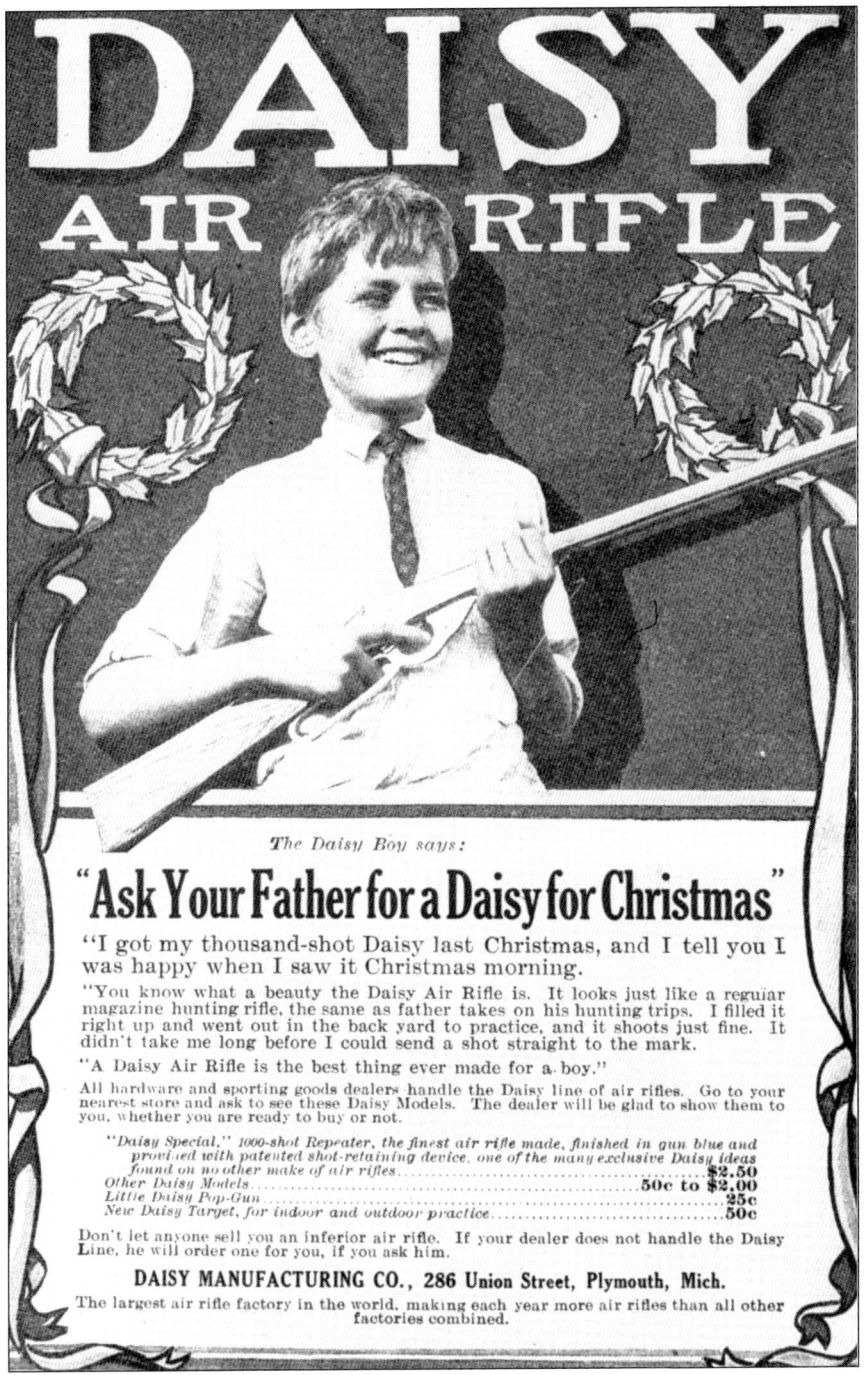

According to *Daisy's Diary*, this was Daisy's first full-page advertisement in a magazine, but there is a discrepancy about when the ad appeared. The book states it was in the October 1907 issue of *American Boy*, but the Little Daisy Pop Gun advertised here was not manufactured until 1908. But *Daisy, It All Starts Here* states the photo shoot was in 1913. This boy, known as "The Happy Daisy Boy," was Rockford Aloysius Reaume, born in 1898 in Michigan. He appeared in many Daisy ads.

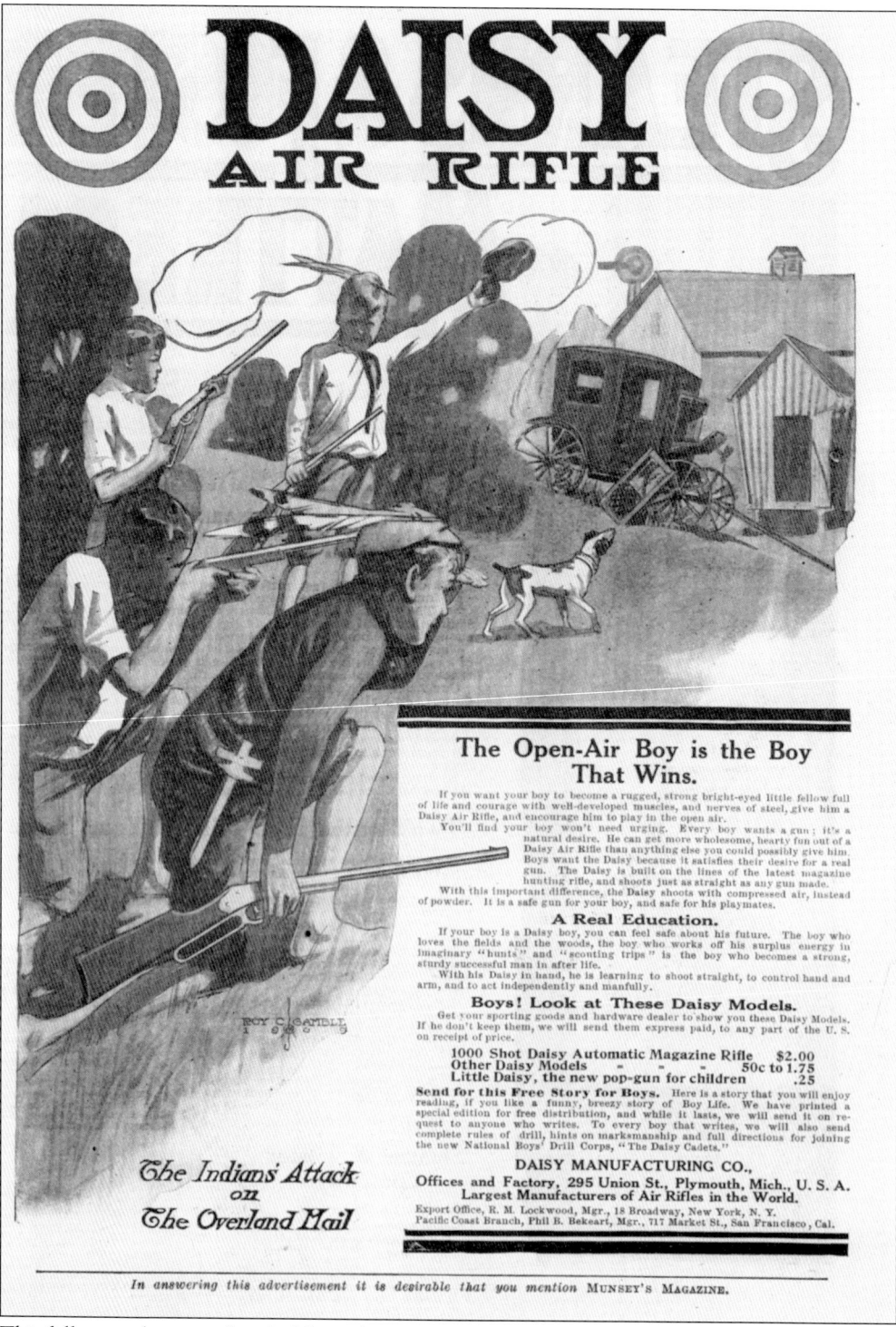

This full-page ad appeared in the November 1909 *Munsey's Magazine*. According to *The Encyclopedia of Science Fiction*, *Munsey's* revolutionized popular magazines when it slashed its price from 25¢ to 10¢. It was published from 1889 until 1929, when it merged with *Argosy*.

A young boy poses coyly with his Daisy Model C air rifle. This gun was manufactured from about 1910 to 1914. (Courtesy of Wesley Powers.)

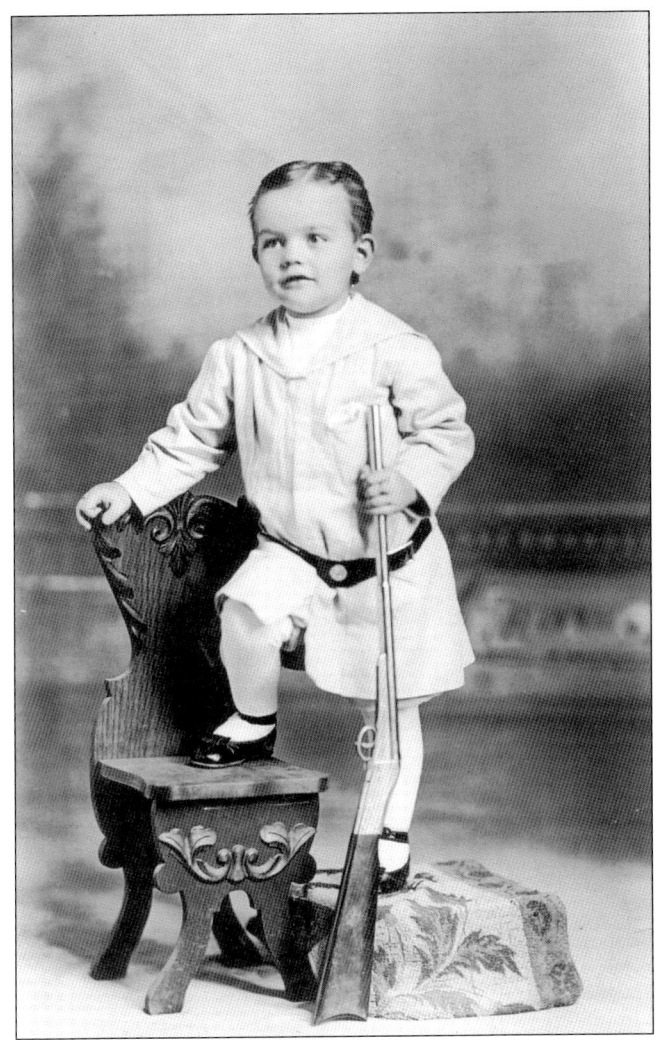

"The Christmas Tree and Toys" was a stereographic image printed by Keystone View Company. The book in the photograph, *Wood Folk at School*, was first published in 1903. A Daisy Model 25 Pump Gun was already opened by the children and is propped up against the wall. The images date to about 1914, when the Model 25 Pump Gun was introduced. (Courtesy of Wesley Powers.)

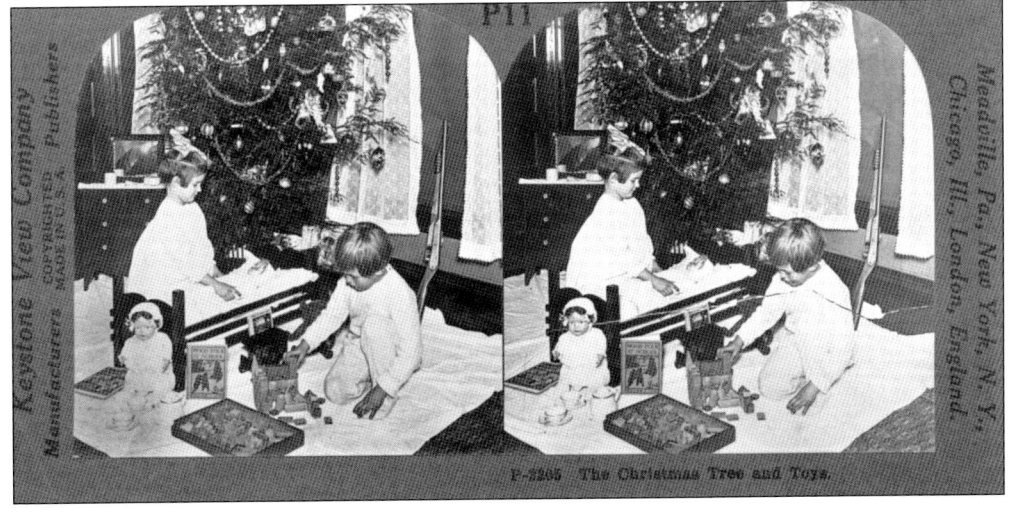

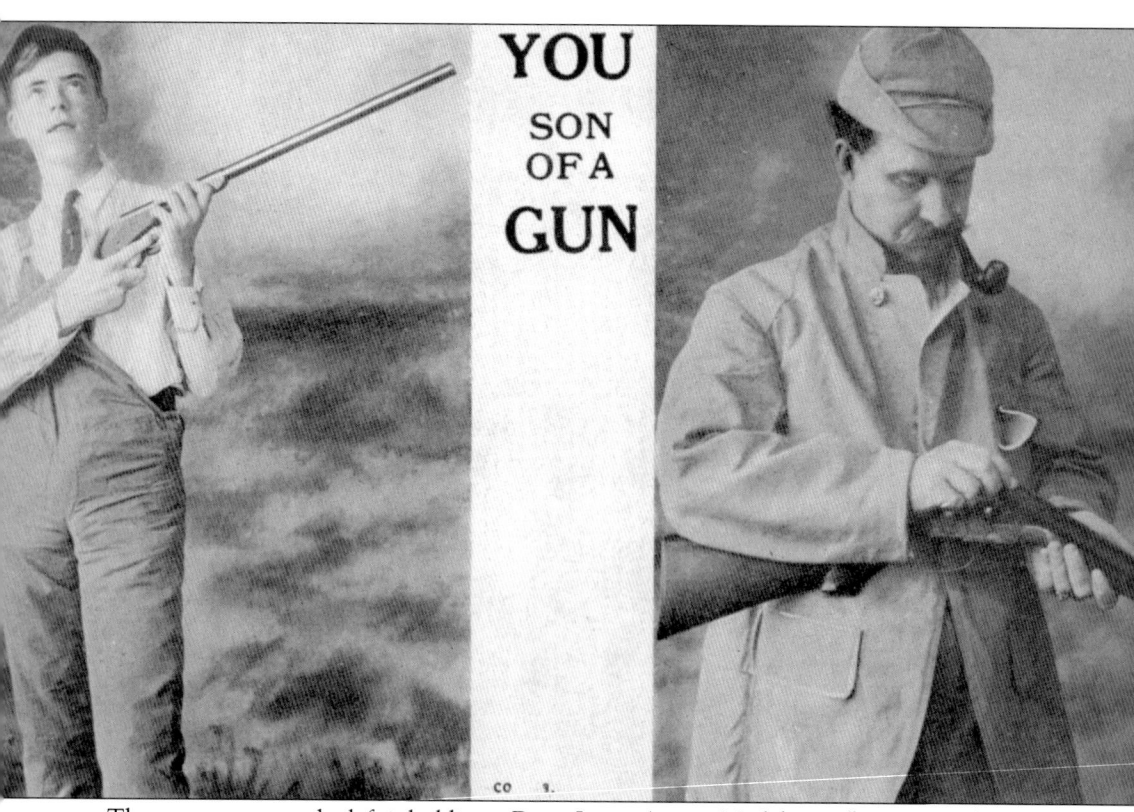

The young man on the left is holding a Daisy Lever-Action Model air rifle, apparently dreaming of the day that he can join his father, who is loading his shotgun. Lever-action guns have a lever under the stock. This type of gun was manufactured beginning in 1903. (Courtesy of Wesley Powers.)

This boy is dressed in a replica World War I–era Army uniform and holds a Daisy Lever-Action gun. (Courtesy of Wesley Powers.)

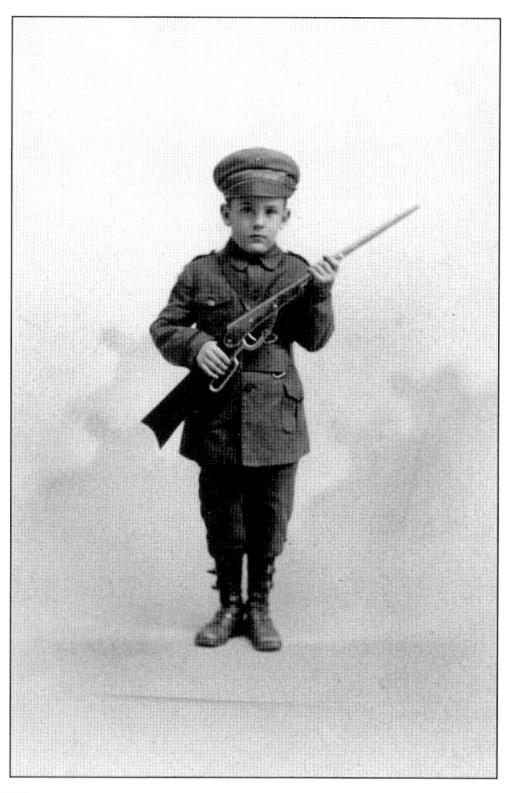

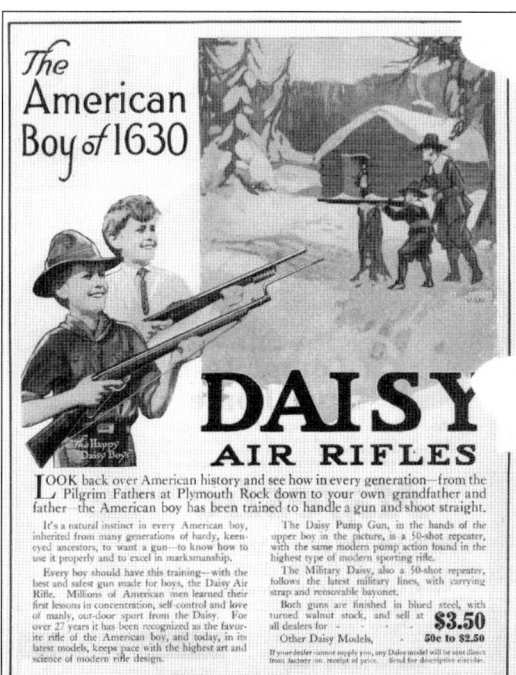

According to *Daisy's Diary*, Daisy began designing a Military Model air rifle in 1914 after World War I began in Europe. The company introduced the new Military Model in January 1916. The twist with this model is that it came with a detachable bayonet. The gun was an instant success, retailing for $5. The steel bayonet with a rubber tip was a first for Daisy, as was the attached sling. This full-page ad appeared in the March 17, 1917, issue of *The Literary Digest*, a weekly magazine published by Funk and Wagnalls. It is interesting to note that the two boys holding guns on the left are the same boy, Rockford Reaume, who appeared in Daisy's first ad. The military-like uniform of the boy in front has been drawn on and the Military Daisy replaced the gun from the original photo shoot. Similarly, the boy in back holds a Daisy Pump Gun, not the Little Daisy Pop Gun he held in the first ad. The words "The Happy Daisy Boys" is superimposed over the boy in front.

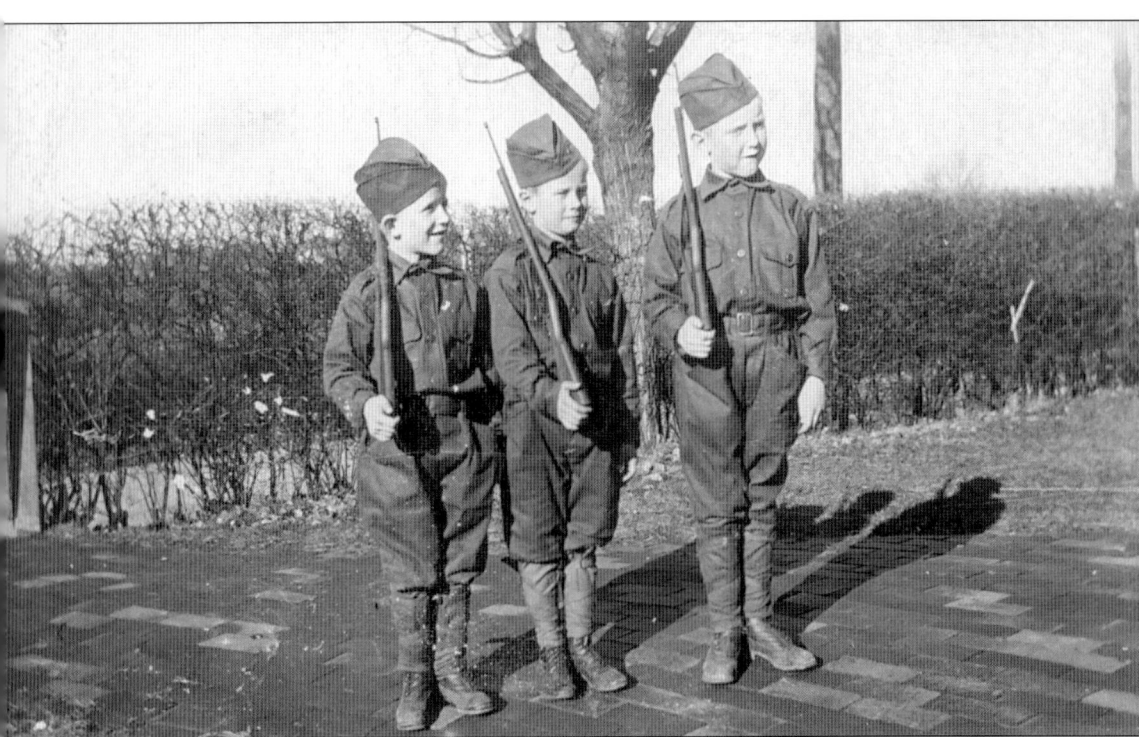

"The Home Guard" is written on the back of this photograph. These boys are, from left to right, Walter ?, Harold Rapp, and Harold ?. All three boys, dressed in World War I–era uniforms, are holding Daisy Military No. 40 air rifles, and all three guns still have bayonets on them. Because the bayonets were detachable, they were easily lost or damaged and are rarely seen in photographs or by collectors. Another reason they disappeared was because parents were not enamored with boys playing with steel bayonets, even with a rubber tip. (Courtesy of Wesley Powers.)

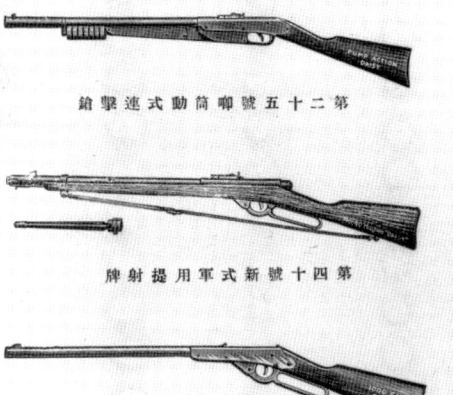

This ad for Daisy products appeared in a Chinese catalog in November 1920, showing how global the company had become by this time.

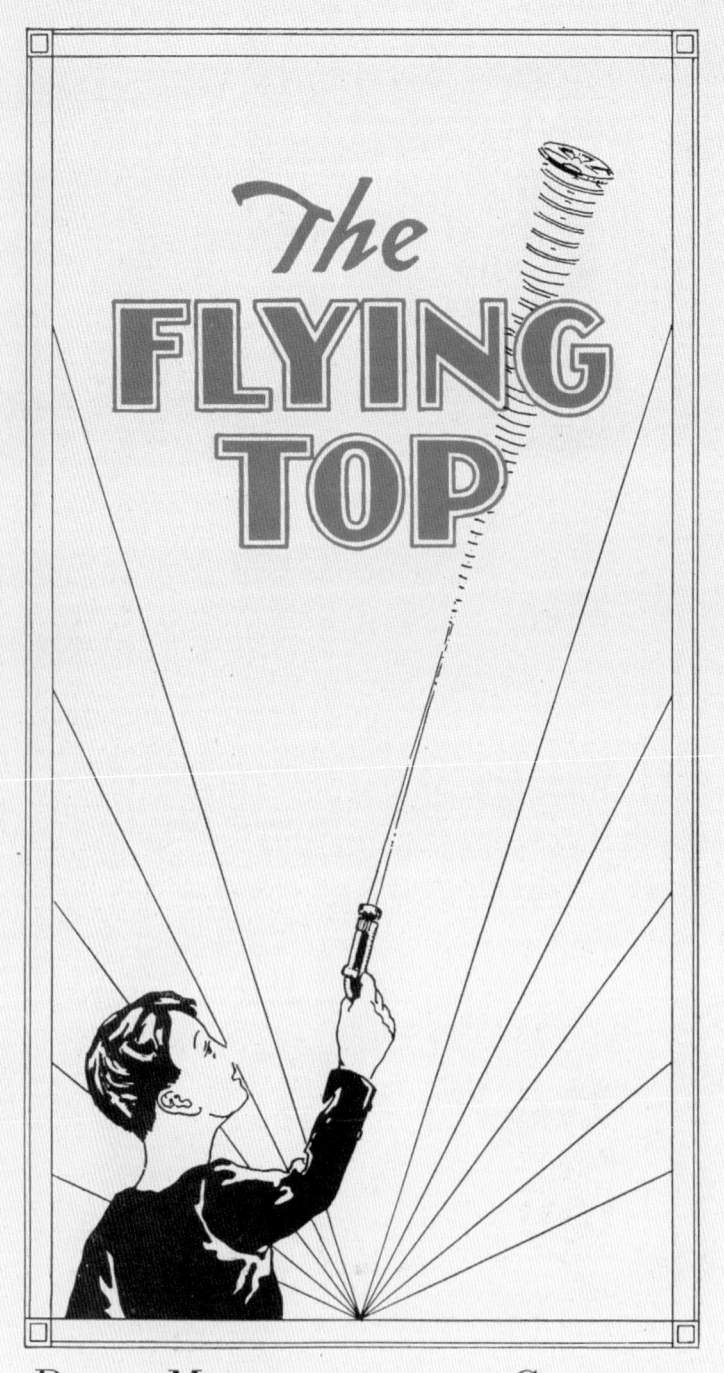

The Daisy Flying Top was available in the early years of the Great Depression, from 1932 to 1934. It sold for 25¢ and could be used indoors and outdoors. It was billed as "a scientific novelty" that "operates upon the same principle as the new Auto-Giro Airplane" in this brochure made available to jobbers. It did not sell well and was sold to General Mills Company for use as a premium in Wheaties cereal.

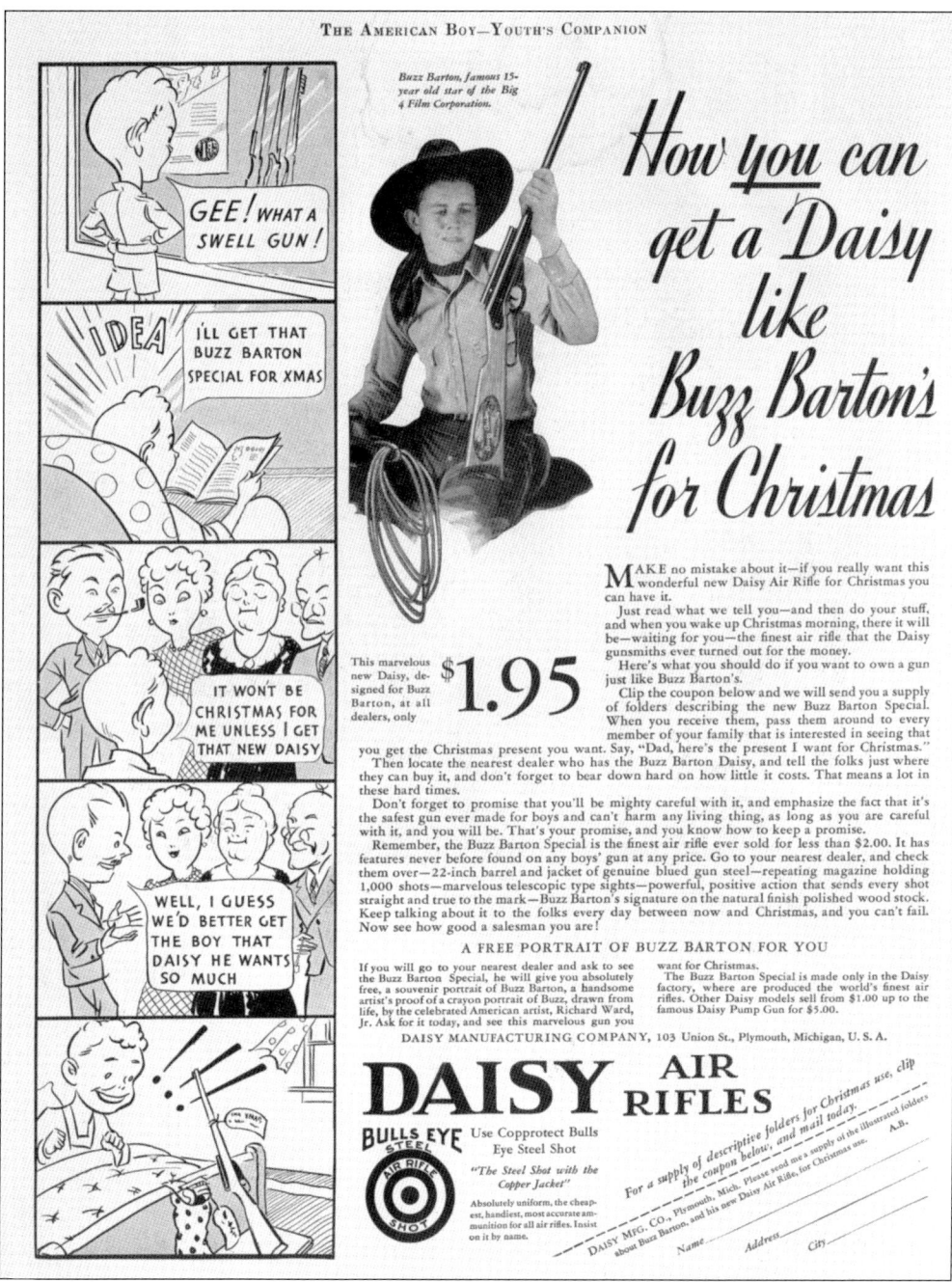

Cass Hough began showing his promotional genius when he signed a contract with the parents of 15-year-old circus hero Buzz Barton—with no royalties. The first Daisy Buzz Barton gun was introduced in 1932. This December 1932 ad from *The American Boy—Youth's Companion* included a coupon for boys to send in to receive literature to share with parents for a Christmas gift idea. The gun was an instant success during the early Depression years.

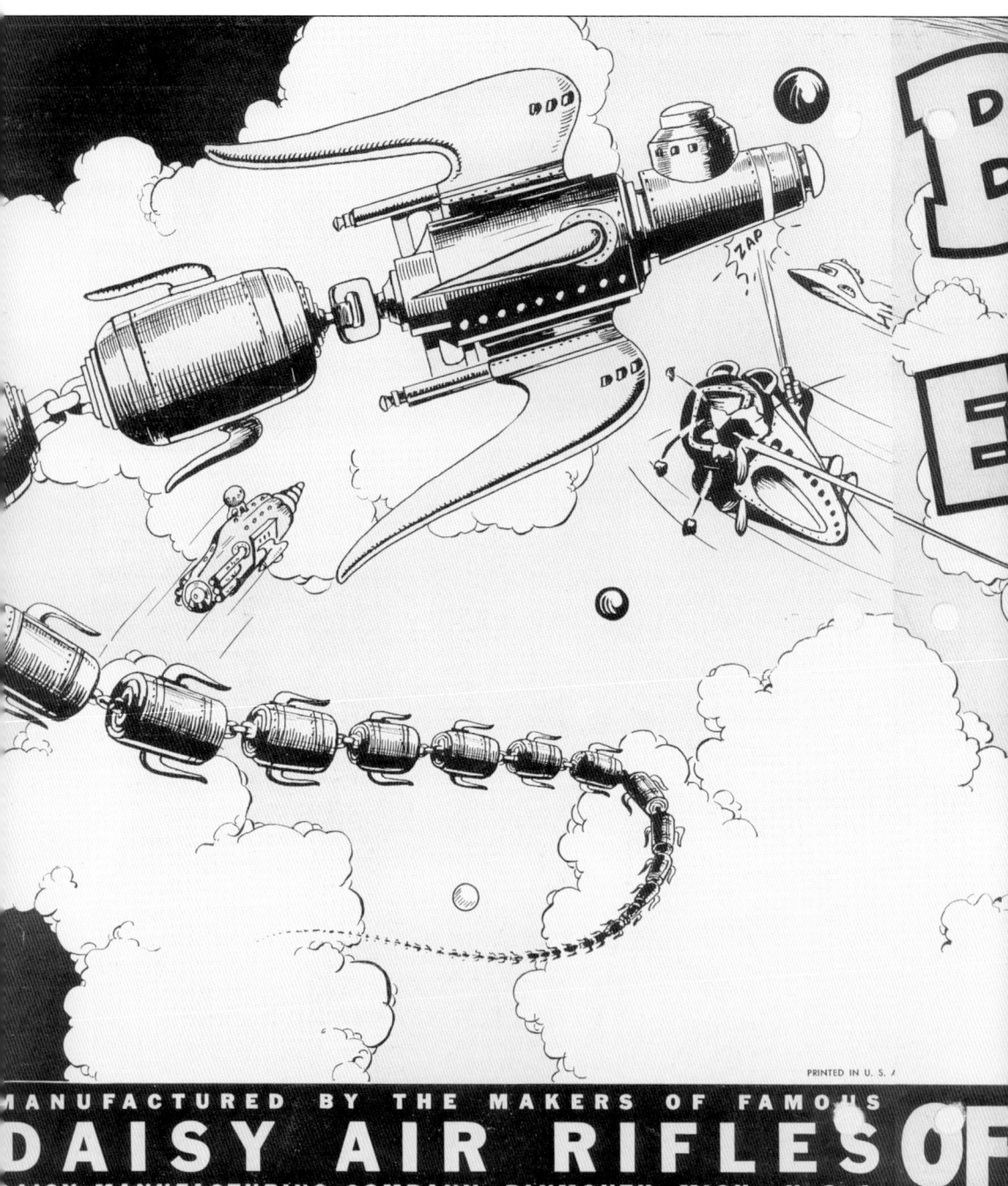

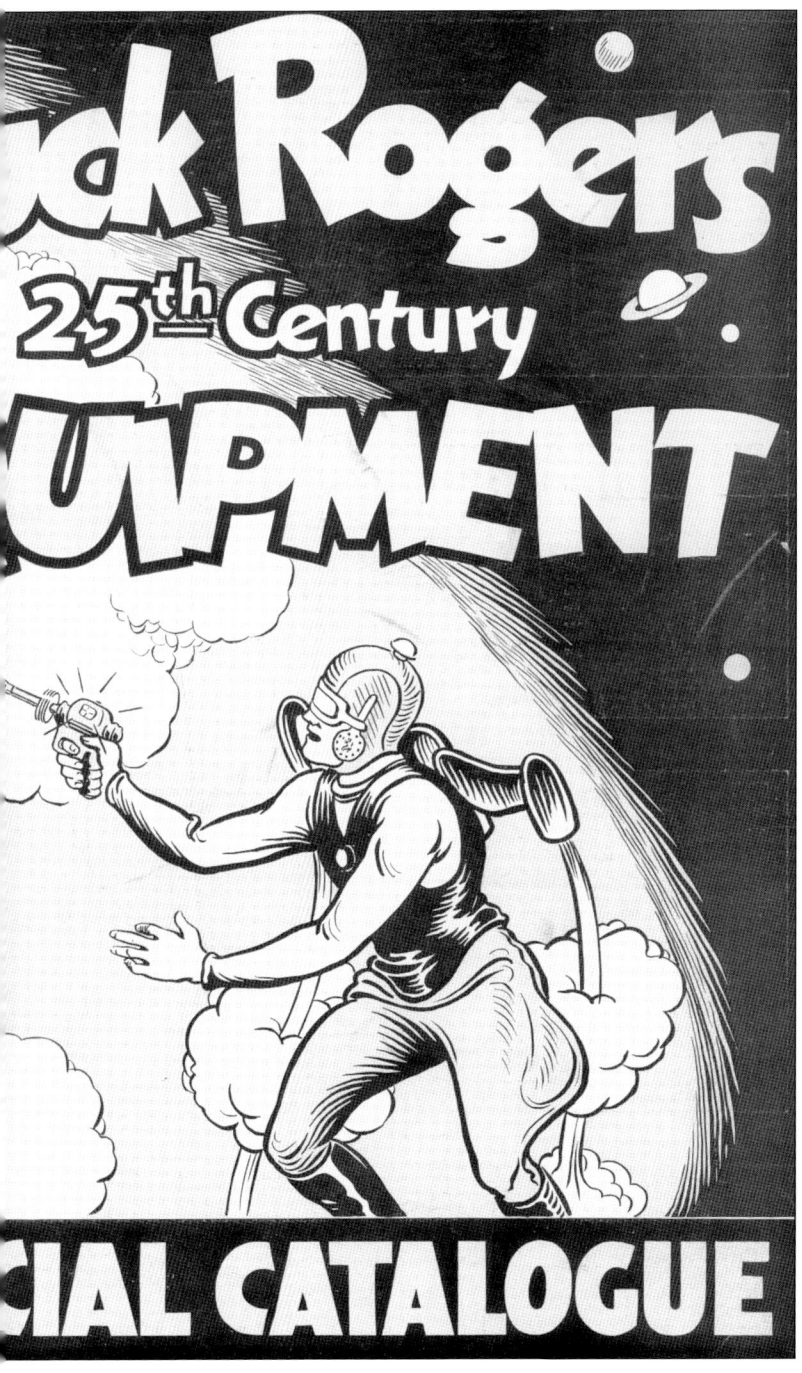

Buck Rogers was a space-travelling cartoon-strip hero from 1929 to 1968. Daisy capitalized on the fictional character's popularity by introducing a line of Buck Rogers, 25th-Century equipment. This is the cover of a four-page catalog from 1935 showing the Buck Rogers line to jobbers. The essential space equipment Daisy sold at that time included two versions of a Buck Rogers Rocket Pistol, a Buck Rogers Disintegrator, Buck Rogers Holsters to go along with the pistols and disintegrator, two different Buck Rogers Helmets, and Buck Rogers Combat Sets with various combinations of the individually sold items. The series was so popular that Daisy issued a "Liquid Helium" Water Pistol in 1937. By 1941, the fad had passed and these items were no longer manufactured.

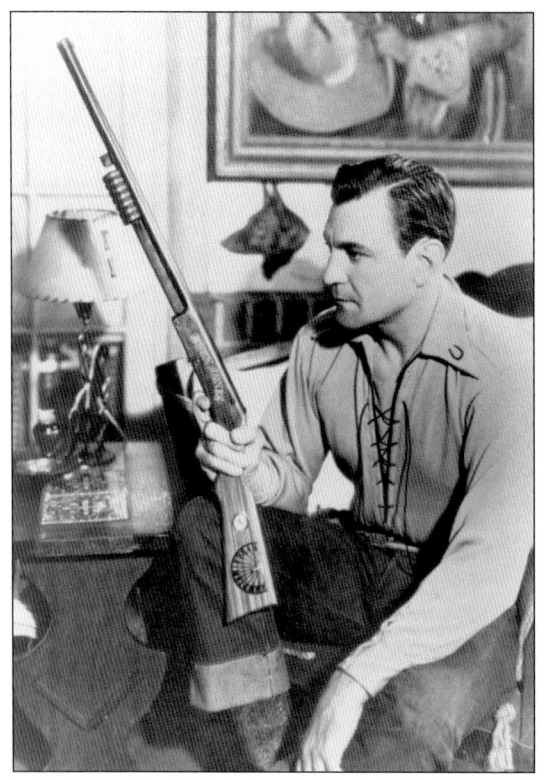

Buck Jones was a motion picture star in popular western movies between the 1920s and the early 1940s. His real name was Charles Frederick Gebhart, who hailed from near Vincennes, Indiana. Continuing to appeal to the imaginations of youngsters during the Great Depression, Daisy turned to Buck in 1934, who agreed to lend his name to several Daisy products, including the Buck Jones Special that Jones is holding at left. The gun was a pump-action repeater with a compass inlaid in the stock and a sundial burned into the stock. Daisy's sales doubled from 1933 to 1934 after the introduction of all of these promotional items. The Buck Jones ad below appeared in *The American Boy—Youth's Companion* in May 1937. (At left, courtesy of Wesley Powers.)

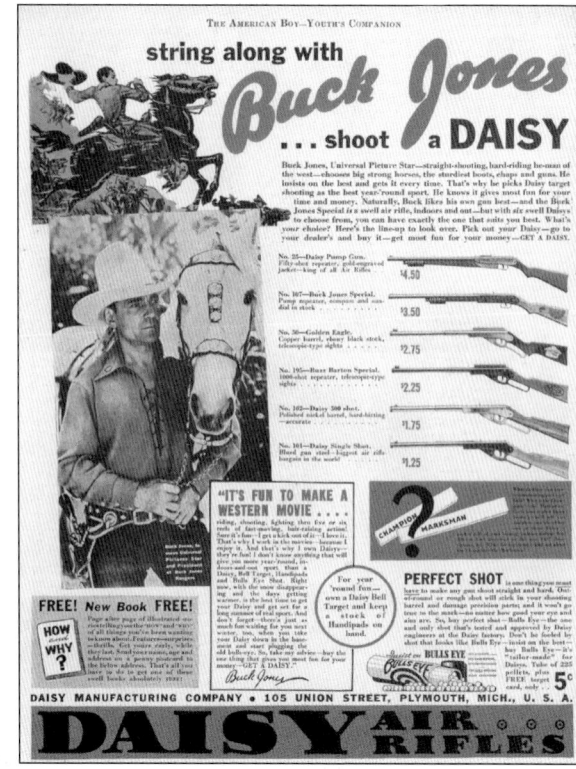

Daisy was also quite successful in the play gun arena. This flyer, from about 1940, advertises the new Squirt-O-Matic 6 Shot Repeater: a combination water and pop pistol. It retailed for a mere quarter and was produced from 1940 to 1941 and 1946 to 1948.

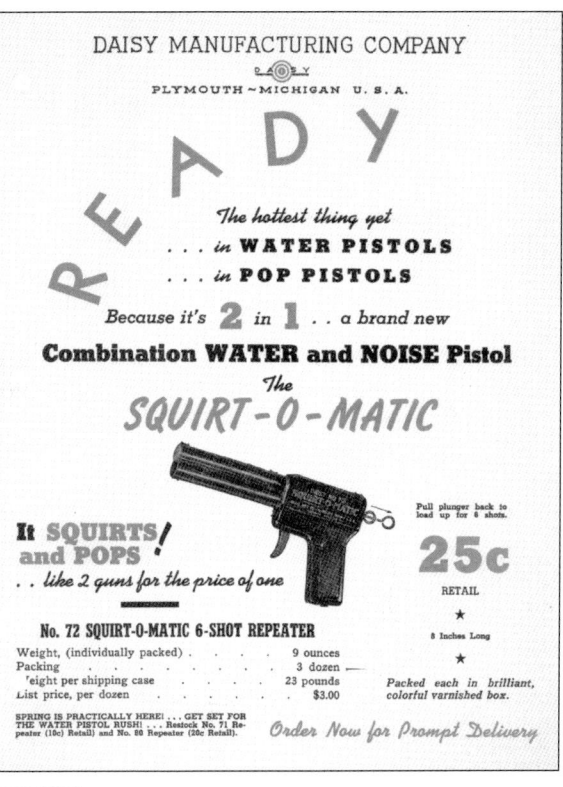

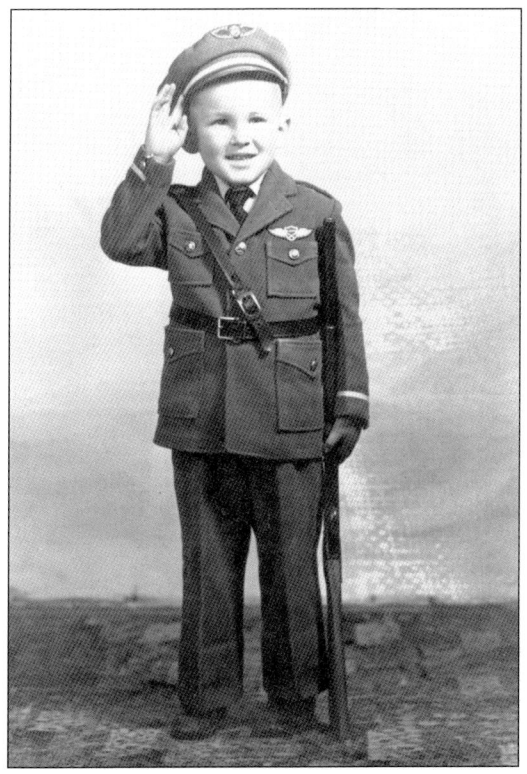

A young boy gives a hearty salute in his World War II–style military aviator uniform. In his left hand, he holds a Daisy air rifle. (Courtesy of Wes Powers.)

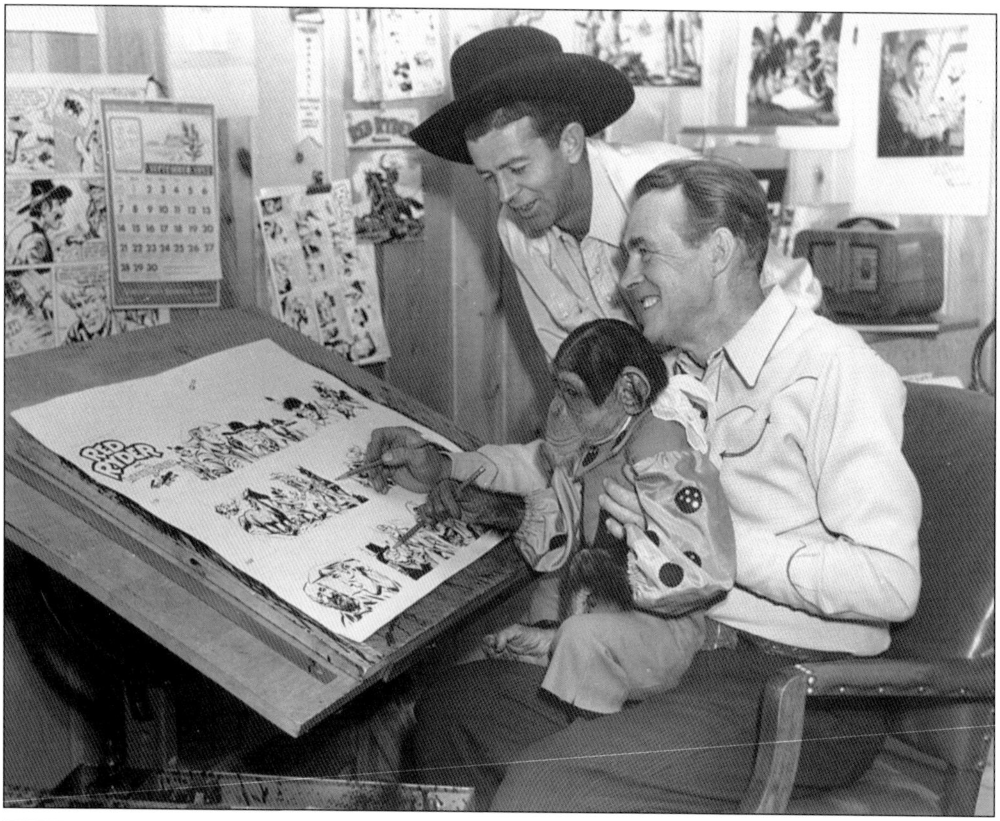

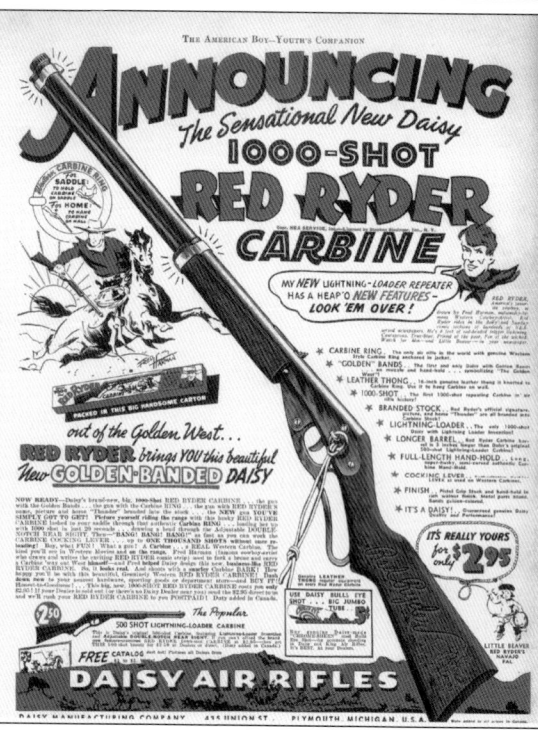

Artist Fred Harman (right) and promoter Stephen Slesinger developed the comic-strip character Red Ryder in 1938. The comic became very popular and worked well with the marketing strategy of Daisy. In October 1939, the company signed a contract with Harman and Slesinger to use the name Red Ryder for a new air rifle. According to *Daisy's Diary*, "Thus began the biggest and most profitable of all air rifle promotions up to 1958."

This is one of the first full-page ads announcing the 1,000-shot Red Ryder Carbine. It appeared in the May 1940 issue of *The American Boy—Youth's Companion*. Daisy's newest air rifle took off like wildfire. By the time production of the gun stopped in 1942 because steel was needed for the war effort, Daisy had sold 628,002 Red Ryders according to historian Gary Garber. Production resumed in late 1945 and was discontinued in 1954.

Daisy ads were designed to help young people approach their parents about getting a Daisy BB gun for Christmas. The company continued that trend with the popular Red Ryder marketing campaign sent to jobbers and department stores in October 1940. These little handouts were included in the campaign, encouraging retailers to give them to children with a mail-in coupon for a "Copyrighted Christmas Reminder Kit."

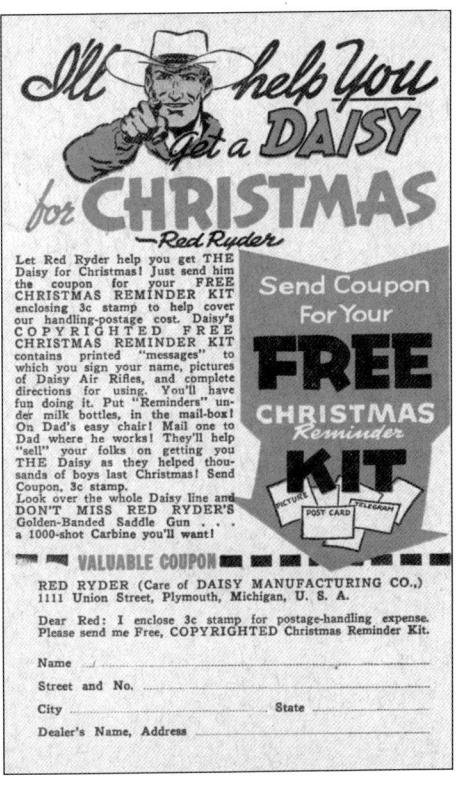

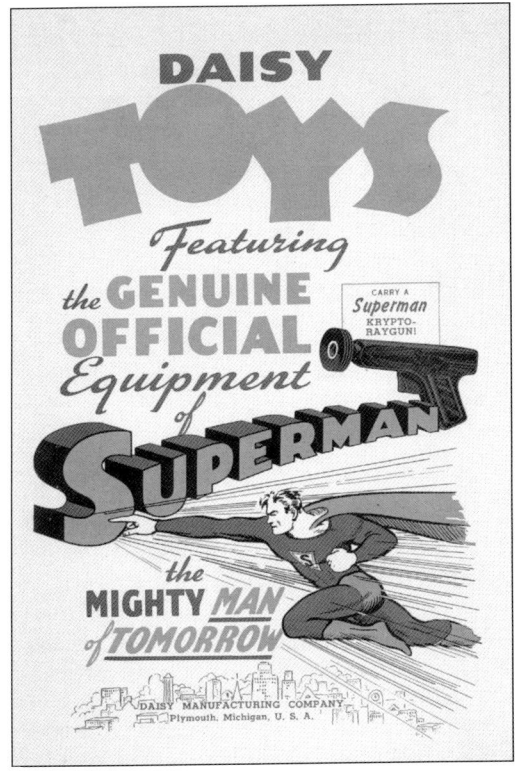

In April 1940, Daisy signed an agreement to use the cartoon superhero Superman on a Superman Krypto Ray-Gun, according to *Daisy's Diary*. This brochure announces the new toy. Pulling the trigger projected a "full-length picture story of Superman's thrilling adventures" onto the wall. Daisy also sold a Projector Pistol and a Peep-Show Pistol. The latter did not project, but had a lens in the rear for watching a picture show inside the gun.

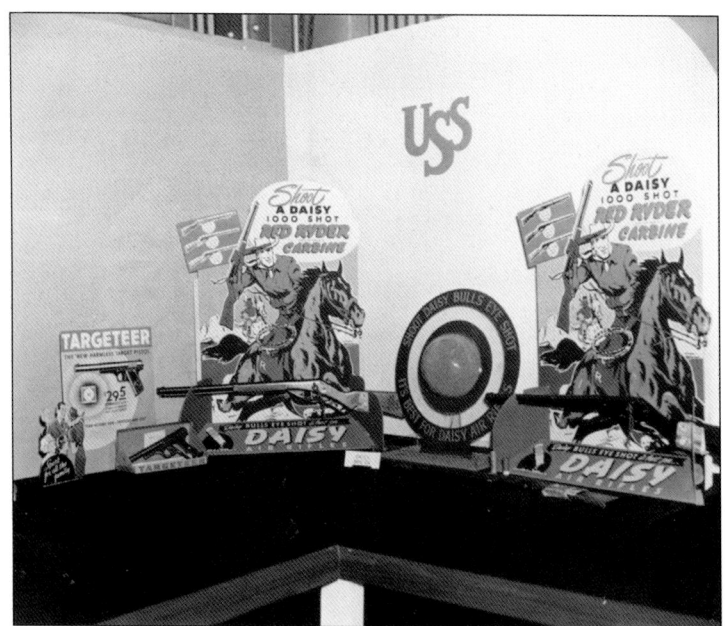

This display at a post–World War II toy trade show shows some of Daisy's late-1940s products, the Daisy Targeteer pistol and the 1,000-shot Red Ryder Carbine.

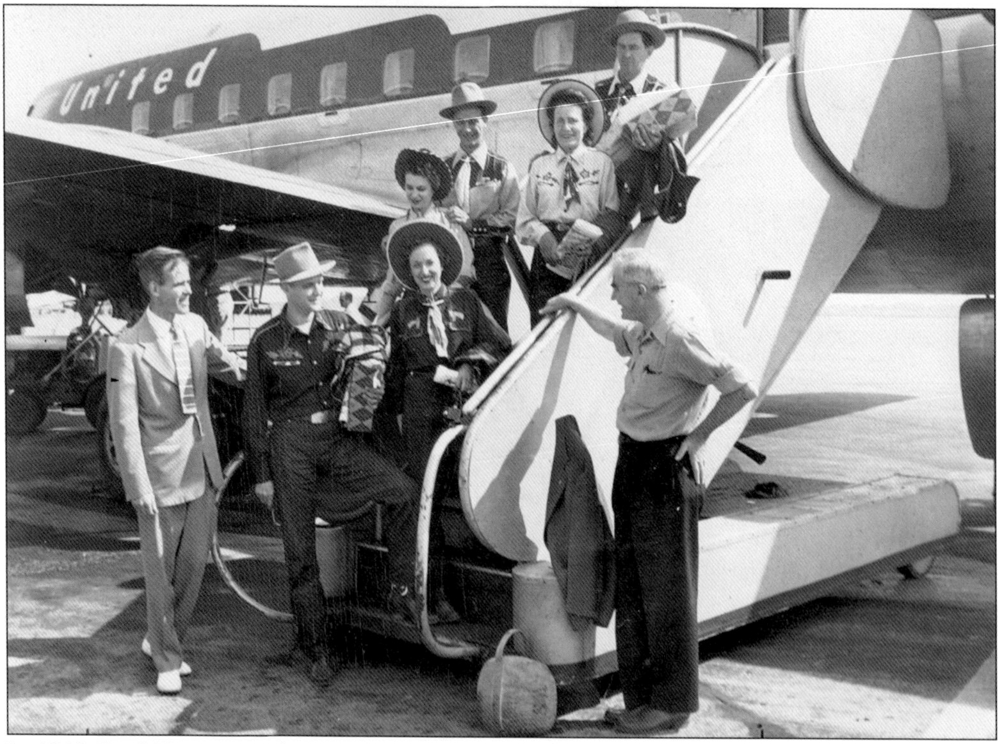

In 1949, Fred Harman and Daisy began sponsoring a 10-day, all-expenses-paid trip to the Red Ryder Ranch outside of Pagosa Springs, Colorado. The trip recipients eligible for the contest were Daisy employees and spouses. The 1950 contest winners seen here are Gerald and Betty Hosier, Don and Jess Schaufele, and Earl and Virginia Dickens. The winners arrived at Willow Run Airport in Ypsilanti, Michigan, all "duded up" and were greeted by Daisy's personnel officer, Tom Kent (far left).

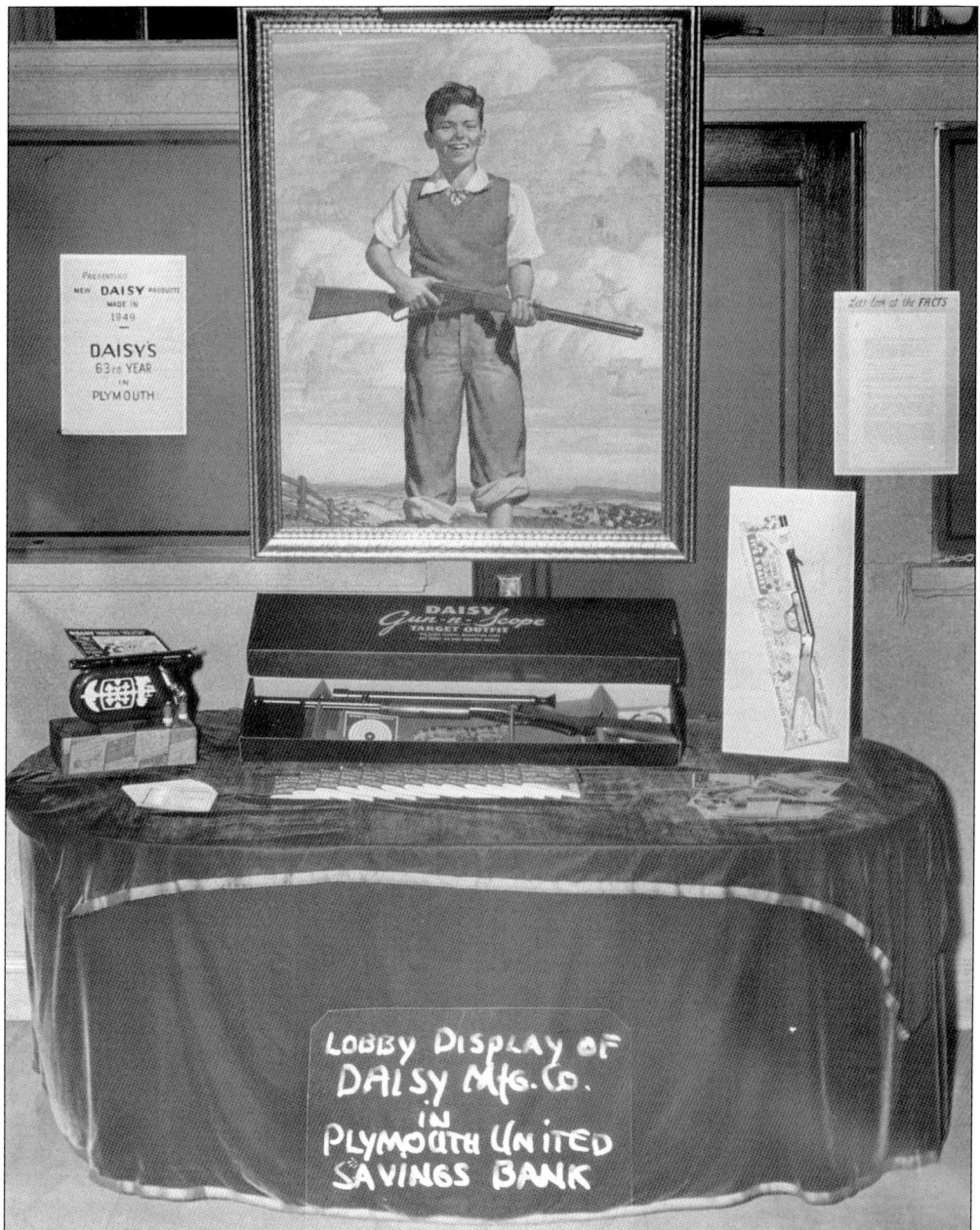

In 1949, Daisy set up a display in the lobby of the Plymouth United Savings Bank showing its new products for the year. The display also served to remind browsers that it was Daisy's 63rd year in Plymouth. At some point (based on Daisy's acquisition of Markham Air Rifle Company), Daisy's advertising began claiming 1886 as its founding rather than the company's start date of 1882 as the Plymouth Iron Windmill Company.

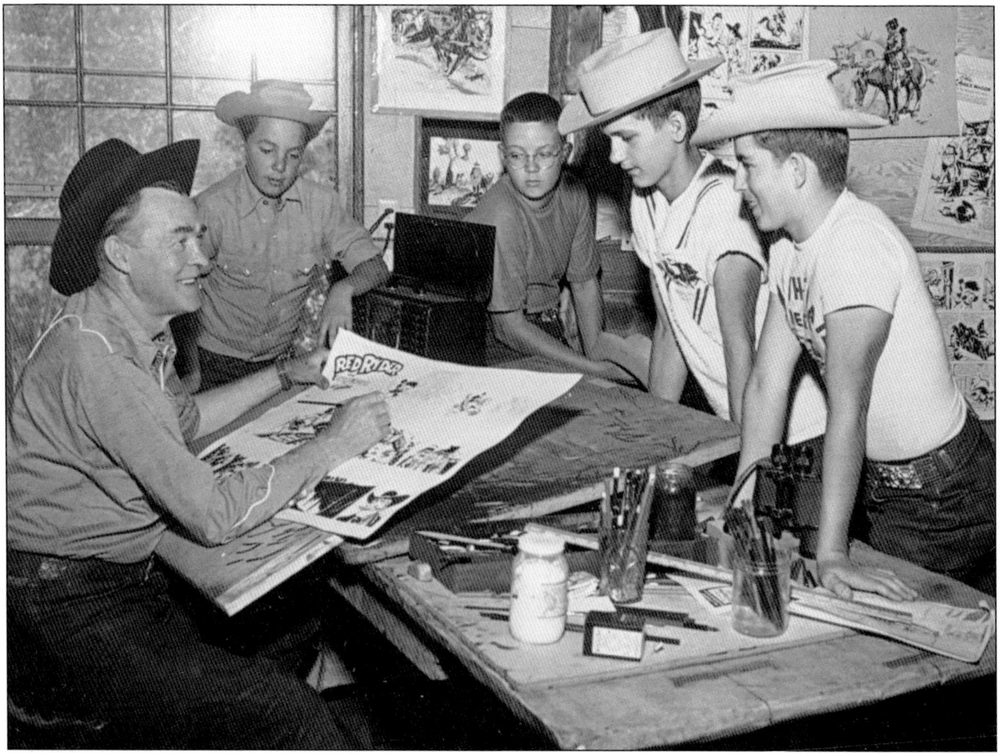

In addition to the Daisy employee trips to the Red Ryder Ranch, there was a Red Ryder Roundup Rodeo held in Pagosa Springs, Colorado, each year, beginning in 1949. Winners of another contest spent a week at the ranch over the Fourth of July. Contest winners spend time with Fred Harman, the Red Ryder cartoon artist, in his studio (above) and out on the ranch (below), experiencing all that ranch life had to offer. The two boys in the photograph below are holding Red Ryder Carbines. The Red Ryder Roundup Rodeo is still held each year in July. Harman died in 1982 in Phoenix, Arizona.

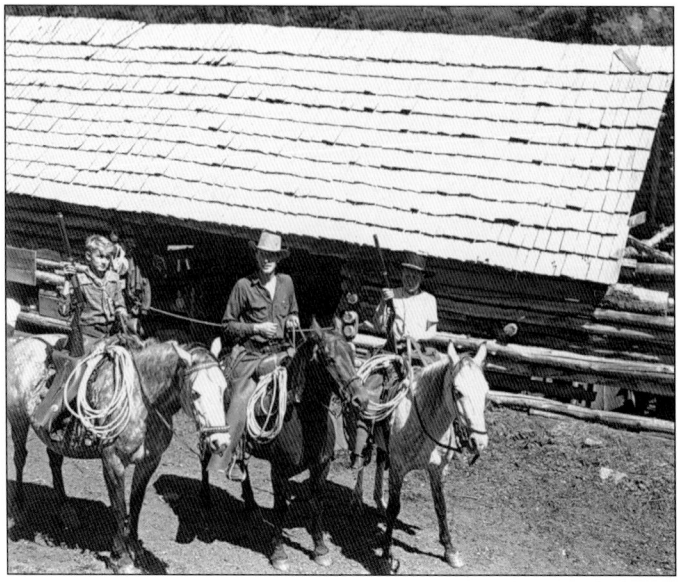

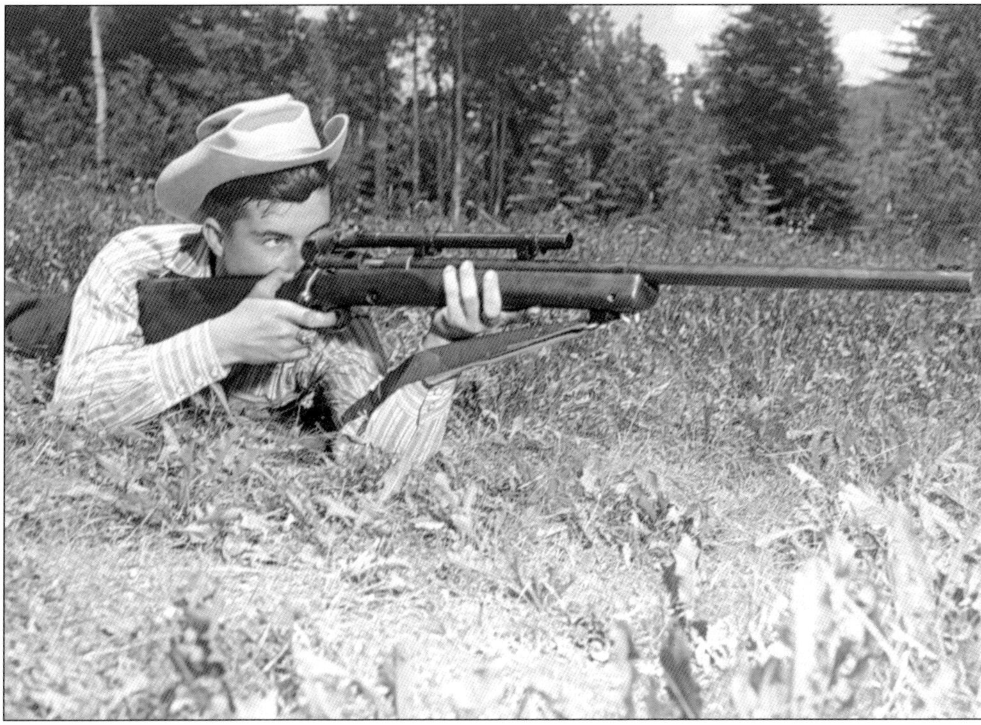

Contest winners participated in many activities during their week on the ranch, including marksmanship training (above) and relaxation in a "saloon" (below).

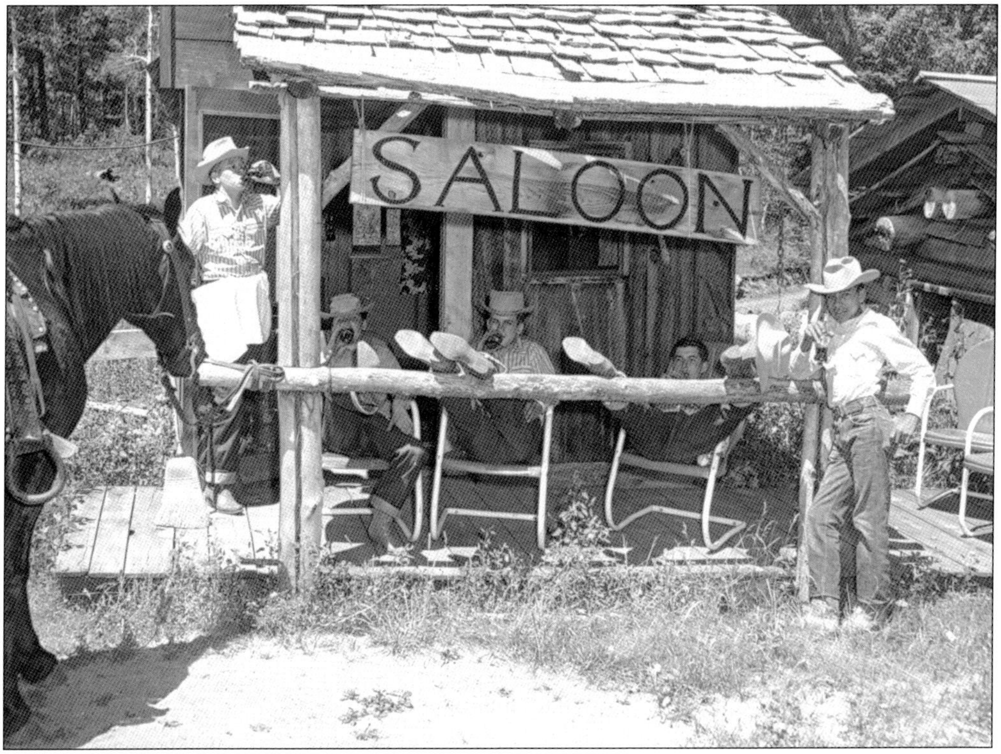

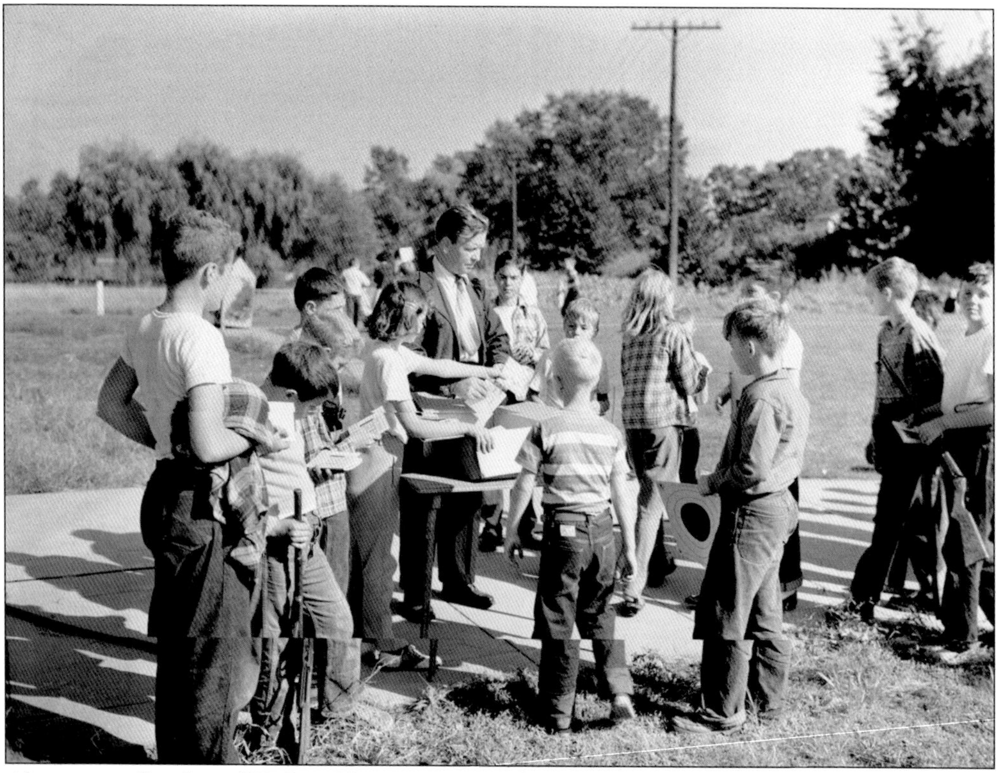

Above, an official at a BB Gun Shoot in Ann Arbor, Michigan, hands out *Daisy Handbooks* to children getting ready to shoot. The event, sponsored jointly by the Fox Tent and Awning Company and the Ann Arbor Police Department, took place in August 1949. All the contestants used Daisy air rifles. Below, participants take aim on one of the firing lines at the shoot; more than 100 boys and girls too part. Daisy had a "Shoot Safe Buddy" campaign at the time, encouraging children to use the guns for training and learning the basic principles of safety. Today, the company remains focused on youth shooting-education programs, reaching as many as one million young people annually and hosting the Daisy National BB Gun Championship Match each year.

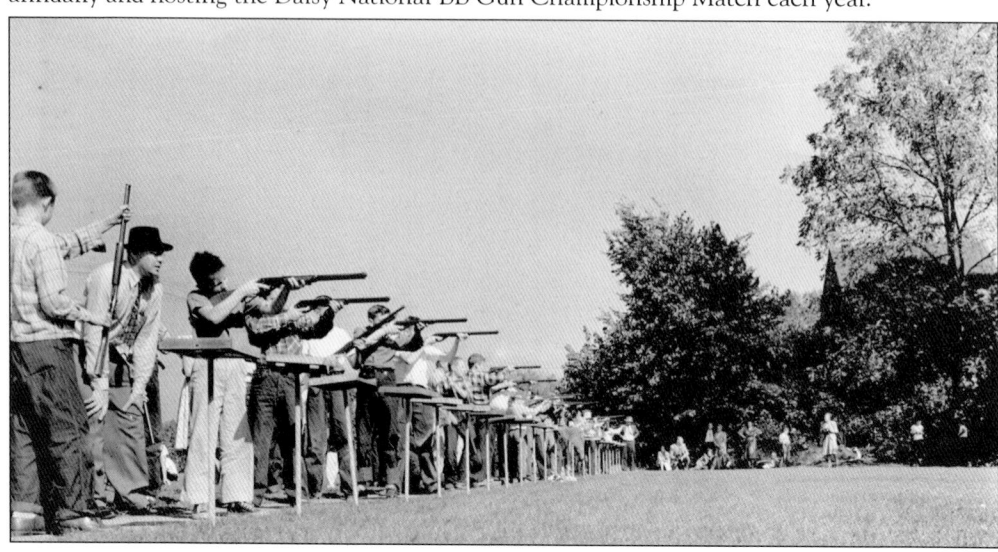

The first two prize winners in both the boys' and girls' division won the newest gun on the market, the Daisy Gun-n-Scope Target Outfit, which included a Red Ryder BB gun with scope and a bell target. The young lady at right had one of the top two scores in the girls' division. The boy below had one of the top two scores in the boys' division. This gun was a coveted prize among all the contestants. Additional prizes for other winners included BBs, Daisy Single Shots, and Shooting Galleries.

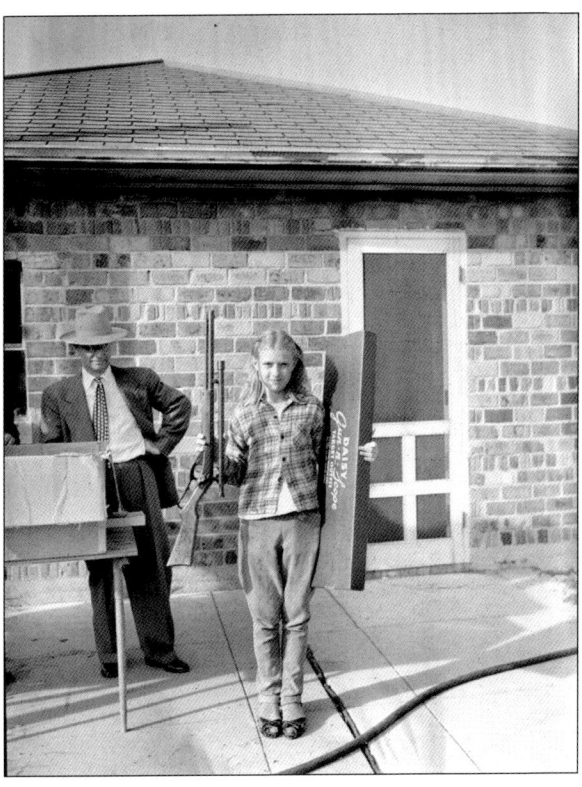

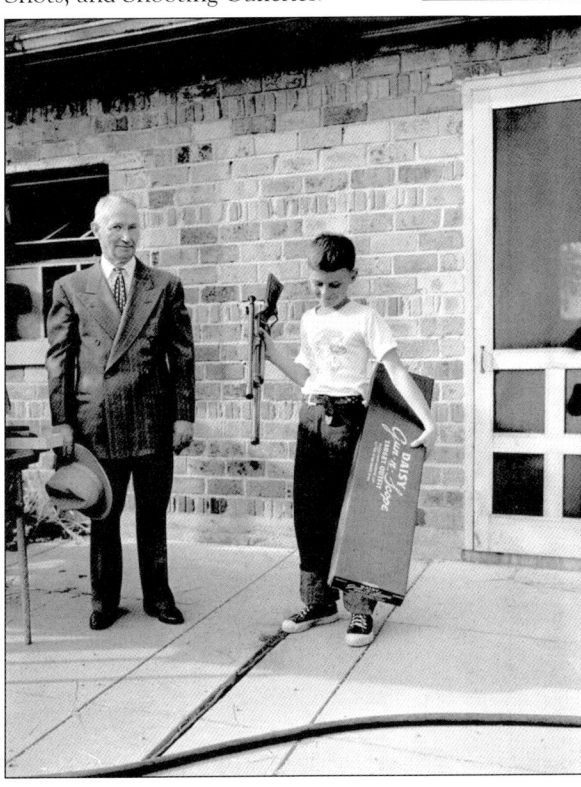

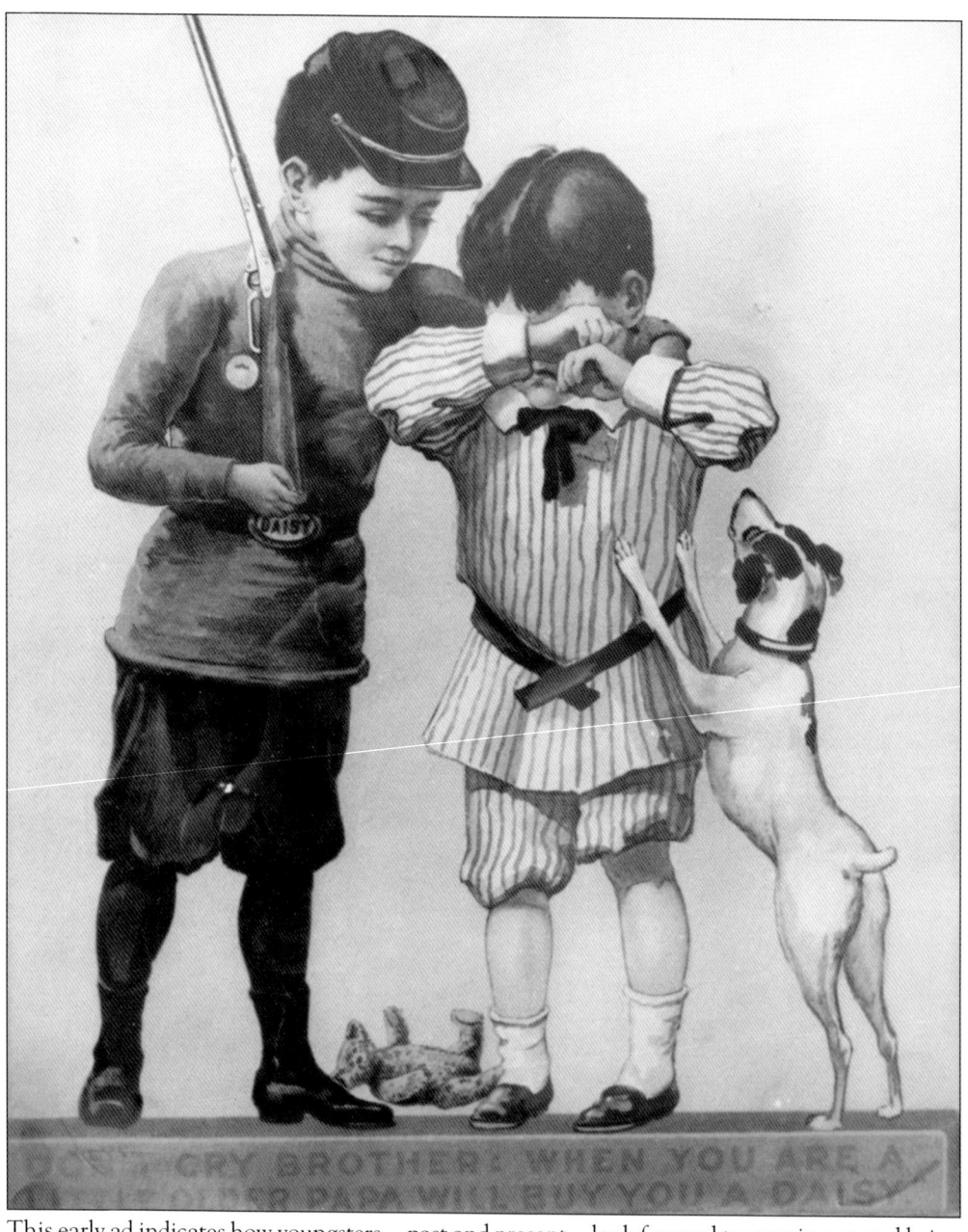
This early ad indicates how youngsters—past and present—look forward to growing up and being old enough to shoot a Daisy.

Eight
Clarence Eyes the Boys' Rifle Market

Clarence Hamilton must have gotten restless at Daisy, because in April 1897 he began a new endeavor with his son Coello. There was a small machining workshop at Clarence's home at 311 Depot Street for many years. By 1897, the workshop was equipped to take on new business from Dr. Abram Pelham, a Plymouth dentist who had invented and patented the Pelham's Pneumatic Plugger. The April 2, 1897, *Plymouth Mail* stated, "The 'Plugger' is being manufactured in the shop owned and operated by Clarence Hamilton. It is for its size probably the best equipped shop in the state of Michigan, as Mr. Hamilton has spared neither time nor expense in fitting it up." Later, in the same month, Clarence and Coello signed articles of agreement forming the partnership of C.J. Hamilton and Son "for the purpose of manufacturing dental pluggers, mechanical novelties, and doing machine work." Clarence provided the factory furnished with machinery and tools plus financial support, while Coello became the superintendent of the factory. On December 14, 1898, Clarence sold his Daisy stock and severed his ties with the company. The Hamiltons introduced a .22-caliber rifle in February 1899, for which they received a patent in 1900. The rifle, called the No. 7, was all metal with a skeleton frame and proved to be very popular. Redesigned rifles were issued on a regular basis for the next 45 years, with each new model's number increasing by four, (No. 11 was issued in 1900, No. 15 in 1901, etc.). Clarence died suddenly on December 16, 1902, at age 53, leaving Coello to carry on the business and the inventive genius. C.J. Hamilton and Son was "the most prolific of the boys' rifle manufacturers," according to historian Jim Perkins. Production did not slow down—except for a few lean years during the Great Depression—until World War II when the factory had to convert to manufacturing tank track components. When the war was over, Coello retired and sold the machinery and patents to John Hoban, who produced rifles for a short time in Salem Township, Michigan.

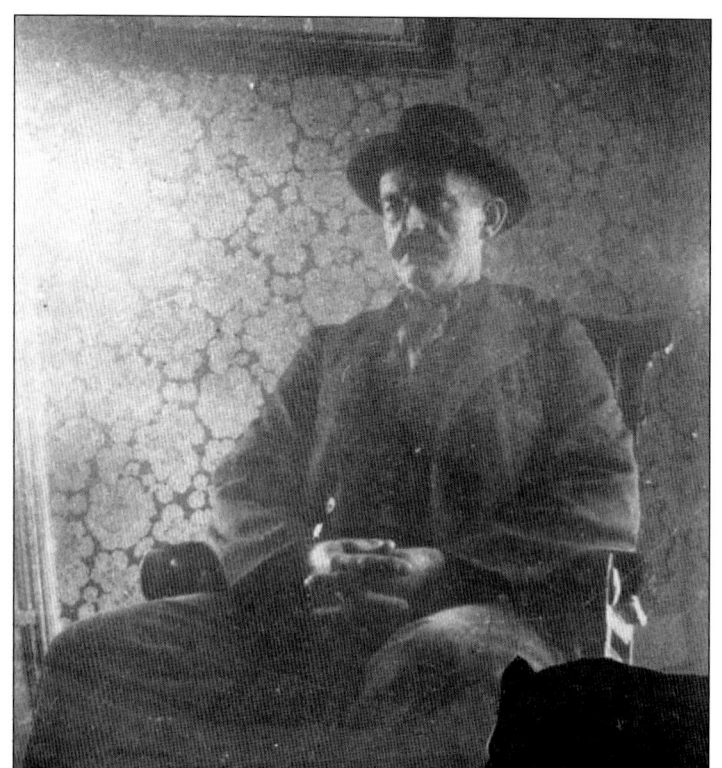

Clarence Hamilton continued his inventive streak with the introduction of a .22-caliber, all-metal rifle in 1899. If he had not died suddenly in 1902 at age 53, he would probably have introduced more innovations to the world. In addition to the patents mentioned earlier in this book, Hamilton also had patents for an improvement in washing machines (1872), a pump (1883), and a stovepipe attachment (1885), among others.

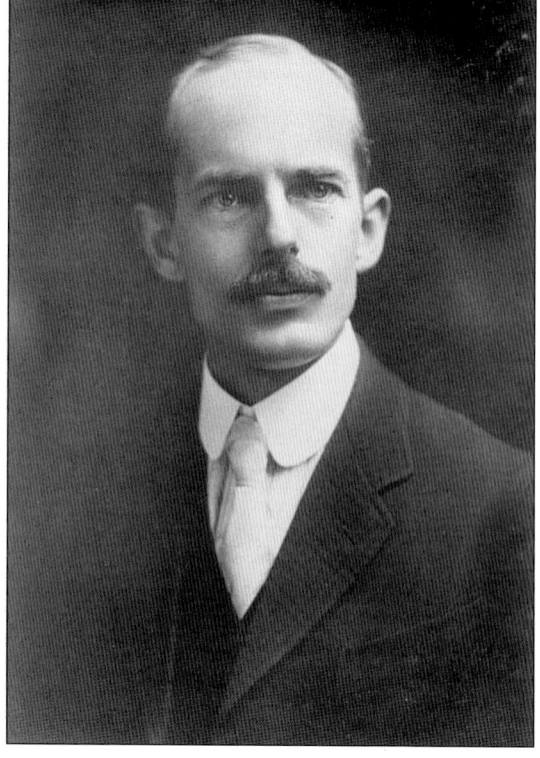

Coello Hamilton (1872–1967) moved with his family to Plymouth when he was two. According to his granddaughter Rita Hogan, "When Coello was barely in his twenties, Clarence told him if he were to become a master mechanic, trained in the tool and die trade, together they would form their own company. Coello would spend the next several years studying . . . in Detroit, Windsor [Ontario], Cleveland, and Chicago." (Courtesy of Rosemary Steele.)

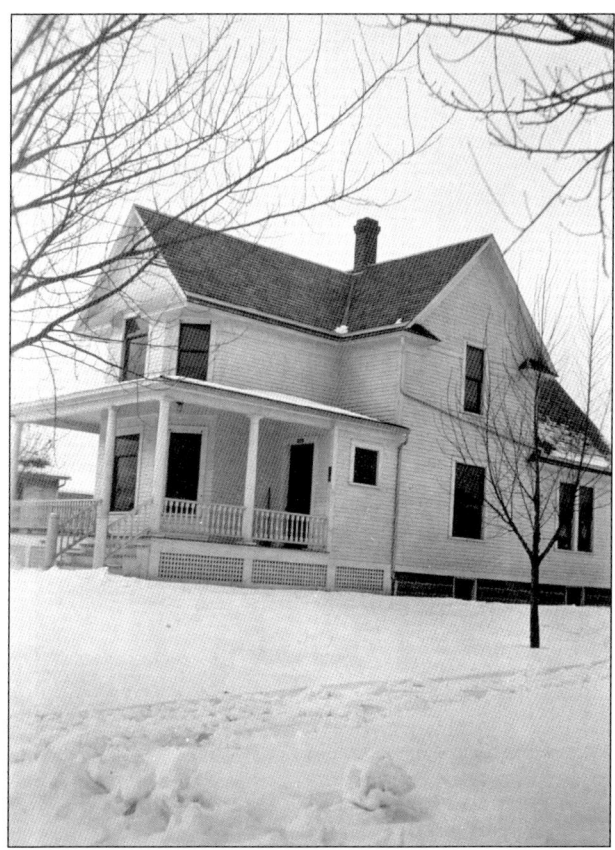

At right, Clarence Hamilton built his Gothic Revival home at 311 Depot Street (now Hamilton Street) in 1877. He had brought his family to Plymouth from Holly, Michigan, in 1874, and the family rented a home on Main Street until this house was completed. Below, after Clarence's death in 1902, Coello and his family moved into the home at 311 Depot Street with his stepmother, Emma Chase Hamilton. In 1926, after Emma's death, Coello spent $10,000 to remodel the home. The house still stands today. (At right, courtesy of Rosemary Steele.)

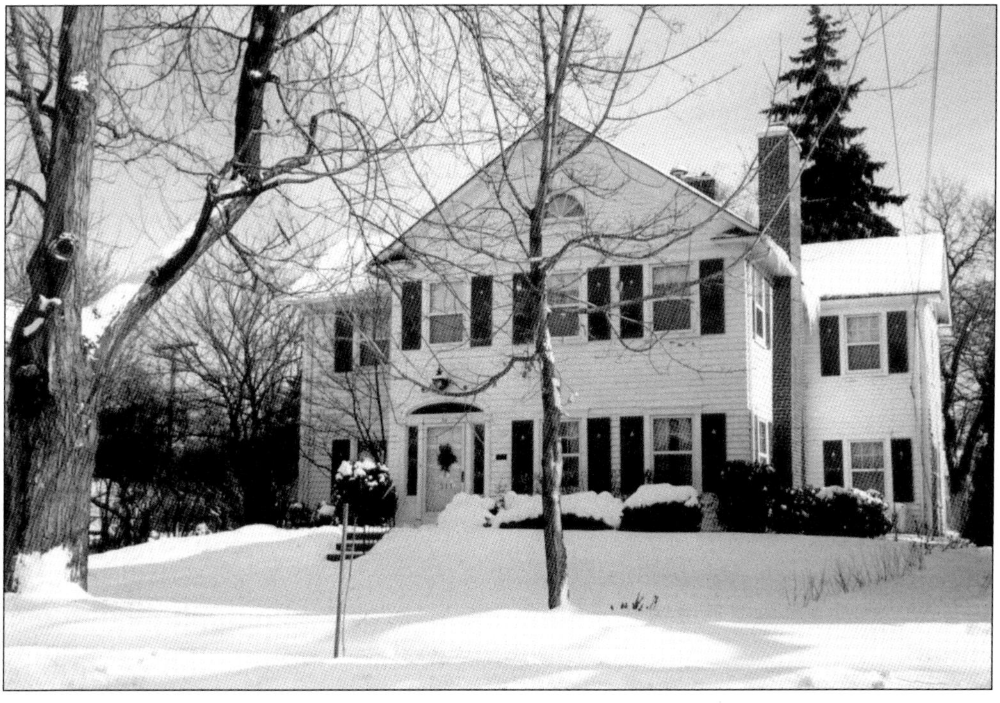

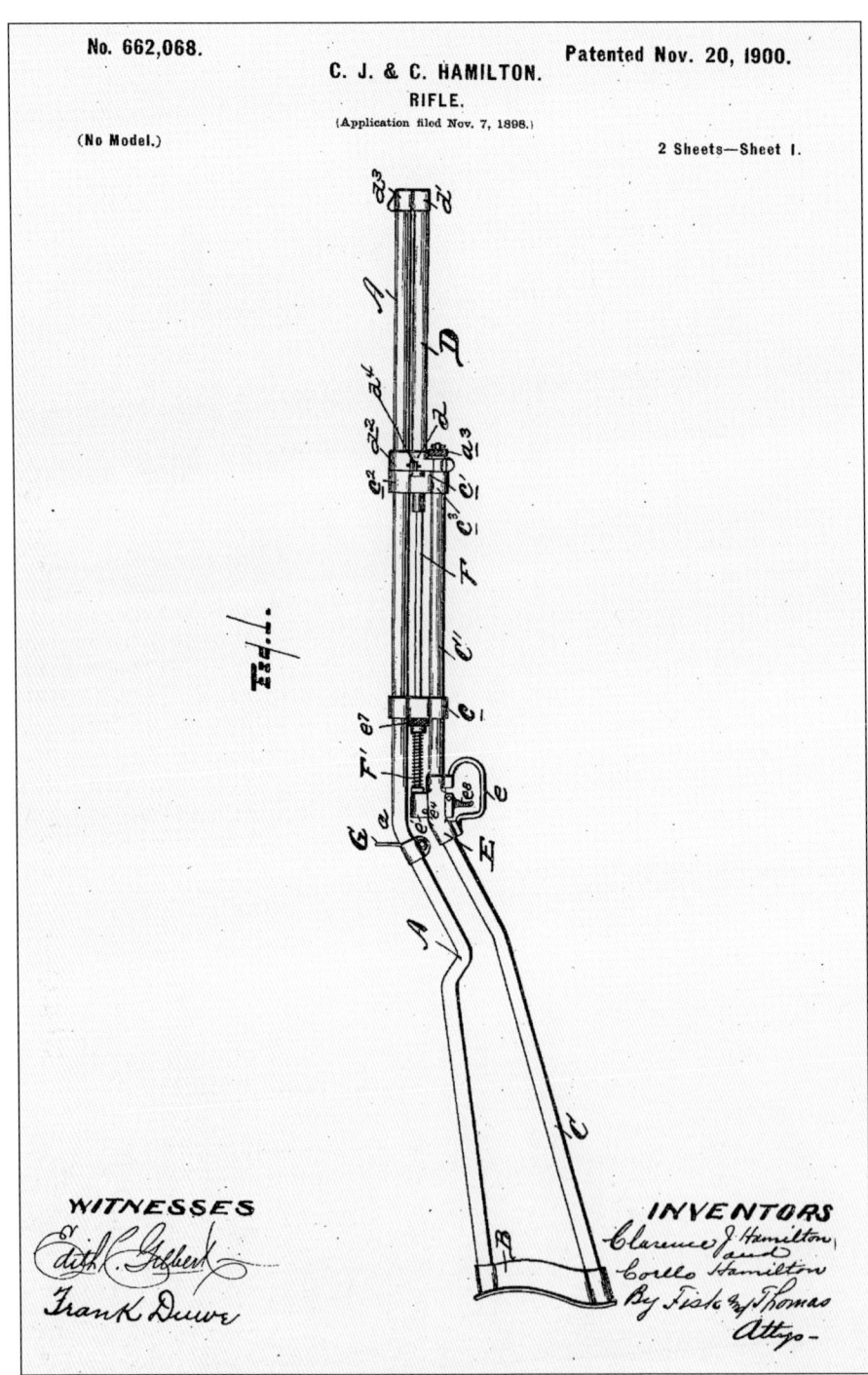

According to the *Plymouth Mail* of February 3, 1899, "The [.22] rifle is a product of Mr. Hamilton's brain and was designed with a view to simplicity, durability, accuracy, and cheapness. . . . This is an all metal rifle, finely nickel plated, is 32 inches long and weighs two pounds." Clarence and Coello applied for the rifle patent on November 7, 1898, and patent no. 662,068 was granted on November 20, 1900. The first shipment of rifles was ready to go on November 4, 1899.

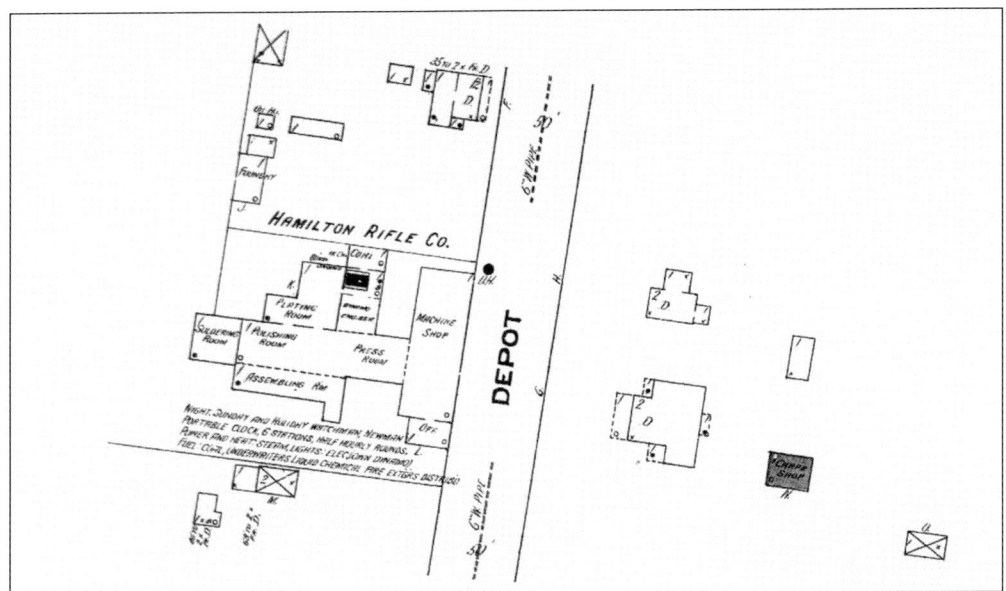

In late March 1897, Clarence Hamilton purchased three lots from S.W. Kellogg immediately across the street from his home at 311 Depot Street. His intent was to move his machine shop to the new property if business warranted. The February 3, 1899, *Plymouth Mail* indicated, "As soon as the weather permits work will be begun on an addition to their shop which was built last spring and is located on Depot Street. When finished they will have a factory 24 feet wide and 100 feet long." Above, this Sanborn Fire Insurance map of 1909 shows the factory and foundry situated right across the street from Hamilton's home, where he still had a carpenter shop. The factory was only a few blocks from Daisy. Below, in 1905, the front of the factory faces Depot Street, while employees stand outside of the building. (Above, courtesy of Environmental Data Resources; below, Jim Perkins.)

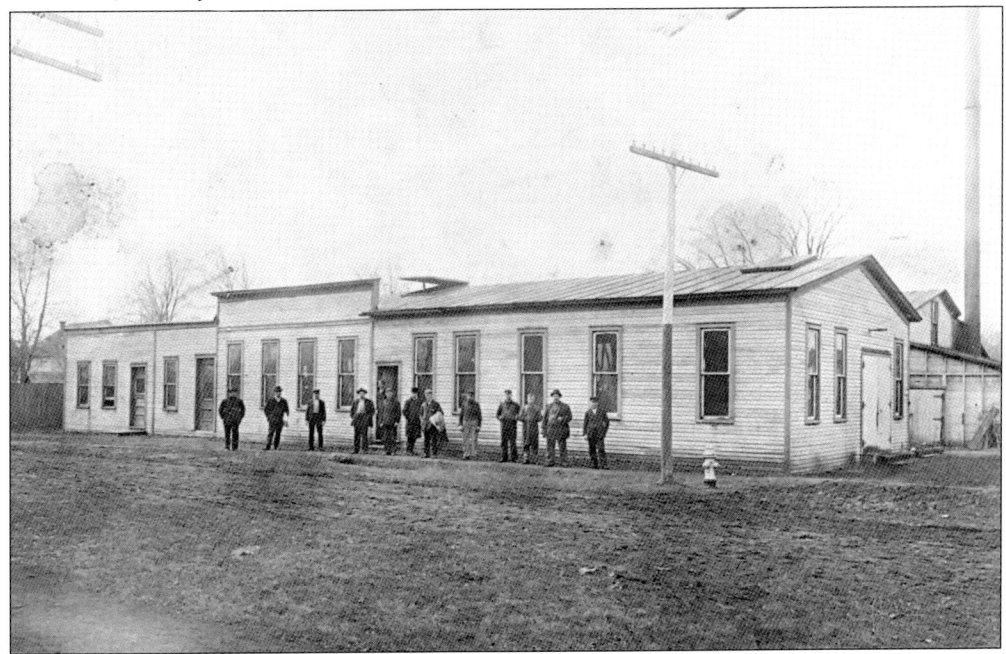

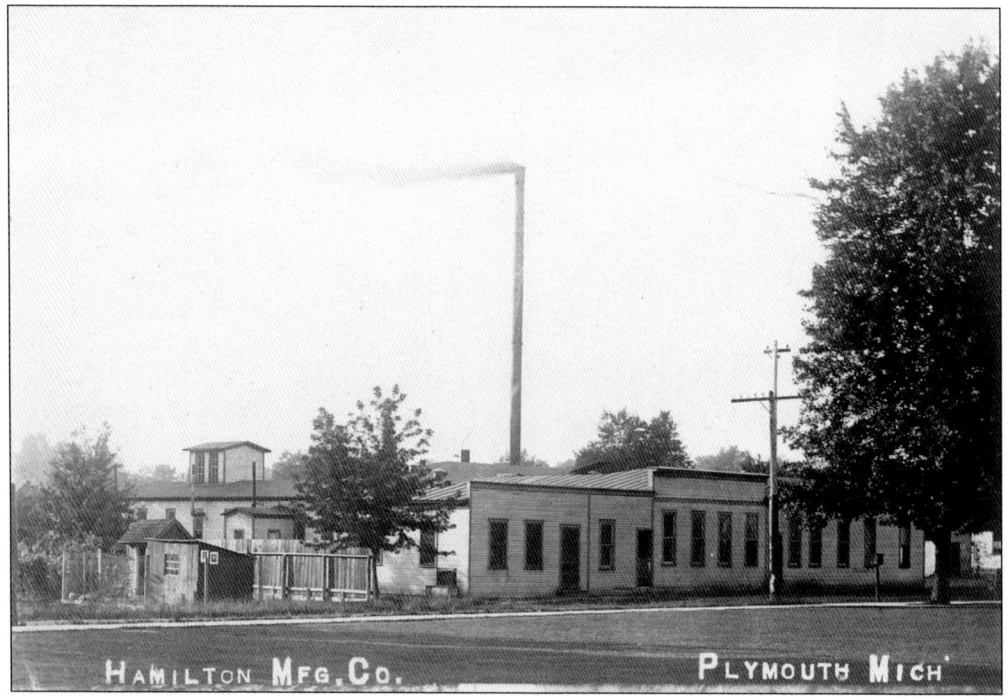

Above is a view of the factory, looking at it from the southeast around 1910, after another addition to the complex. By 1915, sales had increased so much that a major factory renovation was required. The scene below, during construction, shows that the renovation was conducted over the existing buildings. According to historian Jim Perkins, "Rifle production continued unhampered as the new building's walls and roof went up, and the old walls and roof were torn down." (Above, courtesy of Michael Pappas; below, Jim Perkins.)

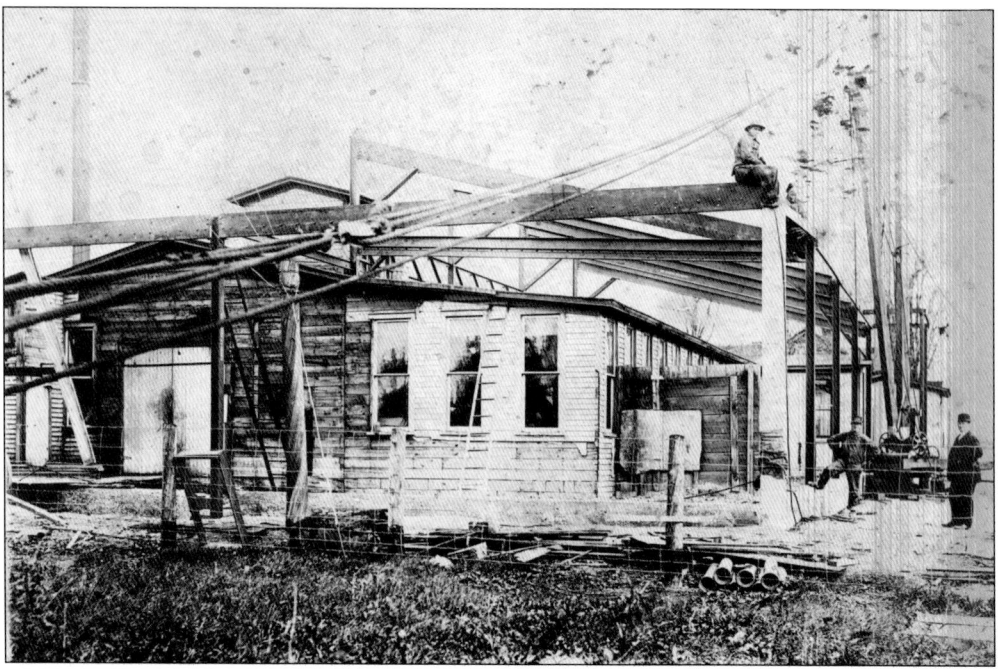

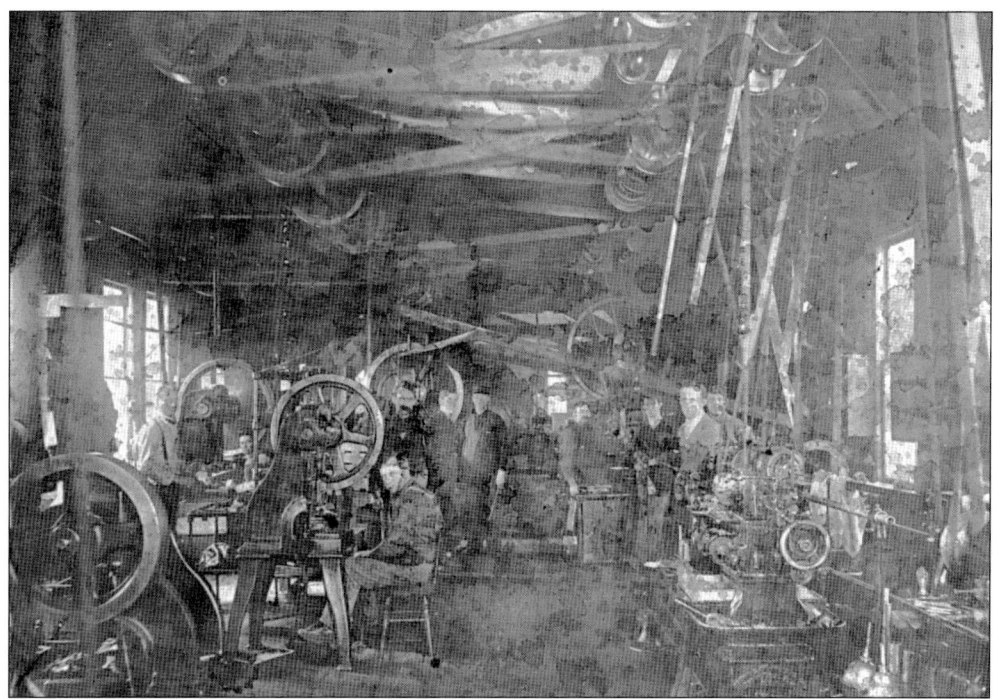

Both of these images were taken inside the Hamilton Rifle Factory around 1905. The view above is probably of the pressroom. Below, Coello Hamilton is standing on the far right (in a suit) in a shot of the machine shop. (Above, courtesy of Jim Perkins.)

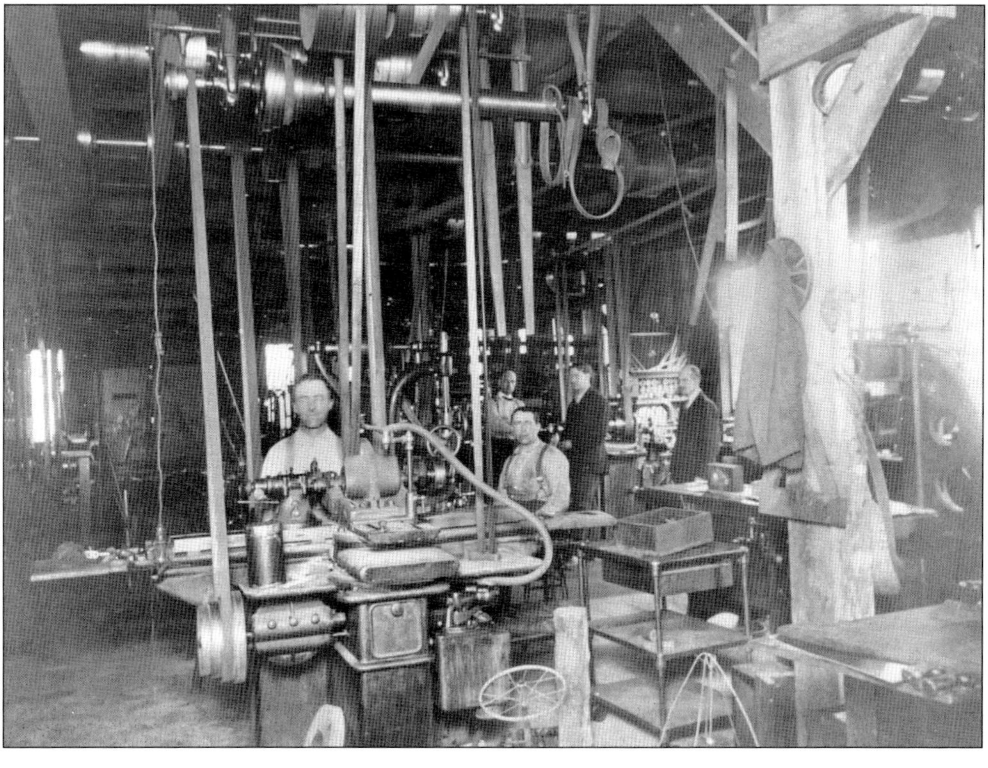

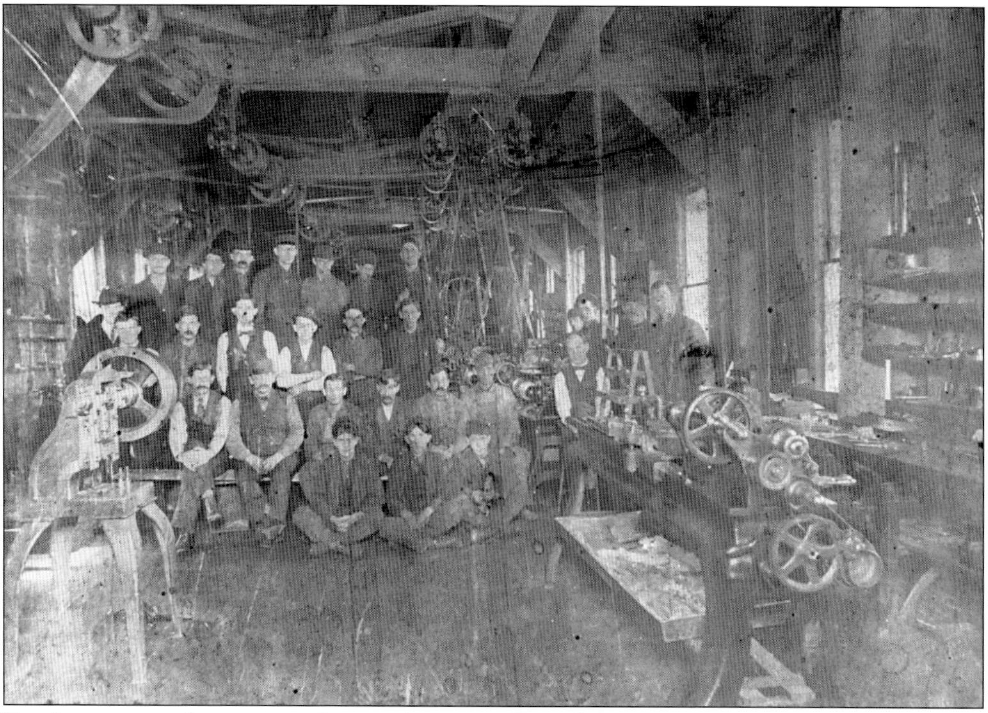

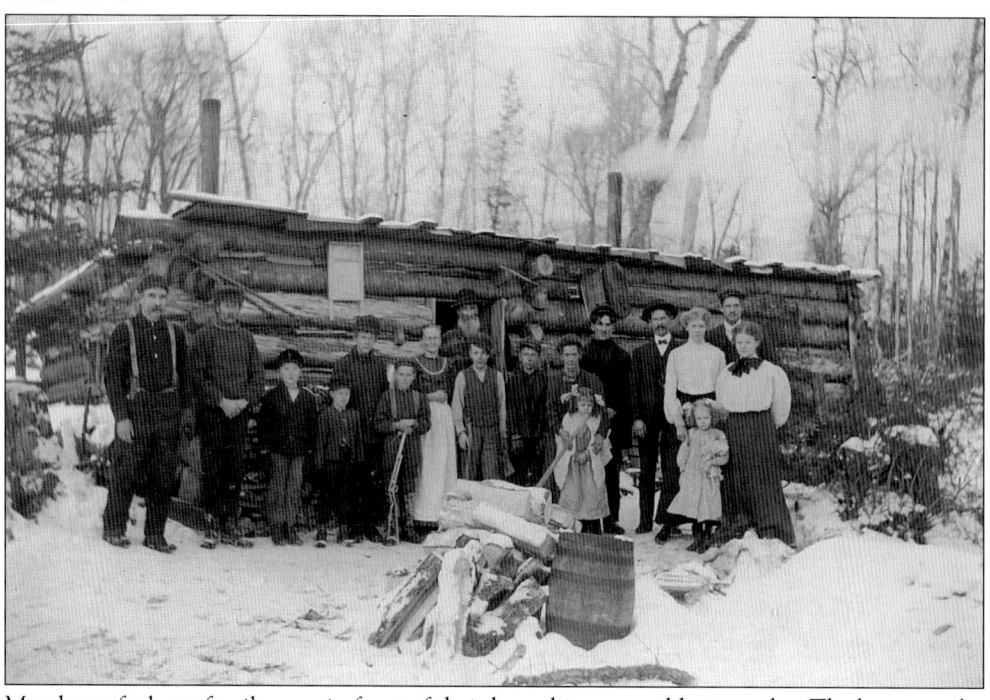

Employees pose for a group shot in the pressroom of the Hamilton Rifle Factory, perhaps around 1905.

Members of a large family pose in front of their log cabin on a cold winter day. The boy near the center is holding Hamilton Rifle No. 7. Even though the No. 7 was commercially successful, it was only manufactured until June 29, 1901. (Courtesy of Wesley Powers.)

A little girl and boy have their portrait taken with their dog. The boy is holding a Hamilton Rifle No. 15. The no. 15 sold for $1.50 beginning in August 1901. (Courtesy of Wesley Powers.)

A little boy poses on top of a donkey with a Hamilton Rifle No. 27 attached to the saddle. Itinerant photographers traveled from town to town with their props, making money photographing people along the way. The No. 27 rifle was Hamilton's best-selling design; it was manufactured beginning in December 1906. (Courtesy of Wesley Powers.)

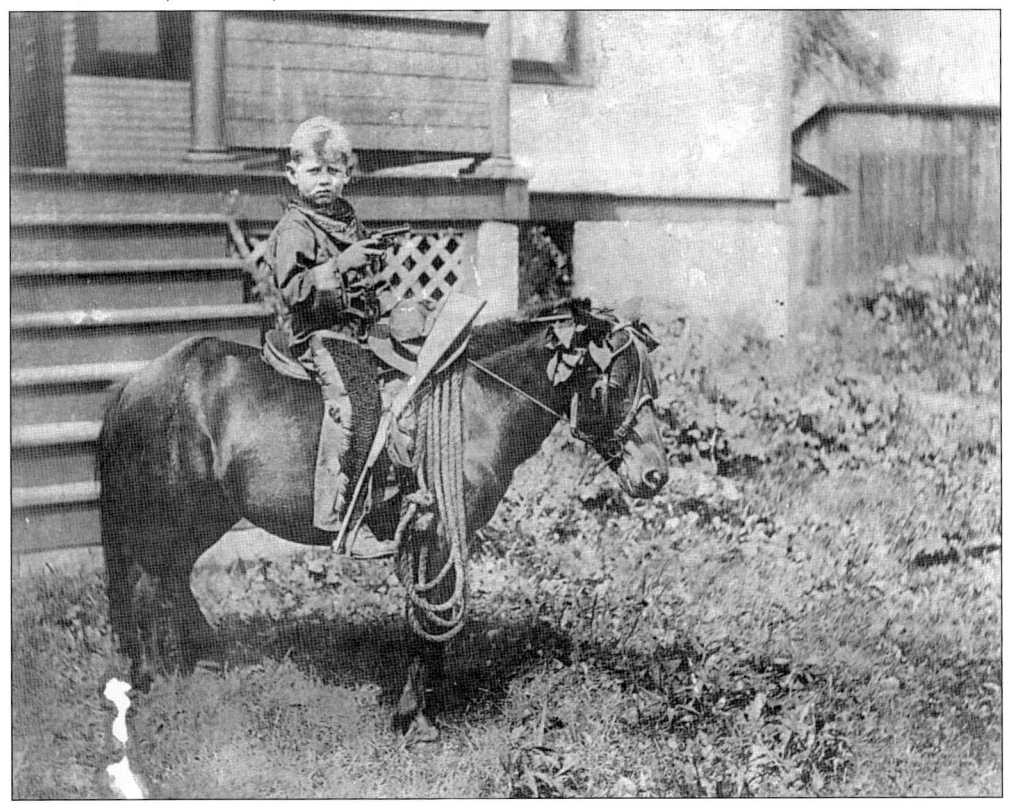

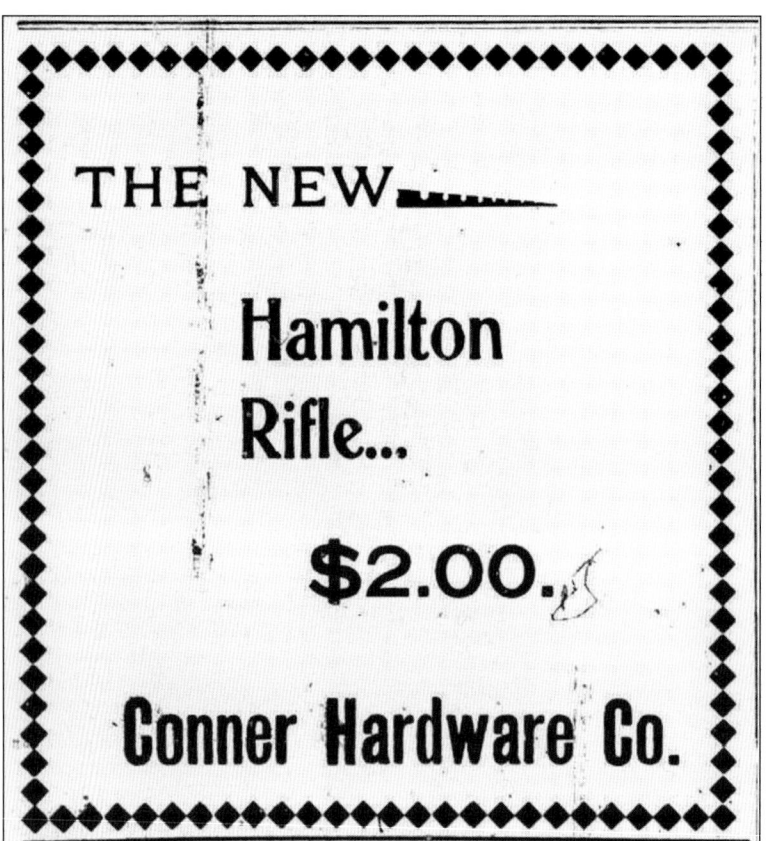

The first ad for a Hamilton rifle appeared in the December 8, 1899, *Plymouth Mail*. The ad promoted the fact that the rifle was sold at Conner Hardware on Main Street in Plymouth and was most likely paid for by Conner Hardware, not the Hamiltons. The ad came out just before Christmas, hoping to attract the attention of little boys making out their wish lists.

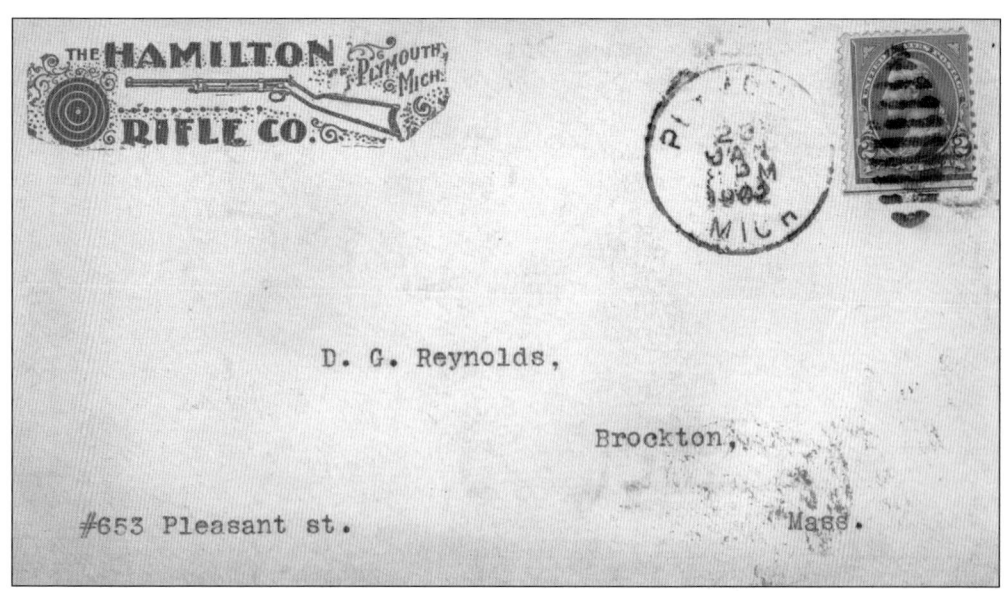

Even though the Hamiltons signed an agreement in 1897 to name their company C.J. Hamilton and Son, the company also went by Hamilton Rifle Company at various times. Rifles were marked with both names, and there was no consistency in the markings. (Courtesy of Michael Pappas.)

C.J. Hamilton and Son advertised its rifles in boys' magazines, such as *Boys Life*. The rifles were also offered as premiums by mail-order companies trying to get boys to sell their products. This ad appeared in October 1913. (Courtesy of Wesley Powers.)

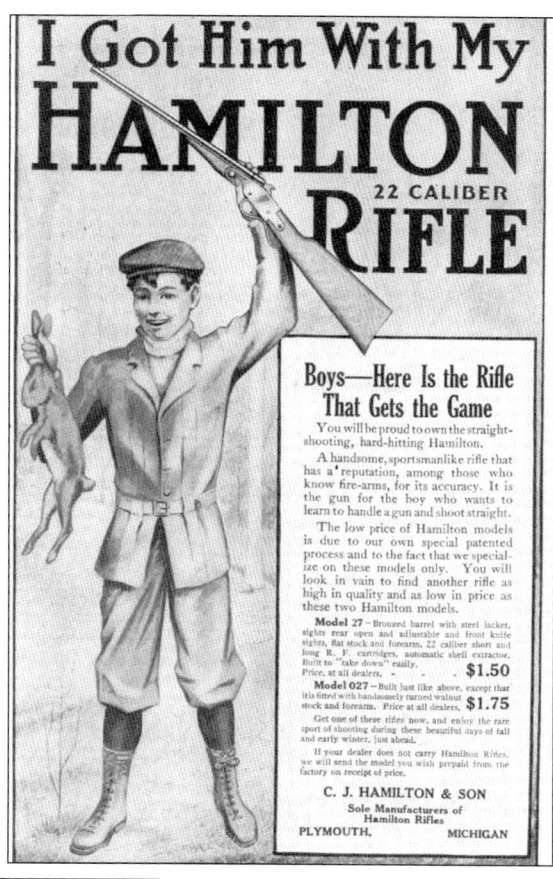

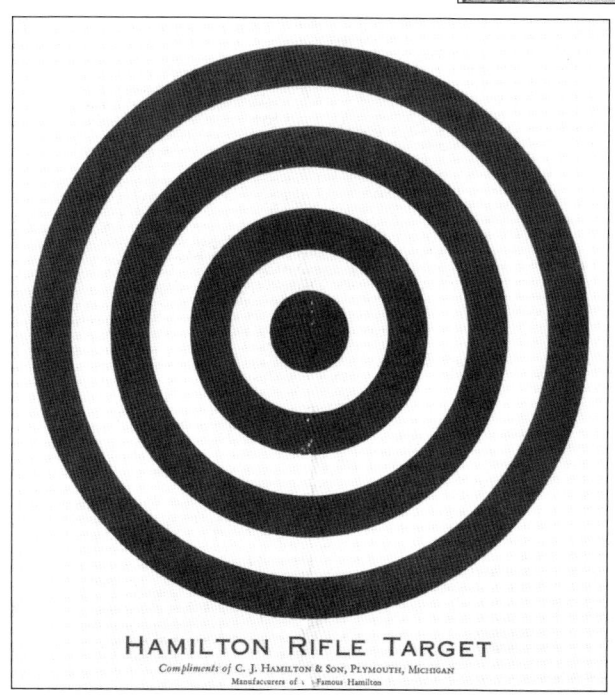

C. J. Hamilton and Son offered a complementary rifle target with the purchase of a rifle. (Courtesy of Wesley Powers.)

BIBLIOGRAPHY

Daisy Manufacturing Company. *Daisy's Diary: 80 Years of Progress.* Rogers, AR: self-published, 1976.
Garber, Gary. *An Encyclopedia of Daisy Plymouth Guns.* Collierville, TN: self-published, 2007.
Hogan, Rita. "Show Me the Daisies," *The Ledger* (May 2005): 12–13.
Hough, Cass S. *It's a Daisy.* Rogers, AR: Victor Comptometer Corporation, 1976.
Markham Air-Rifle Company. *The Story of the Air-Rifle.* Plymouth, MI: self-published, 1913.
Murfin, Joe C. *Daisy, It All Starts Here.* Rogers, AR: Daisy Outdoor Products, 2011.
Perkins, Jim. *American Boys' Rifles, 1890–1945.* Pittsburgh, PA: RTP Publishers, 1976.
———. "Captain Markham's Dream," *The Gun Report* 45 (November 1999): 20–30.
———. "The Hamilton Rifle Company," *The Gun Report* 48 (January 2002): 18–31.
Plymouth Historical Museum Archives.
Plymouth Mail. 1887–1958.
Powers, Wesley. "The Plymouth Air Rifle Company," *American Rifleman* 146 (February 1998): 40–41, 57.

About the Friends of the Plymouth Historical Museum

The Friends of the Plymouth Historical Museum is a privately funded membership organization dedicated to preserving, teaching, and presenting history through the operation and support of the Plymouth Historical Museum. The friends (also known as the Plymouth Historical Society) was organized in 1948 with 52 original members. It owns and operates the Plymouth Historical Museum, which opened its doors to the public on February 14, 1976; an addition was completed in 2001. The museum is housed in a beautiful, 26,000-square-foot building, donated to by Miss Margaret Dunning in memory of her parents. Miss Dunning turned 103 in June 2013 and is still an active and permanent member of the board of directors. The Plymouth Historical Museum is located at 155 South Main Street in Plymouth. It features a late-19th-century Victorian re-creation of Main Street, tracing the growth of the small town from the railroad depot to the general store. The largest Lincoln collection exhibited in the state of Michigan is housed in a separate room off of Main Street. A Timeline of Plymouth is in the lower level, featuring displays of Ford Village Industries, the Alter Motor Car, World War II, communication history, and the subject of this book—Plymouth's air rifle industry. The museum has three special exhibits each year to highlight the depth of the collections and to spotlight Plymouth as a microcosm of small-town America.

Discover Thousands of Local History Books
Featuring Millions of Vintage Images

Arcadia Publishing, the leading local history publisher in the United States, is committed to making history accessible and meaningful through publishing books that celebrate and preserve the heritage of America's people and places.

Find more books like this at
www.arcadiapublishing.com

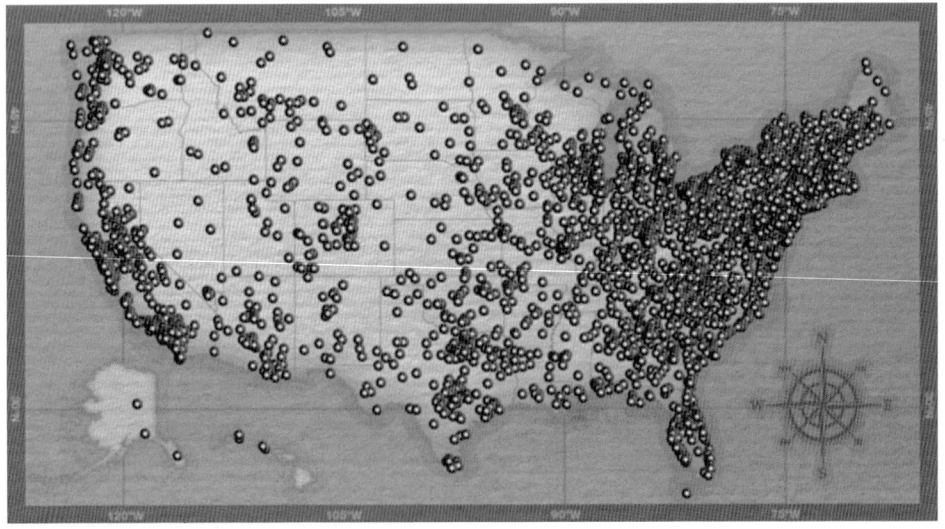

Search for your hometown history, your old stomping grounds, and even your favorite sports team.

Consistent with our mission to preserve history on a local level, this book was printed in South Carolina on American-made paper and manufactured entirely in the United States. Products carrying the accredited Forest Stewardship Council (FSC) label are printed on 100 percent FSC-certified paper.

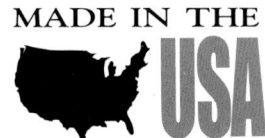